MW00837396

PHOTOSHOP® TECH SUPPORT

PHOTOSHOP® TECH SUPPORT

Ken Oyer, Sean Cavanaugh, and Ted Padova

IDG Books Worldwide, Inc.
An International Data Group Company

Foster City, CA ■ Chicago, IL ■ Indianapolis, IN ■ Southlake, TX

Photoshop® Tech Support

Published by

IDG Books Worldwide, Inc.

An International Data Group Company

919 E. Hillsdale Blvd.

Suite 400

Foster City, CA 94404

www.idgbooks.com (IDG Books Worldwide Web site)

Copyright ©1997 IDG Books Worldwide, Inc. All rights reserved. No part of this book, including interior design, cover design, and icons, may be reproduced or transmitted in any form, by any means (electronic, photocopying, recording, or otherwise) without the prior written permission of the publisher.

Library of Congress Catalog Card No.: 96-76252

ISBN: 0-7645-4000-9

Printed in the United States of America

10 9 8 7 6 5 4 3 2

1E/QZ/QX/ZX/FC

Distributed in the United States by IDG Books Worldwide, Inc.

Distributed by Macmillan Canada for Canada; by Transworld Publishers Limited in the United Kingdom; by IDG Norge Books for Norway; by IDG Sweden Books for Sweden; by Woodslane Pty. Ltd. for Australia; by Woodslane Enterprises Ltd. for New Zealand; by Longman Singapore Publishers Ltd. for Singapore, Malaysia, Thailand, and Indonesia; by Simron Pty. Ltd. for South Africa; by Toppan Company Ltd. for Japan; by Distribuidora Cuspide for Argentina; by Livraria Cultura for Brazil; by Ediciencia S.A. for Ecuador; by Addison-Wesley Publishing Company for Korea; by Ediciones ZETA S.C.R. Ltda. for Peru; by WS Computer Publishing Corporation, Inc., for the Philippines; by Unalis Corporation for Taiwan; by Contemporanea de Ediciones for Venezuela; by Computer Book & Magazine Store for Puerto Rico; by Express Computer Distributors for the Caribbean and West Indies. Authorized Sales Agent: Anthony Rudkin Associates for the Middle East and North Africa.

For general information on IDG Books Worldwide's books in the U.S., please call our Consumer Customer Service department at 800-762-2974. For reseller information, including discounts and premium sales, please call our Reseller Customer Service department at 800-434-3422.

For information on where to purchase IDG Books Worldwide's books outside the U.S., please contact our International Sales department at 415-655-3200 or fax 415-655-3295.

For information on foreign language translations, please contact our Foreign & Subsidiary Rights department at 415-655-3021 or fax 415-655-3281.

For sales inquiries and special prices for bulk quantities, please contact our Sales department at 415-655-3200 or write to the address above.

For information on using IDG Books Worldwide's books in the classroom or for ordering examination copies, please contact our Educational Sales department at 800-434-2086 or fax 817-251-8174.

For press review copies, author interviews, or other publicity information, please contact our Public Relations department at 415-655-3000 or fax 415-655-3299.

For authorization to photocopy items for corporate, personal, or educational use, please contact Copyright Clearance Center, 222 Rosewood Drive, Danvers, MA 01923, or fax 508-750-4470.

LIMIT OF LIABILITY/DISCLAIMER OF WARRANTY: AUTHOR AND PUBLISHER HAVE USED THEIR BEST EFFORTS IN PREPARING THIS BOOK. IDG BOOKS WORLDWIDE, INC., AND AUTHOR MAKE NO REPRESENTATIONS OR WARRANTIES WITH RESPECT TO THE ACCURACY OR COMPLETENESS OF THE CONTENTS OF THIS BOOK AND SPECIFICALLY DISCLAIM ANY IMPLIED WARRANTIES OF MERCHANTABILITY OR FITNESS FOR A PARTICULAR PURPOSE. THERE ARE NO WARRANTIES WHICH EXTEND BEYOND THE DESCRIPTIONS CONTAINED IN THIS PARAGRAPH. NO WARRANTY MAY BE CREATED OR EXTENDED BY SALES REPRESENTATIVES OR WRITTEN SALES MATERIALS. THE ACCURACY AND COMPLETENESS OF THE INFORMATION PROVIDED HEREIN AND THE OPINIONS STATED HEREIN ARE NOT GUARANTEED OR WARRANTED TO PRODUCE ANY PARTICULAR RESULTS, AND THE ADVICE AND STRATEGIES CONTAINED HEREIN MAY NOT BE SUITABLE FOR EVERY INDIVIDUAL. NEITHER IDG BOOKS WORLDWIDE, INC., NOR AUTHOR SHALL BE LIABLE FOR ANY LOSS OF PROFIT OR ANY OTHER COMMERCIAL DAMAGES, INCLUDING BUT NOT LIMITED TO SPECIAL, INCIDENTAL, CONSEQUENTIAL, OR OTHER DAMAGES.

Trademarks: All brand names and product names used in this book are trade names, service marks, trademarks, or registered trademarks of their respective owners. IDG Books Worldwide is not associated with any product or vendor mentioned in this book.

is a trademark under exclusive license to IDG Books Worldwide, Inc., from International Data Group, Inc.

ABOUT IDG BOOKS WORLDWIDE

Welcome to the world of IDG Books Worldwide.

IDG Books Worldwide, Inc., is a subsidiary of International Data Group, the world's largest publisher of computer-related information and the leading global provider of information services on information technology. IDG was founded more than 25 years ago and now employs more than 8,500 people worldwide. IDG publishes more than 275 computer publications in over 75 countries (see listing below). More than 60 million people read one or more IDG publications each month.

Launched in 1990, IDG Books Worldwide is today the #1 publisher of best-selling computer books in the United States. We are proud to have received eight awards from the Computer Press Association in recognition of editorial excellence and three from *Computer Currents*' First Annual Readers' Choice Awards. Our best-selling ...*For Dummies*® series has more than 30 million copies in print with translations in 30 languages. IDG Books Worldwide, through a joint venture with IDG's Hi-Tech Beijing, became the first U.S. publisher to publish a computer book in the People's Republic of China. In record time, IDG Books Worldwide has become the first choice for millions of readers around the world who want to learn how to better manage their businesses.

Our mission is simple: Every one of our books is designed to bring extra value and skill-building instructions to the reader. Our books are written by experts who understand and care about our readers. The knowledge base of our editorial staff comes from years of experience in publishing, education, and journalism — experience we use to produce books for the '90s. In short, we care about books, so we attract the best people. We devote special attention to details such as audience, interior design, use of icons, and illustrations. And because we use an efficient process of authoring, editing, and desktop publishing our books electronically, we can spend more time ensuring superior content and spend less time on the technicalities of making books.

You can count on our commitment to deliver high-quality books at competitive prices on topics you want to read about. At IDG Books Worldwide, we continue in the IDG tradition of delivering quality for more than 25 years. You'll find no better book on a subject than one from IDG Books Worldwide.

John Kilcullen
John Kilcullen
CEO
IDG Books Worldwide, Inc.

Steven Berkowitz
Steven Berkowitz
President and Publisher
IDG Books Worldwide, Inc.

VIII WINNER

*Eighth Annual
Computer Press
Awards ≥1992*

IX WINNER

*Ninth Annual
Computer Press
Awards ≥1993*

*Tenth Annual
Computer Press
Awards ≥1994*

X WINNER

XI WINNER

*Eleventh Annual
Computer Press
Awards ≥1995*

IDG Books Worldwide, Inc., is a subsidiary of International Data Group, the world's largest publisher of computer-related information and the leading global provider of information services on information technology. International Data Group publishes over 275 computer publications in over 75 countries. Sixty million people read one or more International Data Group publications each month. International Data Group's publications include: **ARGENTINA:** Buyer's Guide, Computerworld Argentina, PC World Argentina; **AUSTRALIA:** Australian Macworld, Australian PC World, Australian Reseller News, Computerworld, IT Casebook, Network World, Publish, Webmaster; **AUSTRIA:** Computerwelt Osterreich, Networks Austria, PC Tip Austria; **BANGLADESH:** PC World Bangladesh; **BELARUS:** PC World Belarus; **BELGIUM:** Data News; **BRAZIL:** Annuário de Informática, Computerworld, Connections, Macworld, PC Player, PC World, Publish, Reseller News, Supergamepower; **BULGARIA:** Computerworld Bulgaria, Network World Bulgaria, PC & MacWorld Bulgaria; **CANADA:** CIO Canada, Client/Server World, ComputerWorld Canada, InfoWorld Canada, NetworkWorld Canada, WebWorld; **CHILE:** Computerworld Chile, PC World Chile; **COLOMBIA:** Computerworld Colombia, PC World Colombia; **COSTA RICA:** PC World Centro America; **THE CZECH AND SLOVAK REPUBLICS:** Computerworld Czechoslovakia, Macworld Czech Republic, PC World Czechoslovakia; **DENMARK:** Communications World Danmark, Computerworld Danmark, Macworld Danmark, PC World Danmark, Techworld Danmark; **DOMINICAN REPUBLIC:** PC World Republica Dominicana; **ECUADOR:** PC World Ecuador; **EGYPT:** Computerworld Middle East, PC World Middle East; **EL SALVADOR:** PC World Centro America; **FINLAND:** MikroPC, Tietoverkko, Tietovikko; **FRANCE:** Distributique, Hebdo, Info PC, Le Monde Informatique, Macworld, Reseaux & Telecoms, WebMaster France; **GERMANY:** Computer Partner, Computerwoche, Computerwoche Extra, Computerwoche FOCUS, Global Online, Macwelt, PC Welt; **GREECE:** Amiga Computing, GamePro Greece, Multimedia World; **GUATEMALA:** PC World Centro America; **HONDURAS:** PC World Centro America; **HONG KONG:** Computerworld Hong Kong, PC World Hong Kong, Publish in Asia; **HUNGARY:** ABCD CD-ROM, Computerworld Szamitastechnika, Internetto online Magazine, PC World Hungary, PC-X Magazin Hungary; **ICELAND:** Tolvuheimur PC World Island; **INDIA:** Information Communications World, Information Systems Computerworld, PC World India, Publish in Asia; **INDONESIA:** InfoKomputer PC World, Komputek Computerworld, Publish in Asia; **IRELAND:** ComputerScope, PC Live!; **ISRAEL:** Macworld Israel, People & Computers/Computerworld; **ITALY:** Computerworld Italia, Macworld Italia, Networking Italia, PC World Italia; **JAPAN:** DTP World, Macworld Japan, Nikkei Personal Computing, OS/2 World Japan, SunWorld Japan, Windows NT World, Windows World Japan; **KENYA:** PC World East African; **KOREA:** Hi-Tech Information, Macworld Korea, PC World Korea; **MACEDONIA:** PC World Macedonia; **MALAYSIA:** Computerworld Malaysia, PC World Malaysia, Publish in Asia; **MALTA:** PC World Malta; **MEXICO:** Computerworld Mexico, PC World Mexico; **MYANMAR:** PC World Myanmar; **NETHERLANDS:** Computer! Totaal, LAN Internetworking Magazine, LAN World Buyers Guide, Macworld Netherlands, Net, WebWereld; **NEW ZEALAND:** Absolute Beginners Guide and Plain & Simple Series, Computer Buyer, Computer Industry Directory, Computerworld New Zealand, MTB, Network World, PC World New Zealand; **NICARAGUA:** PC World Centro America; **NORWAY:** Computerworld Norge, CW Rapport, Datamagasinet, Financial Rapport, Kursguide Norge, Macworld Norge, Multimediaworld Norge, PC World Ekspress Norge, PC World Nettverk, PC World Norge, PC World ProduktGuide Norge; **PAKISTAN:** Computerworld Pakistan; **PANAMA:** PC World Panama; **PEOPLE'S REPUBLIC OF CHINA:** China Computer Users, China Computerworld, China InfoWorld, China Telecom World Weekly, Computer & Communication, Electronic Design China, Electronics Today, Electronics Weekly, Game Software, PC World China, Popular Computer Week, Software Weekly, Software World, Telecom World; **PERU:** PC World Profesional Peru, PC World SoHo Peru; **PHILIPPINES:** Click!, Computerworld Philippines, PC World Philippines, Publish in Asia; **POLAND:** Computerworld Poland, Computerworld Special Report Poland, Cyber, Macworld Poland, Networld Poland, PC World Komputer; **PORTUGAL:** Cerebro/PC World, Computerworld/Correio Informático, Dealer World Portugal, Mac*In/PC*In Portugal, Multimedia World; **PUERTO RICO:** PC World Puerto Rico; **ROMANIA:** Computerworld Romania, PC World Romania, Telecom Romania; **RUSSIA:** Computerworld Russia, Mir PK, Publish, Seti; **SINGAPORE:** Computerworld Singapore, PC World Singapore, Publish in Asia; **SLOVENIA:** Monitor; **SOUTH AFRICA:** Computing SA, Network World SA, Software World SA; **SPAIN:** Communicaciones World España, Computerworld España, Dealer World España, Macworld España, PC World España; **SRI LANKA:** Infolink PC World; **SWEDEN:** CAP&Design, Computer Sweden, Corporate Computing Sweden, Internetworld Sweden, it.branschen, Macworld Sweden, MaxiData Sweden, MikroDatorn, Nätverk & Kommunikation, PC World Sweden, PCaktiv, Windows World Sweden; **SWITZERLAND:** Computerworld Schweiz, Macworld Schweiz, PCtip; **TAIWAN:** Computerworld Taiwan, Macworld Taiwan, NEW ViSiON/Publish, PC World Taiwan, Windows World Taiwan; **THAILAND:** Publish in Asia, Thai Computerworld; **TURKEY:** Computerworld Turkiye, Macworld Turkiye, Network World Turkiye, PC World Turkiye; **UKRAINE:** Computerworld Kiev, Multimedia World Ukraine, PC World Ukraine; **UNITED KINGDOM:** Acorn User UK, Amiga Action UK, Amiga Computing UK, Apple Talk UK, Computing, Macworld, Parents and Computers UK, PC Advisor, PC Home, PSX Pro, The WEB; **UNITED STATES:** Cable in the Classroom, CIO Magazine, Computerworld, DOS World, Federal Computer Week, GamePro Magazine, InfoWorld, I-Way, Macworld, Network World, PC Games, PC World, Publish, Video Event, THE WEB Magazine, and WebMaster; online webzines: JavaWorld, NetscapeWorld, and SunWorld Online; **URUGUAY:** InfoWorld Uruguay; **VENEZUELA:** Computerworld Venezuela, PC World Venezuela; and **VIETNAM:** PC World Vietnam. 3/24/97

Credits

Acquisitions Editor
Michael Roney

Development Editor
Stefan Grünwedel

Technical Editor
Don Day

Copy Editors
Robert Campbell
Carolyn Welch

Project Coordinator
Katy German

Graphics and Production Specialist
Mario F. Amador

Proofreader
Dave Wise

Indexer
Liz Cunningham

Book Designer
Margery Cantor

About the Authors

Ken Oyer has been working in the graphics industry for nearly 20 years in a diverse range of environments from service bureaus to advertising agencies to lithographers. He currently works for Reprints, a large lithography house in San Marcos, California, as a designer and production artist. Ken started working on the Macintosh in 1986. He saw the first releases of all the major graphic programs available today and beta tested the first couple of versions of Photoshop. Ken also serves as a curriculum advisor for Platt College of San Diego and teaches seminars on advanced Photoshop and digital prepress.

Sean Cavanaugh is the creative director for Title Wave, Inc., of Carlsbad, California, a multimedia development and consulting firm specializing in Internet applications and CD-ROM development. Sean is the author of four books. His most recent book is *Digital Type Design Guide* (Hayden Books). A professional user of many applications, Sean also specializes in cross-platform integration, OS-level scripting, and desktop publishing. Sean is a graduate of Montana State University, where he studied English literature and creative writing.

Ted Padova is a managing partner of The Image Source Digital Imaging/Photofinishing Centers of Ventura, California. He is a coauthor of *Using Photoshop 3.0, Special Edition* (Macmillan Computer Publishing) and the author of over 20 journal articles on Photoshop. He has also been technical editor for *Macworld Photoshop 4 Bible* and *Photoshop 4 for Windows For Dummies* (both from IDG Books Worldwide). He has spoken at the ThunderLizard Photoshop conferences and has taught Photoshop classes for the University of California, Santa Barbara, since the first release of Photoshop in 1989.

PREFACE

A great many books have been written on Adobe Photoshop, ranging from quick-starts and introductory tutorials to all manner of handbooks, full-color guides to professional techniques, and even a Bible! Photoshop users can't seem to get enough of these tomes, and the thirst for ever more Photoshop information seems to be unlimited. This is a tribute to Photoshop, one of the biggest "killer apps" ever—a powerful, deep, and elegant program that virtually drives the digital graphic arts industry.

Although publications exist on almost every aspect of Photoshop, one key area has been largely overlooked. Few books have dealt with the *technical* side of this delightful but highly complex tool. We all know that where complexity exists, ample opportunity also arises for things to go wrong, especially when one is dealing with multidimensional color spaces and high-resolution, multimegabyte files!

Photoshop Tech Support was created with these technical issues in mind. It exists to provide Macintosh and Windows users alike with critical, hard-won information that will not only help you troubleshoot problems when they occur but also give you the knowledge you need to *avoid* many of the most common time-wasting surprises to begin with.

Each chapter in this book addresses a major task area in Photoshop, beginning with installation and continuing through topics such as memory management, file formats and color modes, color corrections, using Photoshop with other applications, output, system issues, and more. Within each of these chapters you'll find sections dedicated to understanding and troubleshooting problem-prone areas related to the overall topic, including the most common problems encountered by virtually every user of the program.

And there's more to this package. *Photoshop Tech Support* includes a dual-platform CD-ROM featuring a searchable Adobe Acrobat version of the book along with numerous utilities, royalty-free art files, and product demos that will further increase your creative potential while decreasing the time you spend dealing with problems.

What's in the Book

You'll find these pages packed with problem-avoiding tips and techniques gleaned from years of real-world experience. The first two chapters serve as orientations to Photoshop setup and familiarization. Subsequent chapters bring to bear an extensive technical background and range of techniques to help you avoid the most common and vexing Photoshop problems.

Chapter 1, "Installing Adobe Photoshop," discusses Photoshop installation options and issues and how to avoid particular problems related to the installation (or reinstallation) process. It is valuable whether you're new to the application or are installing Photoshop 4 for the first time. Even if you have not experienced problems installing Photoshop, you may want to check out this chapter for an explanation of what exactly is installed by the Photoshop installation program, including complete file information. This chapter, coupled with the complete installation directories listed in Appendix B, should be very helpful in familiarizing you with all of the Photoshop components.

Chapter 2, "Adapting to Photoshop 4.0," covers the significant changes in Photoshop's latest revision—of which there are many. We have read a few reviews of Photoshop 4 saying that this version isn't really a major upgrade deserving of the new number, and that Adobe may as well have numbered this version Photoshop 3.5. We completely disagree with these statements. Adjustment layers alone present an enormous advancement in photo manipulation and warrant the upgrade price. Add to that the performance enhancements, and you can't go wrong with the new version, *unless* you get confused by all of the significant menu and tool changes. This chapter helps you get up to speed with *all* of the changes in version 4.

Chapter 3, "Avoiding Memory Problems," demonstrates how to avoid memory problems and provides some solutions when memory for a given job is limited. Regardless of the amount of RAM installed in your computer, Photoshop will always want more. Photoshop uses, and benefits from, as much memory as you can give it, and you can't have too much.

Chapter 4, "Dealing with Color Modes and File Formats," describes the different file formats and color modes found in Photoshop and shows how to avoid problems while getting predictable results. By understanding some of the key issues in this area, such as what happens when you combine a file format or color mode with a particular application or output device, you can avoid time-wasting glitches.

Chapter 5, "Achieving Good Color Correction," covers some basics we've picked up using Photoshop as a color correction tool. It discusses some of the problems to avoid and issues to consider when your final output is the printed document.

Chapter 6, "Avoiding Common Image Editing Problems," contains procedures and concepts that make working with Photoshop images easier and more productive, including the tricks and traps of working with selections, gradients, transparencies, and more.

Chapter 7, "Using Photoshop with Other Programs," examines some of the ways in which you can combine Photoshop and other applications with optimal efficiency and minimal hassle. Taken alone, both Photoshop and Adobe Illustrator are powerful programs providing a multitude of useful features, but in tandem they become even better—even more powerful. Still, using two or more programs together can also create unexpected problems.

Chapter 8, "Assuring Reliable Output," provides tips and techniques for avoiding many common printing problems related to transformed images, clipping paths, halftones, color separations, and corrupted files.

Chapter 9, "Macintosh System Errors," and **Chapter 10, "Windows System Errors,"** cover the most common error messages you can expect to encounter: what they mean and what to do about them. Eliminating possible OS problems or changing wrongly configured system settings can greatly enhance Photoshop's performance. And we all can use that, can't we?

Appendix A, "Organizing Your Files Our Way," addresses a crucial but often overlooked area—data tracking and management. In this appendix, we discuss how to create an organization scheme that will help you keep track of your data. Our recommendations can help you save time, work efficiently with other people in a department, and avoid some aggravating moments.

Appendix B, "Photoshop's Installation Folders and Files," presents a complete hierarchy of every file installed by Photoshop for both Macintosh and Windows.

Appendix C, "Designer's Guide to Digital Prepress," offers a road map to guide you through high-end print reproduction. If you follow the rules here, you may wind up saving time, money, and much frustration.

Appendix D, "About the CD-ROM," details the contents of the CD-ROM you'll find at the back of the book. (Read onward.)

What's on the CD-ROM

As we mentioned, this book also comes with a dual-platform CD-ROM, which includes a fully searchable, on-screen version of the book in Adobe Acrobat/PDF format. The CD-ROM also includes numerous utilities and exclusive software tools—actions; brushes; demos and tryouts from Adobe, Equilibrium, MetaTools, and others; Photoshop techniques, plug-ins, updaters, and utilities; Web bookmarks (containing pointers to a number of Photoshop-related Web sites); royalty-free images; Acrobat Reader; and more.

Cross-Platform Book Conventions

Photoshop is definitely a cross-platform application, with virtually identical tools and commands under both the Macintosh and Windows operating systems. This nearly seamless identity makes it easy for authors like us to write a book suitable for both Macintosh and Windows users—which we've attempted to do. Where appropriate, we've noted specific Macintosh and Windows issues where they occur, which is mostly in the areas of file formats and operating systems. Throughout the book we've primarily used Macintosh-based screen shots, with a few Windows examples included when what you see in Windows is significantly different from what you see on the Macintosh.

The major difference between working in the Macintosh environment and in the Windows environment lies in the key commands used to invoke certain tools and operations. Happily, there are equivalent keys on either system:

Macintosh Key	Windows Key
Command	Ctrl
Option	Alt

Wherever we give specific key commands throughout the book, we use the convention *Macintosh key/Windows key,* as in "Command/Ctrl+A."

The Goal

Our goal in all of this is to save your time, money, and sanity when working in Photoshop. We've worked for years in high-pressure, deadline-sensitive environments where technical hassles can sometimes get in the way of creativity and efficiency. We know from experience how one or two solid, proven precautions can be worth their weight in gold, so we've tried to provide a book full of them here. We're confident that you'll find some nuggets in these pages.

ACKNOWLEDGMENTS

Ken Oyer would also like to thank Adobe for their continual assistance, without which this book would not have been possible. Don Day at Adobe was always available with the answers to all of our questions. A special thanks goes out to one of my coauthors, Sean Cavanaugh. This is the second project that we have collaborated on, and I know I couldn't have done either one without him. I hope we still have a few more books in us. I would like to thank IDG Books Worldwide for the opportunity to create such a book. Finally, I would like to thank my two children, Taylor and Megan, for allowing Dad to dip into their play time and go write a book. Now we can go to the park.

Sean Cavanaugh would like to thank all the cool people at Adobe for developing such great products and for providing us with so much assistance. Especially Don Day, Photoshop support guru extraordinaire. Thanks also to the IDG Books editorial staff — in particular Stefan Grünwedel, the development editor for this book — and to my agent Margot Maley at Waterside Productions.

Ted Padova wishes to extend his appreciation to the following companies and individuals who assisted him in contributing to this book: Ray Hennessy of Applied Concepts and Christopher Zsarnay of Z-Studios, who contributed images for the color plate section; Sandy Fox for her artwork contribution in the color plate section; Tony Hallas for his outstanding photography and Michael Bacon for his digital imaging work, both of which are contained in the color plate section; Kirk Lyford of Vivid Details for contributing stock images and contents for the CD-ROM; and Andromeda Software for their generous contribution of filter samples included on the CD-ROM.

CONTENTS AT A GLANCE

CONTENTS

CHAPTER ONE

INSTALLING
ADOBE PHOTOSHOP

If you're about to install Adobe Photoshop, this chapter will offer you some invaluable advice. If, on the other hand, you're new to Photoshop but you have already installed it, you may still wish to review this chapter. Installation poses some alternatives that affect the final configuration or that you must evaluate to avoid particular problems related to the installation or reinstallation process itself. This chapter deals with Photoshop installation options and issues. Even if you have not experienced problems installing Photoshop, you may want to read on to learn what exactly is installed by the Photoshop installation program.

Preparing for the Installation

The Adobe Photoshop installation process is streamlined and efficient. The install program options are fairly obvious, and errors and incompatibility problems with it are rare. In fact, it's a fairly safe bet that if you are experiencing difficulty *installing* Adobe Photoshop, you will run into problems *using* it. Before running the install program, you should ask yourself the following questions:

Do I have enough memory?

Photoshop is the mother of all memory hogs in your computing universe. Your first encounter with memory issues comes with the installation process. You need to be certain that you have enough hard drive space to install the program, as well as enough to work on your Photoshop files. We'll briefly mention the former problem in this chapter, and we've devoted Chapter 3 to discussions related to memory requirements when working in Photoshop.

The first memory issue to be aware of is that Photoshop requires approximately three to five times the amount of free hard disk space as that the image file you are working with takes up. Therefore, if you are working with a 10MB file, be certain to have 30–50MB free. As a matter of habit, you should always plan on having five times the file size available. After you install Photoshop, double-check your hard drive for the amount of free space. If you know the file sizes of the images you edit, then be certain that five times the largest of those values is available.

Do I have enough disk space?

A full installation requires approximately 45 megabytes of free hard disk space. Of course, you will need more than 45MB of free space to actually install and *use* Photoshop, but the exact amount varies according to the sizes of the images with which you are working.

You can better free up space and avoid memory problems by using larger-capacity external storage devices. If you are a new Photoshop user and don't have an external storage drive, your first purchase should be such a device. The most affordable of these devices is the Iomega Zip Drive. You can purchase a Zip drive for less than $200 and use cartridges capable of holding 100 megabytes of data. The cartridges themselves run less than $20 for the 100MB capacity disks. If you are a Mac user, you will inevitably purchase a SCSI Zip drive. As a Windows user, you have a choice of using a SCSI drive, for which you'll need a SCSI adapter card, or a parallel drive that can be plugged into your parallel port. If you're a serious Photoshop user who frequently edits large files, you will find that the parallel interface is extremely slow, and you will be much better off with the SCSI drive.

Other types of storage devices include SyQuest drives, Iomega Bernoulli drives, Iomega Jaz drives, and optical and tape backup systems. The serious Photoshop user may wish to opt for the Iomega Jaz Drive, which holds up to one gigabyte of storage. The drive and cartridges are more costly than the Zip but can be a real time saver when you are transporting large documents to the local service center.

Regardless of which external device you use, you have several options for space conservation on your local hard drive. You can back up less frequently used applications to a cartridge and free up your local hard drive space, keep large data files on external cartridges, or work on a Photoshop file from the external media. If this last approach is absolutely necessary, a word of caution is needed. Many of the newer drives are manufactured with energy conservation mechanisms that power down the drive when it is idle for any given period of time. Some manufacturers offer software controls to determine the idle period. If you work on a Photoshop file from an external drive, be certain to set the power-off period to never or an hour or more. You can run into problems if the drive powers down while you're working and you then wish to save your file or perform some operation requiring writing to the disk. At the least, it will take much more time to first power up the mechanism and then perform a save or an edit. But note that saving to removable media or over a network is not recommended. Whenever possible, always first save to a local hard drive and then copy the file somewhere else if need be.

Do I have the serial number handy?

You won't need your serial number to install Photoshop, but you will need it to complete the online registration (which is optional), as well as to start Photoshop for the first time. The serial number is printed on the registration card and on the title page of the *User Guide*. (The number on the outside of the box is not the complete serial number.)

You can also use serial numbers from previous versions of Photoshop (such as version 3.0), in case you've misplaced your version 4 serial number or *User Guide*. For this reason, you may want to write the serial number on the CD jacket.

Do I have the next five minutes free?

Depending on the speed of your computer and CD-ROM drive, the installation requires between three and five minutes, longer if you plan on registering online.

Am I prepared to restart the computer after running install?

The full Photoshop installation, which includes the Kodak PhotoCD color management system, requires that you restart your computer when it has finished. Be sure to quit any open applications before running the install program.

If you are performing a custom install, a restart may not be required.

Do I want to register Photoshop electronically?

To register Photoshop online, you will need your serial number handy, and of course, you will also need a modem connection. The registration program configures your modem automatically, and the number it dials is toll-free, so you have little left to worry about besides making sure that your modem is connected to your computer and a phone line, and that it is turned on.

If for some reason you cannot register online, the problem is most likely with your modem connection or phone line. Make sure your modem is connected to your computer, that the phone lines are properly connected, and that the modem is turned on. Online registration can be completed at a later time — you don't have to complete it immediately following Photoshop installation. You don't have to complete it at all for that matter. You can always send in your registration card via snail mail, or you can fax the form to Adobe Systems. Do register, however, as this is the only way you'll qualify for technical support and future upgrades.

Installing Photoshop

The Photoshop CD-ROM comes with installers specifically tailored to your computer's processor, whether you're working on a Macintosh or a PC.

Choosing the appropriate installer: Macintosh

You probably know whether your Mac uses a 68K processor or a PowerPC processor (we hope you do anyway — if you don't, choose the Easy Install option), but what is the "universal" option, you ask. The universal application contains code for both 68K and PowerPC Macs. It can run on either platform. Universal applications are also referred to as *fat binary* applications, and they are always larger in file size than 68K-only applications. In fact, they're about the same size as the PowerPC applications, in this case about 9.8MB.

So why would you want to install a universal application?

Say you have a 68K Mac — a Quadra 950, for example — that has been upgraded to a PowerPC using a removable add-in board such as the DayStar PowerPro 601. If there's a chance that the board will not permanently reside in your machine (perhaps you share it with other users), this may mean that your Mac is sometimes a 68K machine and sometimes a PowerPC. In such a scenario, you would be wise to install the universal version of Photoshop because you could run it regardless of whether the PowerPC upgrade board was installed in your 950 or not.

Network administrators may also consider installing the universal version on networks used by both 68K and PowerPC Macs.

Choosing the appropriate installer: Windows

If you're a Windows user, you don't need to be concerned with the type of Photoshop application that will be installed. In 32-bit environments such as Windows 95 and Windows NT, or 16-bit operating environments such as Windows 3.1, the Photoshop installer will detect your operating system and install the appropriate files. When you are installing Photoshop from the CD, a startup installer screen will automatically appear. If you do not have a CD and are installing Photoshop from floppies, use the Windows Explorer or Program Manager to locate the Setup.exe file on Disk 1 and double-click the mouse button. The installer will proceed and prompt you to insert the series of disks during the installation.

Easy Install versus Custom Install

After you've started the program named "Install Adobe Photoshop 4.0" from the CD drive, your next step is to decide whether to use the Easy Install or Custom Install option. Windows users will have a choice between the *Typical Install, Compact,* or *Custom.* So which one should you use?

Easy Install

We recommend the Easy Install option for the Mac, or Typical Install for Windows, if this is the first time you are installing Photoshop.

For the Macintosh, choose Easy Install (as shown in Figure 1-1) to let the installer decide the appropriate application — 68K or PowerPC — for the Mac users. The Easy Install option knows what type of processor you have and installs the appropriate application for it. In other words, if you have a Quadra 840AV, for instance, it won't install the PowerPC application, but rather the 68K application.

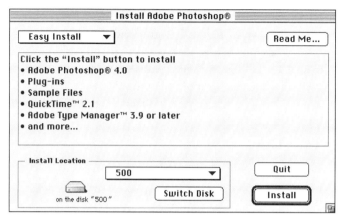

Figure 1-1
The Adobe Photoshop installation program has this appearance
with the Easy Install option selected.

Here's what Easy Install actually installs:

- The Adobe Photoshop application for your Mac (or Windows machine)
- A Read Me file
- The SimpleText application (Mac only, Windows users can read the Read Me files with Windows Notepad)
- All plug-ins
- Sample and tutorial files
- The Goodies folder; Windows users will notice separate folders for the contents of the Mac Goodies folder, which include brushes, calibrate, patterns, plug-ins, and more
- Photoshop help files
- An HTML document linking to the Adobe Web site (and a folder of Photoshop GIF files so that you can view the Photoshop Web page without having to connect to the Adobe site)
- Kodak Photo CD files (Mac only): CMSCP and KPCMS folders (installed in your System folder), Kodak extensions (installed in the System folder's Extensions subfolder), and Kodak Precision Startup (installed in the System folder's Startup Items subfolder)

If you do not want all of these items installed, choose the Custom Install option. The Custom Install lets you install only those items you want or need. For example, if you want to install only the Photoshop application, that is, if you don't want to install the Kodak Photo CD files, the tutorial or sample files, and so on, choose the Custom Install option.

Custom Install

Choose the Custom Install option (shown in Figure 1-2) to decide for yourself those items you want to install. Photoshop enables you to choose whether you wish to install all the elements or selected items. Choose this method if you wish to bypass installing help files, specific filters, Adobe Type Manager, or other such supplements. This installation method enables you to reduce the hard disk requirements by not installing all Photoshop components.

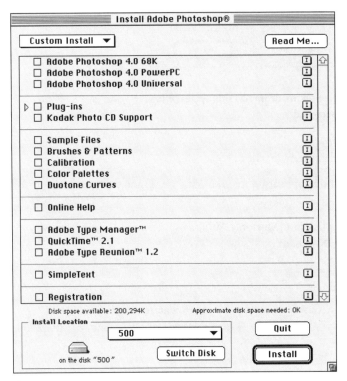

Figure 1-2
The Adobe Photoshop installation program shows the Custom Install option selected.

Designating a Directory or Folder for Installation

Whether you perform an Easy Install or a Custom Install, the installer application provides you with an opportunity to designate the folder or subdirectory on your hard drive to receive the Photoshop folder. In the Install Location section of the installer dialog, a pop-up menu will, by default, display the name of your hard drive. Clicking the pop-up menu will enable you to choose the item Select Folder. When you choose Select Folder, a dialog box appears, enabling you to designate where the Photoshop folder will be installed. We have folders on our hard drives entitled Applications, and all our programs are placed in this folder. It's a good idea to keep all your application files in a folder separate from your data files.

In Windows, Photoshop installs itself into a default directory on your hard drive. You may override this by clicking the Browse button and selecting another directory or typing in a new path.

Entering Serial or Registration Numbers

If you buy a full version of Photoshop and not one that was upgraded from an earlier version of the program, the registration card inside the box should list the serial number. Type this number into the program when you install it. This becomes the number that is registered to this copy of Photoshop.

If you are upgrading from an earlier full version of the program, then you simply use the old serial number. This is when you really need an organized system of tracking your serial numbers for all your programs. We know a few people who open their new software, install it, and then never even keep track of the installation disks, let alone the serial number. This is not the best of practices. When we install new software, the disks are always handled with care and placed back in the original box that they came in. You can also choose to put all original disks in one place for easy access. Either system is fine, but most importantly, keep track of your disks and serial numbers. They may be used for future versions of the software, as is Photoshop.

On your registration card you may see the expression "PS40V." This is not a serial number of any kind. Adobe uses it for tracking purposes.

Upgrading from a Limited Edition (LE) version of Photoshop is slightly different than for a full version. LE serial numbers do not work for full versions of Photoshop. When you upgrade, inform your vendor that you have an LE version of Photoshop and that you need a Photoshop box that has a new serial number inside. Some vendors may not understand that Adobe has this upgrade policy, so be persistent.

By all means, fill out the registration card and send it to Adobe. Registering Photoshop will give you a couple of nice things. First, if you have purchased a full version, registration entitles you to 90 days of phone technical support. If you have purchased an upgrade, you get 30 days of phone support. The clock starts ticking after your first call.

After registering you also get information back from Adobe concerning upgrades and incremental bug-fix versions ("maintenance releases"). Adobe, in our opinion, has always released fairly clean first-round versions of their software. But even under the best of conditions, bugs do get out. When you register, Adobe will be able to inform you about version updates as they become available. If you are connected to the Internet, you should be able to simply download the update file and run it on your current version. Usually the entire process takes about 10–15 minutes. Gone are the days of calling tech support only to be put on hold for a half an hour to ask for the upgrade and then waiting another three to five days for the disks to come in the mail. And sometimes waiting another week after you send them back to get a new set of disks because they sent you the wrong disks.

You also have the option to register your copy of Photoshop immediately using your modem. After installation is complete, the installer program will automatically ask you if you wish to register by modem, as Figure 1-3 shows. If you do have a modem, this is probably the easiest way to register Photoshop.

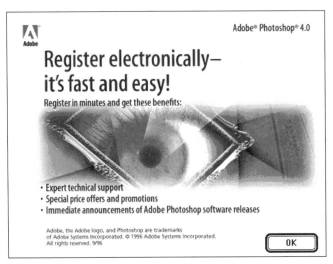

Figure 1-3
If you choose to register Photoshop via your modem, you will
be presented with this screen. Just follow the on-screen
instructions and the program will do the rest.

If you don't choose to register Photoshop in this manner, the installer program informs you that it will remind you after 14 days to register your copy. In order for the reminder to appear after 14 days, a file is placed in the Startup Items folder in your System folder. If you don't want to be reminded, you can trash this file without any fear of performance problems. (This applies to Macintosh users only.)

Files Installed by Adobe Photoshop

Regardless of whether you choose the Custom Install option or the Easy Install option, this section describes files installed on your computer by the Photoshop installer. Depending on whether you have a Macintosh or a PC, these folders may appear in a slightly different arrangement than what you read about here (shown in Figure 1-4).

Adobe Photoshop 4
The file named Adobe Photoshop 4 is the Photoshop application itself.

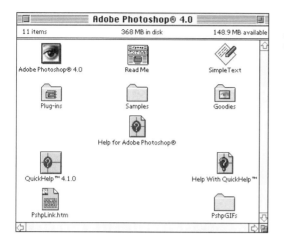

Figure 1-4
A typical Photoshop 4 Macintosh folder shows all items installed.

ReadMe

ReadMe is a SimpleText or Windows Notepad file that contains information about new features, plug-ins, performance issues, and known conflicts with other programs. Required reading for all.

SimpleText

SimpleText is a bare-bones Macintosh text editor of which you probably already have 37 copies. No Windows equivalent is installed.

The Plug-ins folder

Adobe Photoshop installs a whole host of helpful plug-ins.

THE COLORSYNC FOLDER ColorSync is a Mac-only folder. Any applications that involve color in managing their files can hook into the ColorSync Support plug-in.

THE DIGIMARC FOLDER Digimarc is a new plug-in for Photoshop 4. It actually consists of three plug-ins: Embed Watermark, Read Watermark, and Detect Watermark (the last of these can be added manually). Digimarc allows an artist to embed invisible copyright information into images. When a copyrighted image is opened, the plug-in notifies the user that the image has copyright information associated with it. The user can then go to the Digimarc Web site (www.digimarc.com, shown in Figure 1-5) and obtain information about the artist and instructions concerning usage rights for that image.

The digital watermark embedded by the Digimarc plug-in is imperceptible to the human eye and in no way harms the image. Supposedly, the information stays intact even if the image is edited, printed, and rescanned.

Figure 1-5
The Digimarc Web site leads users to information about registered
artwork and instructions for using their copyrighted images.

THE DISPLACEMENT MAPS FOLDER Photoshop places 12 different files in the
Displacement Maps folder to be used as displacement maps. When you choose Filter ⇨
Distort ⇨ Displace, a dialog box appears where you enter parameters specifying how the
image is to be distorted. You're then prompted to select a file, normally referred to as a
displacement map, which distorts the image. Any file except a bitmap file can be used as a
displacement map. Photoshop supplies you with 12 starter files to use or practice with.

THE EFFECTS FOLDER Here is where you will find all the special-effect style filters such as Charcoal, Dry Brush, Glowing Edges, and Neon Paper. Photoshop installs a total of 47 effects filters in this folder. Most of them are new to version 4. The new ones are slightly modified versions of filters previously known as *Adobe Gallery Effects*.

THE EXTENSIONS FOLDER The Extensions folder contains some specialized utilities, depending on your hardware accessories or system capabilities. For instance, Windows color management is handled here, through the Kodak KPCMS system plug-in Ccms.8bx.

DirectBits The DirectBits plug-in was developed by Adobe to accelerate the drawing of paths in Photoshop. The plug-in is not automatically loaded because it may be incompatible with some video cards. If you experience slow performance using the pen tool, install this plug-in to see if it improves performance. To install the DirectBits plug-in, drag the plug-in into the Plug-ins folder. To disable the plug-in, drag it back into its original folder.

DirectCursors The DirectCursors plug-in improves the display of some cursors, making them easier to see. If you notice that a cursor is difficult to see, try loading this plug-in. To load DirectCursors, make sure Photoshop is not currently running. If you have an old version of DirectCursors, trash it and then copy the new version into the DirectCursors folder located within the Extensions folder inside the Plug-ins folder. The next time you open Photoshop, DirectCursors will be active. Photoshop installs this plug-in by default. For Mac users, if you wish to deactivate DirectCursors, place an Option+L character (¬) at the beginning of the folder. The next time you restart Photoshop, it will not install DirectCursors. (No equivalent Windows plug-in exists.)

Multiprocessor Extension The Multiprocessor Extension plug-in is for those lucky few who have computers with more than one processor. Multiprocessor computers utilize two or more CPUs to make Photoshop run faster. This plug-in enables Photoshop to use multiple CPUs if they are present in your system. By default the plug-in is loaded and ready to use. In Windows it's named "Mthread.8bx."

Pressure Support If you are using a graphics tablet such as a Wacom tablet, you need this plug-in to take advantage of the pressure sensitivity of your pen. Pressure-sensitive tools such as the airbrush will change opacity or brush size as you press softer or harder with the pen tip on the tablet. The clone tool is another tool that takes good advantage of pressure sensitivity. By default the plug-in is loaded and ready to use.

Enable Async I/O Using the Enable Async I/O plug-in enables asynchronous file handling and will improve file reading and writing performance. According to the Read Me file associated with the plug-in, it will increase performance on AV and PowerMac computers as well as 68040 machines. This pretty much covers all the Macintosh models that are running Photoshop. The Read Me file also covers such other conditions as system software versions that need to be present in order for this plug-in to work properly. To install the plug-in, remove the Option+L character (¬) at the beginning of the folder name. The next time you open Photoshop the plug-in will be active. To disable it, place an Option+L character (¬) at the beginning of the folder.

Using GWorld Memory GWorld Memory is a type of memory that resides on some video boards and that can accelerate the speed at which graphics are drawn on screen. Screen drawing responsibilities are handled by the video board rather than transferred to the computer, resulting in increased performance. If your video board has GWorld Memory, install this plug-in by removing the Option+L character (¬) before the folder name. The next time you start Photoshop, the plug-in will be installed. How do you know if your video board uses GWorld Memory? Good question, unfortunately the answer is less than scientific: if the video board is compatible, it won't crash when you start Photoshop with the GWorld Memory plug-in enabled; if it doesn't crash, it probably uses compatible GWorld memory. This plug-in is disabled by default.

THE FILE FORMAT FOLDER Photoshop is frequently called upon to open and save images in a multitude of file formats. This is part of Photoshop's appeal. The plug-ins stored in the File Format folder extend Photoshop's ability to write and/or read file types beyond the standard formats (Photoshop binary, EPS, JPEG, PICT, TIFF, PDF, and Scitex). If you know that you will never need to open a Pixar file, for example, then you can remove that plug-in from the folder.

TIP It's a good idea to scan through your plug-ins and remove or disable the ones you don't need. Photoshop loads faster with fewer plug-ins installed.

The Kodak Photo CD Folder A folder containing the Kodak Photo CD plug-in is stored in the Plug-ins File Format subfolder. We suggest that you read the accompanying Read Me file if you plan on editing Kodak Photo CD files in Photoshop. Photoshop can read (but not write) Photo CD files.

The Photoshop installation program places additional Kodak files in your Extensions and Startup Items folders within the System folder. Consult the Read Me file for more info about these files.

To open a Kodak Photo CD image, follow these steps:

1. Double-click Photoshop to open it.

2. Select File ⇨ Open.

3. Select any Photo CD image from the Images folder that is stored in the Photo CD folder, and click Open. The plug-in looks for the appropriate precision transform from the KPCMS database. The Kodak CMS Photo CD plug-in dialog appears and gives you a thumbnail of the image.

4. Select the appropriate options in the Kodak CMS Photo CD plug-in dialog box and click OK.

You have several options for managing plug-ins. We suggest creating a new folder named "Plug-ins (Disabled)" inside the Photoshop folder (not inside the Plug-ins folder but on the same level, as you can see we've done in Figure 1-6) to store all unneeded plug-ins.

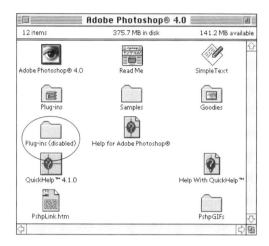

Figure 1-6
Create a folder named "Plug-ins (disabled)" to store those plug-ins you don't want loaded when Photoshop starts up.

Photoshop 4 abandoned some file formats from previous versions of the program and with good reason. Such formats as MacPaint and Amiga IFF are not installed with the new version. If for some rare reason you wish to have access to these formats, you can find them on the version 4 CD-ROM in the Other Goodies folder.

If you are a Mac user, Now Startup Manager 7.0 (from Now Software) allows you to install and uninstall Photoshop plug-ins just as if they were system control panels and extensions (see Figure 1-7).

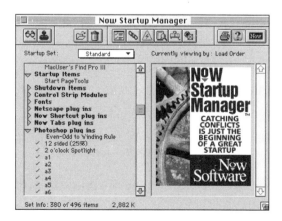

Figure 1-7
Now Startup Manager lets you enable and disable Photoshop plug-ins with a click of the mouse.

MANAGING
PHOTOSHOP
PLUG-INS

(continued)

As a Windows user, you can use the Explorer to locate the Formats subdirectory of the Plugins directory (see Figure 1-8). Like the Mac users, you can create a new directory, label it Disabled, and store all your unused formats there. Regardless of the platform, don't trash the files. You may never need the formats you disable until that one day after you trash them, when someone will want you to export in the format that no longer is available.

Figure 1-8
Windows Explorer enables you to disable plug-ins by relocating them from the Format's folder into a folder called Disabled.

MANAGING PHOTOSHOP PLUG-INS
(continued)

THE FILTERS FOLDER The Filters folder contains more image-modifying plug-ins, such as Crystallize, Extrude, and Pointillize. We really don't know why some plug-ins are stored here rather than in the Effects folder, but we assume Adobe has its reasons. We should talk about two folders inside the Filters folder: Distortions and Displacement Maps. Distortions include nine plug-ins that perform certain types of distortions to an image; among them are Pinch and ZigZag. Displace is also in this list; it's the plug-in that utilizes displacement maps. The second folder contains the Lighting FX plug-in. This plug-in can perform really cool lighting effects on your image. It takes some getting used to but is definitely worth the effort. Inside the folder is another folder that contains some predefined settings for the plug-in to start out with. You can load these settings and then change anything you see fit.

THE IMPORT / EXPORT FOLDER The Import/Export folder contains modules that allow you to open and save certain files that are not found in the standard file formats. Here is a description of each:

■ **Anti-Aliased PICT** imports PICT files from programs like Canvas or MacDraw. It converts the PICT file to an antialiased (smoothed edge) Photoshop file (see Figure 1-9). Since this reads the entire image into memory, some large PICT files may not import in low-memory environments. If the file doesn't import, quit Photoshop, allocate more memory to the program, and try again.

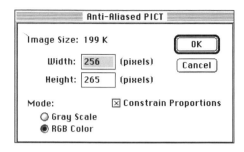

Figure 1-9
The Anti-Aliased PICT dialog box enables you to smooth edges for imported PICT files.

■ **GIF89a** lets you create an 8-bit (256-color) indexed GIF file from any RGB image (see Figure 1-10). GIF files are mostly used for creating images for the Web. This format differs considerably from the CompuServe GIF format found under File ⇨ Save ⇨ CompuServe GIF. The GIF89a format allows you to use selection masks and multiple color selections for creating transparency.

Figure 1-10
The GIF89a Export dialog box provides you with file exports for Web formats, including interlacing and transparency

■ **Paths to Illustrator** allows you to transfer paths back and forth from Photoshop to Illustrator. You can do this by simply copying the desired path to the clipboard in one program and then pasting the path into the other program. When you export a path using this module, Photoshop creates an Illustrator file with the same name as the original Photoshop file but with the .ai extension so that you can open it in Illustrator (as shown in Figure 1-11). The cool thing about this module is that if you have multiple paths in Photoshop, you can export them all at once. This does three things. It exports them all with one command, saving you from having to copy and paste them separately. It saves them with the same bounding box relative to the Photoshop file. It also saves the paths' positions relative to one another. In other words, the positioning of each path is the same in the Illustrator file as it was in Photoshop.

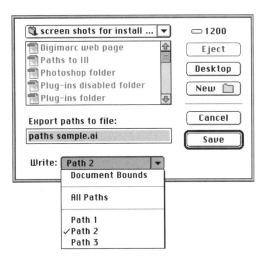

Figure 1-11
The Export Paths dialog box allows you to export paths to Adobe Illustrator.

■ **PICT Resource** is an import module that allows you to grab images from within programs or documents (see Figure 1-12). An example would be a splash or startup screen for a program.

Figure 1-12
PICT Resource export options enable you to create files for start-up screens on the Macintosh.

■ **Quick Edit** is both an import module and an export module (see Figure 1-13). Quick Edit features the ability to open a small portion of a large file, work on just that portion of the image, and save it back into the large file. The original file must be a Photoshop 2.0, Scitex CT, or uncompressed TIFF image for this to work.

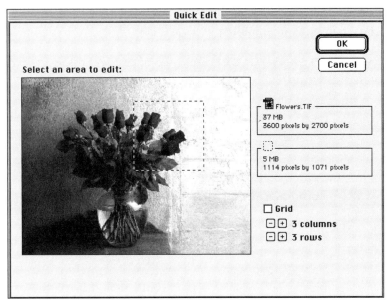

Figure 1-13
**The Quick Edit dialog box allows you to edit small portions of a larger
document area.**

- **TWAIN** (Technology Without an Important Name) is an interface for
  capturing images from digital cameras, scanners, and video frame grabbers. In
  order for it to work properly, the manufacturer of the scanner or frame grabber
  should provide you with a TWAIN data source and a Source Manager.
  Photoshop supports TWAIN, TWAIN32, and TWAIN_32 standards for
  scanning.

THE PARSER FOLDER These modules work in conjunction with the Place command under the File menu. The Adobe Illustrator Paths Parser allows you to open,
place, paste, or drag and drop Illustrator files. After you have placed the image, you can
size, position, and rotate it any way you wish. To complete the Place process, double-
click anywhere inside the bounding box of the image or press Enter. The image will
now be rasterized. Be aware that as you place files in this manner, Photoshop automatically creates a new layer for every new image. The EPS Parser does the same thing with
generic EPS files.

THE SAMPLES FOLDER The Samples folder contains images developed by Adobe
for learning and experimenting with Photoshop.

THE TUTORIAL FOLDER You will need these files to complete "A Quick Tour of
Adobe Photoshop," found in Chapter 1 of the *User Guide*. Other tutorial files are on
the Tutorial CD that came with Photoshop.

THE GOODIES FOLDER Goodies is apparently Adobe's word for Miscellaneous. The Goodies folder contains four other folders:

THE BRUSHES AND PATTERNS FOLDER Four sets of custom brushes are here for you to load into the brush palette:

- **Custom Brushes** contains a basic set of brushes in various sizes and densities, as shown in Figure 1-14.

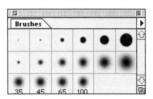

Figure 1-14
Custom brushes contains a basic set of brushes in several sizes and densities.

- **Assorted Brushes** contains an assortment of brushes in various shapes and textures (see Figure 1-15). Some, like the starbursts, are very useful.

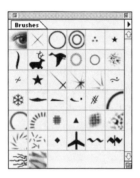

Figure 1-15
Assorted brushes is a set of many textures and icons provided by Adobe when Photoshop is installed.

- **Drop Shadow Brushes** can be used to create drop shadows for boxes using the brush tool (see Figure 1-16).

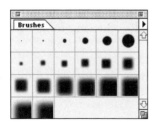

Figure 1-16
Drop Shadow brushes are used to create drop shadows with geometric selections.

- **Square Brushes** contains a series of square brushes instead of the traditional round brushes (see Figure 1-17).

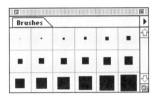

Figure 1-17
Square brushes is an alternative to the default round brush shapes.

- There is a folder on the CD named Ken's Brushes that contains 18 hard-edged and 18 soft-edged brushes ranging from 1 pixel to 300 pixels in size (see Figure 1-18). These brushes were created by Ken Oyer.

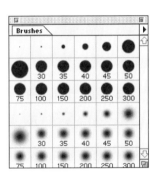

Figure 1-18
Ken's Brushes is a custom set we've included on the CD-ROM.

The PostScript Patterns Folder Adobe supplies 21 Illustrator files that contain unique PostScript patterns for you to use in Photoshop. These files are small patterns (shown in Figure 1-19) that can be tiled together in Photoshop to create large patterns. To use the patterns, follow these steps:

1. In Photoshop, select File ➪ Open.

2. Select one of the 21 PostScript patterns and click Open.

3. In the next dialog box, you can adjust the options to change the size and resolution of the PostScript pattern before you rasterize it. Once you have set up the options click OK.

4. The PostScript pattern will now be opened into a Photoshop file. Select all the text and choose Edit ➪ Define Pattern. This saves the pattern into a buffer for later use.

5. Select the area of the image in which you want to place the pattern. Select Edit ➪ Fill. In the Fill dialog box set Use to Pattern, set the appropriate Blending options, and click OK.

NOTE Any selection can be filled with a pattern. To fill the entire document window, however, you can eliminate a selection. When you choose Fill Pattern from the Fill dialog box without a selection marquee, Photoshop will fill the entire document area.

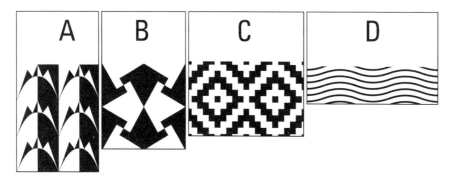

Figure 1-19
Various fill patterns are available: (a) Deco, (b) India, (c) Mayan bricks, (d) Waves.

THE CALIBRATION FOLDER Calibration begins with monitor adjustments using the Gamma control panel. As a Windows user, find gamma adjustments by choosing File ⇨ Color Settings ⇨ Monitor Setup. In the Monitor Setup dialog box notice the button designated Calibrate. When you click the Calibrate button, a dialog box will appear similar to the Mac Gamma control panel device (see Figure 1-20 for the Windows version, Figure 1-21 for the Mac). Mac users need to move this device out of the Photoshop folder after installation and place it in the Control Panels folder.

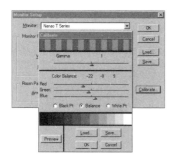

Figure 1-20
Windows gamma control is contained in the Monitor Setup dialog box.

Figure 1-21
The Macintosh Gamma control panel is located in the Control Panels folder.

The three files in this folder — CMYK Colors, Olé No Moiré, and Lab Colors — are also used for monitor calibration. The Photoshop 4 CD includes a high-resolution version of the Olé No Moiré file that can assist you in your monitor calibration. The file can be found in the Other Goodies folder on the CD inside the Calibration folder.

THE COLOR LIBRARIES FOLDER Photoshop provides nine custom color libraries you can use for picking colors. The definitions for these color libraries are stored in the Color Libraries folder. To pick from a custom color library, click once on either the foreground or background color in the toolbox. In the Color Picker click the Custom button on the right. The Custom Colors dialog box appears (see Figure 1-22). Click the Book pop-up menu and select the color library you want to use. The color bar that runs vertically can be used to pick a certain hue. Then you can choose the exact color you want from the list on the left. See the *User Guide* for more information concerning the different custom color libraries.

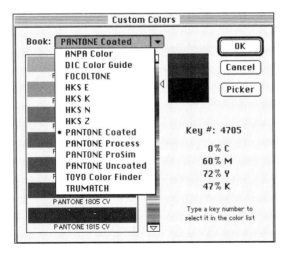

Figure 1-22
Custom Colors dialog box enables you to load many different color libraries.

THE DUOTONE PRESETS FOLDER Duotones are images that use color and grayscale information to increase the tonal range of a grayscale file. Since a printing press can represent about 50 levels of gray and a grayscale image can handle up to 256 levels of gray, a grayscale image will lose some detail when printed using only black ink. A duotone uses the grayscale and one or more colors to represent the image. Using two or more colors for printing an image increases the number of gray levels being represented and therefore increases the amount of detail.

Adobe has developed a series of files that represent varying presets for duotones, tritones, and quadtones. There are three folders in the Duotone Presets folder, one for each of the three types of duotones. Within each of those folders, duotones are further broken down into three more categories: Gray, Pantone, and Process presets. To use one of these presets, follow these instructions:

1. In Photoshop, create a grayscale image.

2. Change the Image Mode to Duotone by selecting Image ⇨ Mode ⇨ Duotone.

3. In the Duotone Options dialog box (shown in Figure 1-23), click the Type pop-up menu and select Duotone. Then click the Load button on the right.

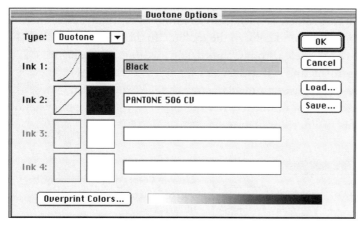

Figure 1-23
The Duotone Options dialog box controls duotone values and curves.

4. Find the Duotone Presets folder inside the Goodies folder and select the Duotones folder. Then select the Process Duotones folder.

5. In that folder you will find a number of different files representing presets of duotone settings. Select any one of the files and click Open.

6. The Duotone Options dialog box changes to reflect the presets it found in the file you selected. Click OK to apply these presets to your image.

This is just a sampling of how to work with duotones. For more information about duotones and how to work with them, see the section on duotones in Chapter 6.

Help Files

Three files are associated with the Help system in Photoshop: Help for Adobe Photoshop (Figure 1-24), QuickHelp 4.1.0 (Figure 1-25), and Help With QuickHelp. Run the QuickHelp application and open the Help for Adobe Photoshop file for online help.

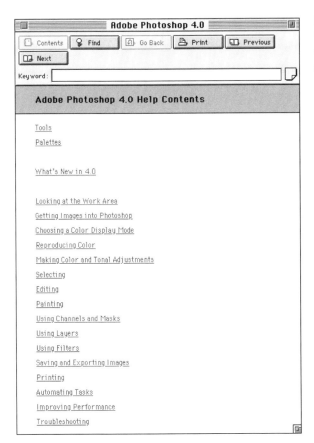

Figure 1-24
The Help dialog box comes up when running the QuickHelp application.

PshpGIFs

The 20 files in the PshpGIFs folder are resource files used when you access the Photoshop Web page. They really don't do anything else. Take a look at them if you are interested in Web page graphics.

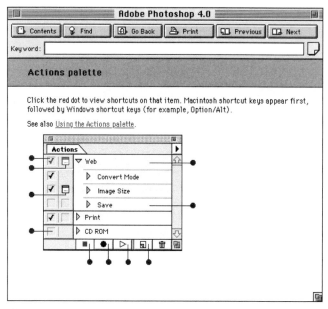

Figure 1-25
The Quick Help dialog box appears when launching the
QuickHelp application program.

If You Have Installer Problems

If for any reason the installation program fails to run properly, try the following measures:

- Restart your computer with no programs, utilities, extensions, or control panels running. You will need to load your CD driver, but you can disable other extensions and control panels using the Extensions Manager. Try running the Photoshop installer again.

- Copy the Photoshop 4 Disk Images folder to the hard drive and reboot the computer with extensions off (Shift+Restart for the Mac) or in Safe Mode (for Windows 95). Then run the installation from the files on the hard drive. (Safe Mode entails selecting Start ⇨ Shut Down ⇨ Restart the Computer and then pressing F8 when you see the message "Starting Windows 95.")

- Try installing Photoshop on another machine. If the problem persists, the Photoshop CD itself may need replacement. Contact Adobe for a replacement CD.

For a complete listing of all installed files, see Appendix B.

New in Photoshop is the ability to link to the Photoshop information on the World Wide Web. To go to this page directly from Photoshop, select About Photoshop from the Apple menu or the Windows Help menu (or click the graphic at the top of the tool box) and then click the Adobe icon in the upper-left corner of the dialog box shown in Figure 1-26. The first time you access the Web page (called PshpLink.htm on your hard drive), Photoshop prompts you to identify your Web browser. If you have Netscape Navigator, Microsoft Internet Explorer, or some other browser, you can navigate to the folder or directory and select the browser you use. Each subsequent time you access Adobe's Web site (shown in Figure 1-27), the browser is automatically launched. If you have your browser configured to connect to the World Wide Web automatically, you are connected directly to Adobe's Photoshop page.

Figure 1-26
The Adobe Photoshop splash screen provides a web link to Adobe's Web site.

(continued)

**LINKING
TO THE
PHOTOSHOP
WEB PAGE**

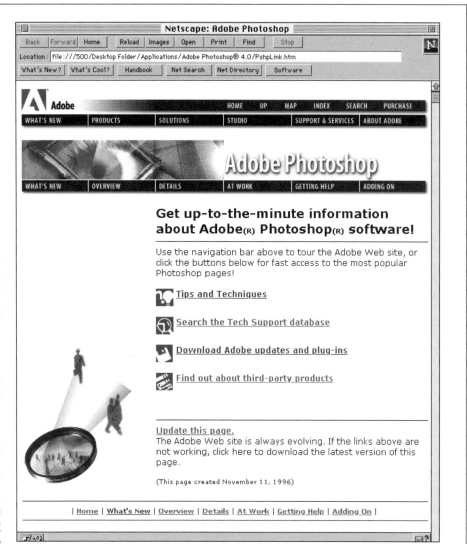

Figure 1-27
The Adobe Systems Web site provides updates and tips for Photoshop users.

CHAPTER TWO

ADAPTING TO
PHOTOSHOP 4.0

If you are familiar with Photoshop 3.*x* and you've just upgraded or are thinking of upgrading to Photoshop 4.0, read this chapter carefully. Here we get you up to speed on the interface and functional changes in version 4.0. Some are minor differences, but most are quite significant. A few of them drastically change the way you work with the program.

This chapter will discuss some of the more important changes experienced in the upgrade. We'll also point out many of the advantages that make upgrading to Photoshop 4.0 worthwhile.

Menus and Tools

Context-sensitive menus are a very powerful new feature in Photoshop. Basically this feature presents you with a pop-up menu when you hold down the Ctrl key on the Macintosh keyboard and click the mouse anywhere on the image or when you right-click the mouse on the PC. The contents of the pop-up menu depend on where you click, which tool you have active, or whether or not you have something selected—in short, the current state of Photoshop.

Selection tools

The marquee, oval, and lasso tools have the same context menu items. In fact they have one set that is shown when you don't have anything selected and a different set when you do (see Figure 2-1).

One good way to conserve monitor space is to get rid of the floating palettes altogether. Wouldn't it be great to turn off all the palettes at once? You can, by pressing the Tab key:

1. Press Tab; all the active palettes disappear. You then have the whole monitor devoted to your image.
2. Press Tab again; the palettes return to their original positions.

By using the Tab key to hide all the palettes and then using the tool keyboard short-cuts to activate different tools, you can accomplish almost anything you want without the clutter of floating palettes on the monitor. We also like to set the screen mode (the three buttons at the very bottom of the toolbox) to Full Screen with the menu bar. Click the middle button at the bottom of the toolbox, or press the F key. With the screen mode set to Full Screen and all the palettes hidden, you can use virtually the entire monitor to view the image.

CONSERVING MONITOR SPACE

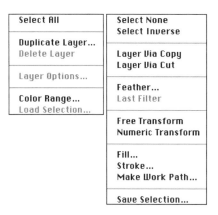

Figure 2-1
The context menu has these contents (left) when nothing is selected and (right) when anything is selected.

The magic wand tool is similar to the other selection tools in that it presents different context menus depending on whether or not you have something selected. The menus are slightly different, though (see Figure 2-2).

Select All	Add To Selection
Color Range...	Subtract From Selection
Load Selection...	Intersect Selection
	Select None
	Select Inverse
	Feather...
	Grow
	Similar

Figure 2-2
This magic wand context menu is shown (left) when nothing is selected and (right) when anything is selected.

The move tool

With the move tool, you can select a different layer by using the context menu. The context menu will give you a list of all the layers that have pixels in the area you have clicked, unless those pixels are transparent. So as you move the cursor around the image and click the mouse with the Command/Ctrl key down, the context menu will display different layer names. To select a new layer, move your mouse over a layer name in the context menu and release the mouse button.

Painting tools

This section describes context menus for the airbrush, paintbrush, eraser, pencil, rubber stamp, smudge, and blur tools. They all display the same four items at the top. These four items change brush sizes or select the first or last brush in the brush palette. The items listed after that change depending on what tool you have selected. The context menu also lists the blending modes available for the current tool. Blending modes change how the tool works when used. They might include, for instance, Dissolve, Multiply, or Hard Light (Figure 2-3).

Figure 2-3
The first four items stay the same for all of the tools mentioned in this section. The remaining items will change depending on the currently selected tool.

The dodge, burn, and sponge tools

These three tools are similar to the painting tools but are slightly different. In fact, the dodge and burn tools are similar to each other (Figure 2-4) in that each adds or deletes brightness values in a type of painting effect. The Sponge tool, on the other hand, saturates or desaturates the applied area (Figure 2-5). This illustrates how Adobe has made an effort to incorporate just the items useful for any particular tool in the context menu. All tools have the same four items at the top of the context menu but differ from there.

Figure 2-4
Both the dodge tool and the burn tool share this context menu.

Figure 2-5
The sponge tool has its own context menu.

The pen tool

The pen tool has no context menu associated with it, because the Ctrl key is used for other functions within the tool. See Chapter 7 on how to deal with pen tool limitations.

The gradient tool

The context menu for the gradient tool allows you to change from linear to radial gradients (Figure 2-6). It also changes the blending mode for the tool.

Figure 2-6
The gradient tool context menu offers a range of choices.

The bucket tool

The bucket tool doesn't have a context menu associated with it. Apparently this tool has no Ctrl key functionality.

The eyedropper tool

The context menu for this tool changes what type of sample is used when reading pixels in an image. You have three types of samples to choose from: Point Sample, 3×3 Average, and 5×5 Average.

```
Point Sample
3 by 3 Average
5 by 5 Average
```

The hand tool

The hand tool context menu switches between three views. They are: Fit on Screen, Actual Pixels, and Print Size.

```
Fit on Screen
Actual Pixels
Print Size
```

The zoom tool

The zoom tool has the same three items as the hand tool but adds Zoom In and Zoom Out at the bottom of the list.

```
Fit on Screen
Actual Pixels
Print Size

Zoom In
Zoom Out
```

The Free Transform Command

The Free Transform command adds new functionality to Photoshop but at the expense of a feature that was available in Photoshop 3. In Photoshop 3, you could select all the nontransparent pixels on a layer by pressing Command+Option+T/Ctrl+Alt+T. This key sequence now brings up the Free Transform command. You still can select all the nontransparent pixels on a layer by Command/Ctrl-clicking the layer. Every pixel on the layer that is not completely transparent will become selected.

Improving Free Transform efficiency

The Free Transform command will allow you to make multiple transformations to your image all at once. In Photoshop 3 if you wanted something resized and rotated, you needed to perform these transformations separately. If you made a mistake on the first transformation and were already on the second or third transformation, you would have to revert to the original image and start over. With the Free Transform, you can perform scale and rotate transformations at the same time. You can keep adjusting each until you are happy with both. To invoke the overall transformation, simply double-click inside the transformation area or press Return/Enter.

When you accept the transformation edits, the image data are interpolated. Photoshop 4 offers us a much improved ability to transform objects, since the interpolation is made only after the edits are accepted. In the earlier versions of Photoshop, every transformation required you to accept the edits individually and therefore resulted in interpolation for each transformation made. One major problem to avoid when performing transformations is not repeating them. In other words, don't make a transformation, press Enter to accept the change, and then go back and repeat the process. When you do so, Photoshop will interpolate each transformation. Your objective should always be to keep interpolations to a minimum.

The Free Transform command allows for five types of transformations. They are Scale, Rotate, Skew, Distort, and Perspective. All five transformations can be accomplished in any combination at one time. And Photoshop does an incredible job of updating the preview, even with large files, to give you quick feedback on the transformations.

To support a more consistent interface, the Free Transform command, the Crop tool, and the Place command have a unified look and behavior.

Creating a Free Transformation

You have a few ways to start the Free Transform process. If you are working on the Background layer (the layer that is automatically created is named "*Background*" in italics), you need to make a selection first and then select Layer ⇨ Free Transform. If you are working on any other layer than the Background layer, all you need to do is select Layer ⇨ Free Transform—that is, assuming you wish to transform the entire layer contents. If you want to transform just a portion of the layer, then you need to make a selection first.

When you do invoke the Free Transform command, a box will appear around your selection or layer with eight small handles on its edges (as in Figure 2-7). See the following paragraphs for an in-depth description on how to use the different Free Transform commands.

After you have made all the transformations, to invoke the overall transformation double-click inside the transformation area or press Enter. If you wish to cancel just the last transformation made, you can do so by pressing Command+Z/Ctrl+Z. If you want to cancel all the transformations, press Esc. Keep in mind that the Esc key or Command/Ctrl+Period takes you out of the Free Transform command. You will need to invoke the command again to start the process over.

If you have the info palette visible while using the Free Transform command, you can see a numerical readout of the transformations.

Modifying points

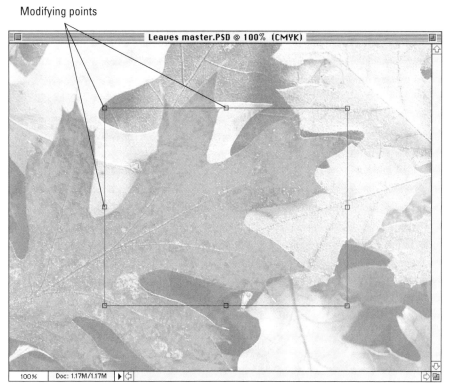

Figure 2-7
The Free Transform command box has eight modifying points.

SCALING To scale an image using the Free Transform command, grab any of the eight handles on the outer edges of the Free Transform box. The handles are represented by small boxes. If you want to scale the image nonproportionally, just grab any of the eight boxes and start pushing and pulling (see Figure 2-8). If you grab the corners, the image will be scaled in two directions. If you grab the sides, the image will be scaled in only one direction. If a proportional scale is required, hold down the Shift key while scaling one of the eight points. In both the proportional and nonproportional scaling techniques, pressing the Option/Alt key will add the ability to scale from center.

Figure 2-8
The scaling process is under way with the Free Transform command.

ROTATION Rotation with the Free Transform command (as illustrated in Figure 2-9) is accomplished by positioning your cursor anywhere outside the selected area. If the entire canvas is selected, you are unable to do this because there is no available area outside the selection. You need to first change the screen viewing mode to the middle icon. The screen mode icons are the last three items in the toolbox. The middle position removes the desktop and replaces it with a neutral gray area. Position the cursor in this gray area, and you will then be able to use the rotation function on an entire image. Hold down the Shift key to constrain rotation to 15-degree increments.

Figure 2-9
The rotation process is shown with the Free Transform command.

SKEW Skewing an image is similar to italicizing text (see Figure 2-10). You can slant the sides while keeping the top and bottom untouched. Or you can slant the top and bottom while leaving the sides alone. To skew an image, hold down the Command/Ctrl key and the Shift key and drag any of the four sides, not the corners, of the Free Transform box. To skew only one side, drag any of the four corners, not the sides, of the Free Transform box.

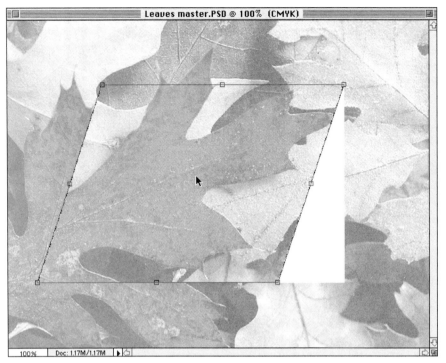

Figure 2-10
The skewing process looks like this with the Free Transform command.

DISTORT You can freely distort an image using the Free Transform command (see Figure 2-11). Hold down the Command/Ctrl key and drag any handle out in any direction. Dragging the corner handles gives you more of a feel of distorting the image than the side points, but all eight handles are available.

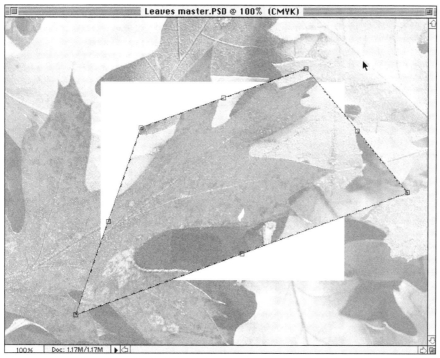

Figure 2-11
The distorting process is shown with the Free Transform command.

PERSPECTIVE With the Command+Option+Shift/Ctrl+Alt+Shift keys held down, you can perform a Perspective transformation by dragging any of the four corners (see Figure 2-12), or you can effect a double-skew function by dragging any of the sides.

You will find it useful to experiment with the new feature with different keys held down. We sat down and played for quite some time before getting comfortable with all of its functions. This is a great addition to a great software product.

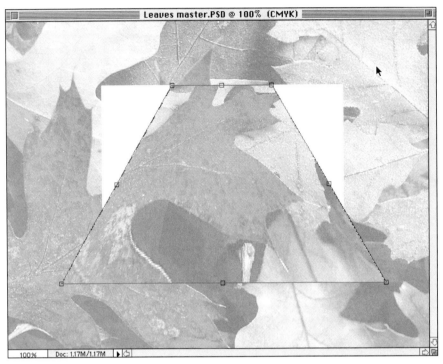

Figure 2-12
The Perspective transformation has this effect with the Free Transform command.

Adjustment Layers

This new function is exactly what the layers palette needed. First let's talk about some terminology that will describe what this feature does. Two types of modifications exist: destructive and nondestructive. *Destructive* modifications are applied directly to the image and forever change the original file. If you lighten an image, all the pixels are lightened and can never be returned to their original condition. *Nondestructive* modifications are applied in such a way that the original pixels are never really modified and can, at any time, be restored to their original condition. Obvious advantages exist to using a nondestructive modification whenever possible.

Adjustment layers allow for nondestructive modifications for the following areas:

- Levels
- Curves
- Brightness/contrast
- Color balance
- Hue/saturation

- Selective color
- Inversion
- Threshold adjustment
- Posterization

You have a couple of ways to create adjustment layers. You can select Layer ➪ New ➪ Adjustment Layer. A new layer will be created, and a dialog box will appear for you to select what kind of adjustment layer you want. You can also Command-click/Ctrl-click the New Layer button at the bottom of the layers palette. The New Layer button is the one in the middle (see Figure 2-13).

Figure 2-13
Clicking the New Layer button makes a regular layer. Command/Ctrl-clicking the same button makes an adjustment layer.

New Layer button

In the Adjustment Layer dialog box, select which type of modification you wish to make. Photoshop even gives you an option to name the layer. This is helpful when you are using several adjustment layers. Click OK, and the appropriate dialog box will appear for you to make the adjustments required (see Figure 2-14). Click OK once you have made them, and they will be applied to the adjustment layer.

Select the type of layer here

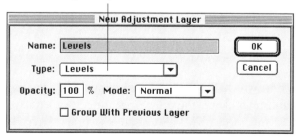

Figure 2-14
The New Adjustment Layer dialog box permits you to select the type of layer you wish to create.

Notice that the adjustment layer looks very similar to a regular layer except for the half-black/half-white circle on the right, which indicates that it is an adjustment layer (see Figure 2-15). All adjustments made to this layer are applied to all layers below it in the layer list. All layers above are untouched. That's one of the strengths of this feature. In Photoshop 3, in order to apply the same modification throughout multiple layers you had to apply the same modification to each layer separately or merge the layers and apply the modification to the merged layer. Either solution had its drawbacks. Now you can simply create an adjustment layer, make the modifications, and you're finished.

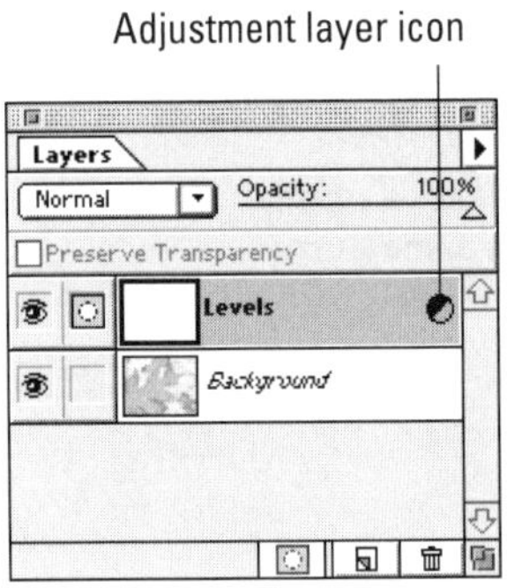

Adjustment layer icon

Figure 2-15
It's easy to distinguish an adjustment layer from a regular layer. The icon shown here appears only on an adjustment layer.

Another strength of this feature is that it offers you the ability to change your mind. This is where the nondestructive modification comes in. Since the modification is applied to a separate layer and not to the pixels of the image, the modification can be further changed or removed at any time. If you wish to change the modification settings, double-click the layer name (if you want to change the layer options, double-click the layer thumbnail). After you double-click the name, the appropriate dialog box will appear. Notice that the settings are exactly as you left them the last time they were changed. If you make an adjustment outside of an adjustment layer, click OK and then return to the dialog box; all the settings will return to their defaults. In an adjustment layer, the settings are as they were when you last changed them. Gone is the need to write down all the settings in the dialog boxes. That should save a forest or two of paper alone.

If you want to see what the image looks like without the adjustment layer, click the eyeball of the adjustment layer to temporarily turn it off. You can turn it on and off at any time for before and after comparisons.

The default adjustment layer is pure white. This means that the entire canvas area of the image will be modified by the adjustment layer. You can change the adjustment layer as you can any grayscale channel. If you create a black box in an adjustment layer, the space that the black box occupies will no longer be affected by the adjustment layer. Where there are white pixels, the adjustment layer will modify the image. Where there are black pixels, the adjustment layer will not modify the image. Grayscale will also affect the image in different ways. If you put a box in the adjustment layer that is 50 percent black or gray, the image will be modified by 50 percent of the modification. For example, if the adjustment layer is set to Invert, all the white pixels in the adjustment layer will allow the image to be inverted at an intensity of 100 percent. Where the pixels are black, the image will be unaffected. Where the pixels are 50 percent gray, the image will be inverted at 50 percent. You have the ability to change the adjustment layer with any tool you can use in any other channel. It can handle grayscale pixels only.

As we mentioned before, an adjustment layer affects all layers below it and leaves the layers above unaffected. As adjustment layers are moved up or down in the layer list, the image will change because the adjustment layer is affecting different layers. But what if you want the adjustment layer to affect only the one layer below it and not the other layers further below? You can set up a clipping group that will accomplish just that effect. First create an adjustment layer above the layer you wish to modify. Make any modifications needed, or just leave the default settings and come back to it after you have set up the clipping layer. With both layers created, the adjustment layer should be just above the layer it is to modify in the layer list. Position the cursor between the two layers. Hold down the Option/Alt key and click the mouse. As you hold down the Option/Alt key, the cursor changes to indicate that you are about to create a clipping layer. After you click, a few visual clues appear to confirm that a clipping layer has just been created. The icon for the adjustment layer shifts slightly to the right, and the solid line between the two layers changes to a dotted line (see Figure 2-16). Oh yeah, your image probably has changed a bit, too. Clipping layers were available in Photoshop 3 and still are present in Photoshop 4, but the adjustment layer just adds another function to them.

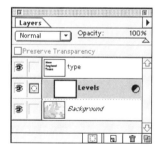

Figure 2-16
Compare the visual differences between the adjustment layer here affecting the layer below it and the adjustment layer in Figure 2-15.

To extend the feature set of adjustment layers further, the opacity and blending modes that are available to regular layers are also available to adjustment layers further. This allows you to further change how the adjustment layer affects other layers. A bonus here is that these two changes, like the adjustment layer itself, are also nondestructive. You can change the opacity and blending modes to whatever you wish and at any time return them to the default settings. All without modifying the original image.

The Digimarc Watermarking Filter

The Watermarking filter allows the author of a Photoshop image or illustration to add copyright and authorship information directly into the image. To find out if any image has a digital watermark, open the image and select Filter ⇨ Digimarc ⇨ Read Watermark. If you have the plug-in Detect Watermark loaded, Photoshop will automatically alert you to any digital watermark information. This plug-in is not loaded during the standard installation of Photoshop, but you can find the plug-in on the installation CD in the Other Goodies folder. Open the Optional Plug-ins folder and then open Digimarc. Grab the Detect Watermark plug-in and put it into your Photoshop Plug-ins folder. If you had Photoshop open while doing this, you must first close Photoshop and then relaunch it for the new plug-in to work properly.

If the filter detects a digital watermark, a dialog box will come up with an ID number of the author (see Figure 2-17). If you are connected to the Internet, click the Web Lookup button. This will load your Web browser and take you directly to the Web page that has contact information concerning the author. If you don't have Internet access, call the number at the bottom of the dialog box. Using this phone number and the creator ID number also found in the dialog box, you can get the same contact information concerning the original author via your fax machine.

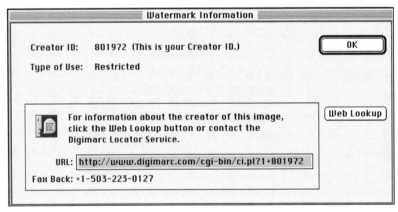

Figure 2-17
The Digimarc Alert dialog box leads to information for a copyrighted image.

Preferences

Most preferences in Photoshop have been bundled together in one main area. You can now flip back and forth between eight different types of preferences without leaving the main preference box—a very nice feature if you like changing preferences from their default settings. We tend to use most of the default settings, but here are a few recommended changes.

General

General Preferences are grouped into the dialog box shown in Figure 2-18. Among them, Show Tool Tips is a very useful setting while you are learning about the new features in Photoshop 4. This will allow Photoshop to display short, one-line descriptions of tools, palette functions, and such. Just position the cursor over an area, and if there is a description to display, it will pop up in a second or two. Again, this is probably a good thing to have around while you are learning the program, but after a while, it may become annoying. If you do find it a bit annoying, then it may be time to turn off this feature.

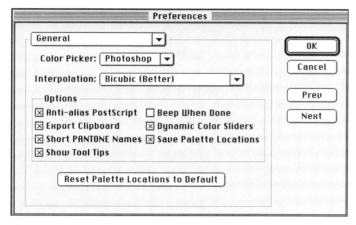

Figure 2-18
These are the general preferences available to you.

Advanced users may find this feature unnecessary and wish to immediately eliminate the display of the Tool Tips. If you are not familiar with *all* the keyboard and modifier key equivalents, however, then the Tool Tips can be a nice aid. Each time a tip is displayed, the equivalent keystroke command is identified within parentheses. If you're a Photoshop whiz, don't be too offended by the simplicity of this feature. It can help you master some important keystroke commands.

Saving Files

The Saving Files section (Figure 2-19) includes a couple of interesting items. First off, note 2.5 Compatibility under Options. If you don't need to open images in Photoshop 2.5, then turn this option off. When 2.5 compatibility is on, Photoshop will save a layered version of your image as it normally would and also save a second version of your image that is flattened, all in one file. This will obviously increase the amount of disk space required to save your image plus add time to the saving process. If you don't need to open an image in Photoshop 2.5, then be certain to turn this option off. It is turned on as a default.

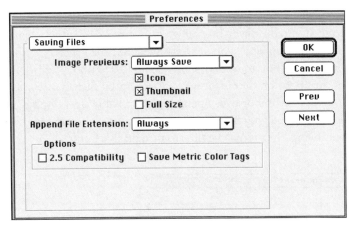

Figure 2-19
These are the Saving Files preferences available to you.

The second item of interest here is the Append File Extension option. It has a pop-up menu with three settings: Never, Always, and Ask When Saving. This option will append appropriate file extensions to the ends of filenames. An image saved as an EPS file will have .EPS at the end of the filename. An image saved as a TIFF image will have .TIF at the end of the filename. Photoshop will highlight the first portion of the filename so you can easily change the name if need be — a nice feature overlooked by many programs. I am always in favor of adding file extensions to virtually all computer filenames. It gives you one more bit of information related to the file.

Display & Cursors

The main item in the Display & Cursors section (Figure 2-20) is Painting Cursors. We always set ours to Brush Size. When Brush Size is selected, and a tool that uses brush sizes is selected, your cursor will display a circle that represents how big the brush size is in relationship to the image. The maximum size brush that will display as a circle at 100 percent is 300 pixels. At 200 percent, all brushes up to 150 pixels will display as circles. So remember that the viewing size of your image determines how big a brush will display as a circle.

Transparency & Gamut

The Transparency & Gamut preference (Figure 2-21) controls how transparency and gamut are displayed by Photoshop. Transparency will display as a checkerboard pattern. You can change the size and color of the pattern. When we first encountered layers in Photoshop 3, we found the strong checkerboard pattern to be annoying. Your inclination may be to turn off the transparency view, which you can do in this preference setting. If None is selected in the dialog, the layer will appear white. Unfortunately, you won't be able to tell the difference between transparency and white pixels.

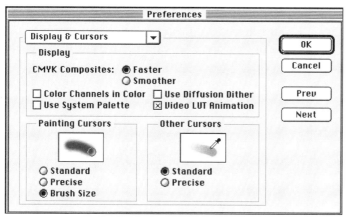

Figure 2-20
These are the Display & Cursors preferences available to you.

TIP Rather than display no transparency, we've found it helpful to make the pattern a bit more subtle. You can accomplish this by clicking the gray swatch displayed in the dialog box that brings the color picker to your screen. If you move the selected neutral gray in the color picker up to a lighter shade, the checkerboard pattern will appear softer and may be more pleasant as you view layers. As with most of the other preference settings, you have control over how you wish to view your Photoshop environment.

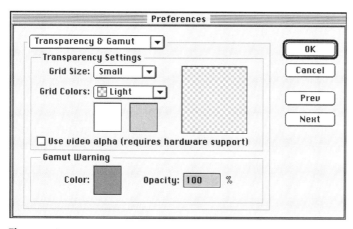

Figure 2-21
These are the Transparency & Gamut preferences available to you.

Units & Rulers

This preferences section is shown in Figure 2-22. Changing the Units setting under Rulers will change what type of unit of measure is represented in many of the dialog boxes found throughout Photoshop. But it's much easier to change this setting in the info palette. At the bottom left in the info palette is an X-Y coordinate area. Just to the left of that, click and hold the mouse on the crosshair icon; a pop-up menu will appear. Select the new unit of measurement you wish to use.

Adobe has added a Point/Pica Size setting at the bottom of this section. We recommend keeping the default setting of "PostScript (72 points/inch)." If you need to use the Traditional option, change over and do the work required. Then change back to the first option before you continue working.

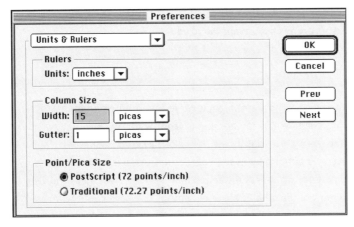

Figure 2-22
These are the Units & Rulers preferences available to you.

Guides & Grid

The only change we make in the Guides & Grid section (Figure 2-23) is to the very last option. Set Subdivisions to 8. This will create a grid that is in one-eighth-inch increments. The reason for using 8 instead of the default setting of 4 (for one-fourth-inch increments) is that the standard bleed measurement is one-eighth inch. When this option is set to 8, you can use the grid to see bleed areas. When you view the grid in Photoshop, the outermost grid segment will represent the bleed area. This feature comes in handy when you are moving items around; using it, you can make sure that you don't accidentally position an element outside the live area and into the bleed area.

TIP If you are viewing a grid on an image that is dominated by one color, you may wish to change the grid lines to another color to better view them. For example, a blue sky may not be the best place to use blue grid lines. But red grid lines will surely get your attention.

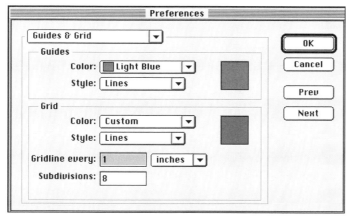

Figure 2-23
These are the Guides & Grid preferences available to you.

Plug-ins & Scratch Disk

Plug-ins and Scratch Disk preferences are shown in Figure 2-24. If your plug-ins are working, you shouldn't need to change the Plug-Ins Folder designation. You should, however, check to see if the Scratch Disks options are set up properly. If you have only one hard drive for your computer, the Primary setting, as a default, is set to Startup. If you have more then one drive, you can define Secondary as another drive. As your primary disk fills up with virtual memory space, Photoshop will start using the next drive. Only two drives can be set at one time.

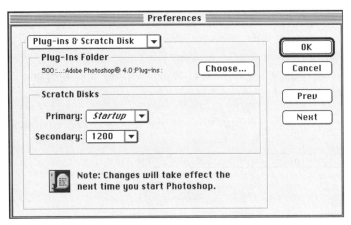

Figure 2-24
These are the Plug-ins & Scratch Disk preferences available to you.

If you have any background in Photoshop, you probably have some awareness of scratch space and what it does. If you are not fortunate enough to have a second hard drive attached to your computer, you may not have looked at this preference setting since first installing Photoshop. This is such an important setting that it deserves some power user tips and a thorough understanding before we leave the topic. Understand that Photoshop continually reads and writes information to your hard disk. When you run low on physical memory, the scratch space is used as an extension of memory so that you can perform operations such as Undo, Define Pattern, and Take Snapshot, not to mention adding layers, adding channels, and opening additional images. This constant reading and writing to your hard disk is pounding it severely. Ideally, it would be beneficial to have a second hard drive so that all this pounding could be handled on the secondary drive. Unfortunately, if you are like most users, you have a single drive where all your applications, system software, and scratch space reside.

If you've purchased a computer during the past few years, you probably have at least a 1.2GB hard drive and maybe a 2.0GB hard drive. If this is the case, here's what we recommend you do to improve performance of both Photoshop and your system:

1. Use a good formatting utility such as FWB Hard Disk Toolkit version 2.0 or above to reformat your hard drive.
2. After formatting, set up a partition with enough space to hold your System folder, applications, utilities, and fonts, leaving several megabytes free.
3. Add a new partition and call it Scratch.
4. Reinstall your system and software on the system partition.
5. Launch Photoshop and set the primary scratch space to your scratch partition and the secondary scratch space to the system partition.

**IMPROVING
SCRATCH DISK
PERFORMANCE**

When you work in Photoshop, all the reading and writing for the scratch space will first go to the scratch partition. This will keep the constant pounding of your hard disk away from system software and your applications.

Ted Padova purchased a 2.4GB Seagate Barracuda 2 hard drive over three years ago and installed it in a Quadra 840AV. He partitioned the drive and kept scratch space away from all the application files on the hard drive. All data files and scratch space resided on the same partition. In over three years he has never rebuilt the desktop, reformatted the drive, or optimized it. We don't recommend you avoid maintaining your drive with desktop rebuilds or optimization. But the point is, you'll get much more out of your drive by keeping your data and scratch space away from the system and application files.

IMPROVING SCRATCH DISK PERFORMANCE

Image Cache

To increase speed performance in Photoshop 4, Adobe added an Image Cache section to the preferences dialog box (see Figure 2-25). This feature will speed redraw of your image when you perform such operations as compositing, layering, scrolling, zooming, and applying color adjustments. Photoshop accomplishes this by drawing a sequence of proxies to the screen. These proxies start at lower resolutions and progress to the highest resolution available. These proxies will not ultimately affect the resolution of the image, just how you may view it on the screen. And only for the small amounts of time it takes to build the high-resolution preview.

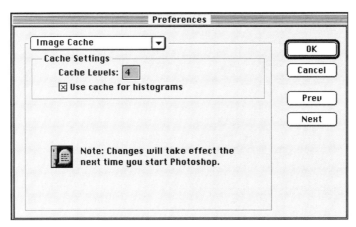

Figure 2-25
These are the Image Cache preferences available to you.

You have the ability to adjust how much Photoshop uses this new feature. The image cache can be set to any number from 1 to 8. Setting it to 1 turns off all image caching, and Photoshop will run as did Photoshop 3. The higher the number, the more proxies will be used as the preview changes to the image. The default setting is 4. If Use Cache for Histograms is turned on, histograms are created with proxies in the same manner as other previews.

 TIP If running out of memory is a constant problem when you work in Photoshop, then set the Image Cache to 1. Lowering the caching is not a solution for avoiding memory upgrades, but it can help conserve memory and get you through many Photoshop sessions.

Extending Images and Paths outside Canvas Size

The capability to extend images and paths beyond the canvas area is a very welcome change in Photoshop 4. As you drag paths off the canvas area, they still are visible and editable (as shown in Figure 2-26). First, switch your viewing mode to the middle icon at the bottom of the toolbox. This will remove the desktop and put in its place a neutral gray background. This is the area in which you can drag and edit paths outside the canvas boundary. In Photoshop 3 you could basically do the same thing, but you were flying blind, since you couldn't see any path that was moved outside the canvas area.

Figure 2-26
Paths dragged outside the canvas area are still
available to you for editing.

Images react in the same manner. If you paste an image that is larger than the canvas, the excess image area from the original image will still be there. If you come back to the image later and move or reposition the image, you will be able to see the areas that were outside the canvas area.

This feature has its advantages and disadvantages. An advantage is that you never lose your image. You can at any time return to the layer and adjust the position of the image, because Photoshop hasn't deleted the excess area as it did in earlier versions. A disadvantage is that, since no information is deleted, the file sizes can be considerably larger than what is really needed. If you paste a 10MB image into a 2MB canvas area, the entire 10MB are saved with the file. If you don't believe you will need the other 8MB of information, then you should delete the excess image data. This will allow you to work more efficiently, since you are not opening, processing, and saving information that is not really needed.

If you have excess information outside any of the layers and wish to remove it to conserve disk space, choose Select ⇨ Select All (Command+A/Ctrl+A) and then Image ⇨ Crop. One thing to keep in mind here is that when you do this procedure, all layers that have excess data will also be cropped. So you will lose all the excess data on all layers. If you want only one layer to be cropped, follow these instructions:

1. Target the layer that has the excess data.

2. Choose Select ⇨ Select All or Command+A/Ctrl+A.

3. Choose Layer ⇨ New ⇨ Layer Via Copy (Command+J/Ctrl+J). The new Layer Via Copy command will duplicate the selected area and place the data on a new layer without using the clipboard, thereby saving precious memory.

4. Delete the layer by dragging the layer name to the Trash Can icon or select the layer in the layers palette and depress the Option/Alt key while clicking the trash icon at the bottom of the layers palette.

Floating Selections

In past versions of Photoshop, the paste command placed the clipboard contents into the currently selected layer and made them a floating selection. In Photoshop 4, all pasted, placed, or dragged-and dropped images become their own layer. You can then use the move tool to reposition the new image. If you then wish to make it part of the layer below it, you can use the Merge Down command in the Layer menu. If you wish to incorporate it with several layers at a time, link all the layers that you wish to make into one and select Merge Linked from the Layer menu. To link layers together, select any of the desired layers and then click in the box between the eyeball and layer icon. All the layers, except the layer selected, should have a little chain link in the box.

At first view, Photoshop 4 will no doubt give you the impression that floating selections no longer exist. After all, the Select menu does not provide the Float option as in earlier versions of the program. Also, Adobe seems to force us to use layers whether we want to or not. Copy/Paste creates a new layer, and text appears on a new layer when you create it. It may not be obvious in your first experiences with Photoshop 4, but you can still create a floating selection. To do so, hold the Command/Ctrl key down and press any one of the four arrow keys. If you want the selected area to remain in the precise position, press the arrow key for the opposite direction after you create the floating selection. When you view the layers palette, you will see the familiar floating selection hovering over the layer from which the selection was created. Defloat the selection by choosing Defloat (Command+E/Ctrl+E) from the Layer menu or Select ⇨ None (Command+D/Ctrl+D) from the Select menu.

TIP If you want to select a portion of a feathered area on a given layer, click the desired image area with the magic wand tool to create a selection. Hold down the Command/Ctrl key and press an arrow key. The selection will become a floating selection containing all the feathered information.

Selection Tool Changes

After a selection is made, you can reposition the selected area by clicking inside the selection and moving it to a new location. The pixels within the selected area will not move with the selection. This was accomplished in Photoshop 3 with the Command/Ctrl key and the Option/Alt key held down. If you do wish to move the pixels with the selection area, hold down the Command/Ctrl key as you move the selection. When you depress the Command/Ctrl key, you will activate the move tool. You can either use the tool from the toolbox or the keyboard modifier to move the selected data.

You can add to any selection by holding down the Shift key while making a new selection. The first selection will remain with the new selection being added to it. To remove part of the selection, hold down the Option/Alt key while making a new selection that intersects the first selection. In all earlier versions of Photoshop, you would hold down the Command/Ctrl key as you used a selection tool to delete from the selected area. Since the Command/Ctrl key became the key to invoke the move tool, Adobe chose the Option/Alt key to remove something from a selection.

A few new functions have been added to the selection tools. Holding down the Shift key and the Option/Alt key will make an intersect selection. This means that only those portions of the new selection that intersect the first selection will remain selected. You can also reposition the rectangle or oval selection tools while you are still drawing by holding down the Spacebar. As you drag out a selection, hold down the Spacebar without letting go of the mouse, and then reposition the selection. When you let go of the Spacebar, the selection will work normally. Pretty cool little feature!

TIP Assume for a moment you wish to create a shape similar to a tire or doughnut. The selection shape will need to appear similar to the "O" character. To create such a selection, you need to first create a circle and then delete from the center of your selection. Let's also assume that you wish to create a perfect circle drawn from center. Photoshop now uses the Option/Alt key to delete from a selection as well as to draw from the center of the object. So here's our dilemma—how do we draw from center while simultaneously deleting from the selection?

Here's how to do it. In a new document window, draw with the elliptical marquee while holding down the Option/Alt and Shift keys. This action will create a perfect circle drawn from center. (If you wish to be precise, you could show rulers and create two guides intersecting at the center of the document window.) Release the mouse button and reposition the cursor to the center of your selection. While the first selection is still active, hold the Option/Alt and Shift keys down and drag a short distance. You'll notice that the circle is now being created from the top-left corner. You should have two selection circles, one inside the other. While keeping the Shift key and mouse button depressed, release the Option/Alt key and then press it again. The second circle will now pop to the center position and enable you to continue with a draw from center.

Moving data between documents is best performed by using the move tool. Position two documents adjacent to each other, click in one document window with the move tool, and drag to the other document window. The new data will appear as a new layer. Photoshop provides for pin registration when moving data in such a manner. Hold down the Shift key and drag one image to the second document. The newly established layer will be precisely center aligned. When you use drag-and-drop methods in Photoshop, you avoid using excessive memory as would be required for copy/paste operations. Dragging and dropping image data does not use the clipboard to hold information in memory.

Zooming through Images

The zoom tool has been greatly enhanced. In Photoshop 3 you could only view an image in 100 percent increments. In Photoshop 4 zooming is in increments of 1/100th of a percent. You can set viewing sizes such as 145.84 percent. At the bottom-left corner of the image box you will find a readout of the current viewing size. You can use the normal ways to change the viewing size. Select the zoom tool or hold down the Command/Ctrl key and Spacebar and click the mouse to enlarge the view to the next preset size. Adding the Option/Alt key will reduce the viewing size. You can also select the number at the lower-left corner (Figure 2-27) and type in any size you wish. The navigator palette contains a slider that can also be used to change viewing size. Maximum viewing size has not changed from 1600 percent, but the minimum is now all the way down to 0.34 percent. That's point-34 percent or less than half of one percent. If you want to see a thumbnail view of your image, try setting the viewing size to .34 percent. That's what we call a thumbnail.

Figure 2-27
The number at the bottom of the window shows the viewing percentage. You can type in any number from 0.34 to 1600 percent.

The Navigator Palette

A new palette has been added to Photoshop 4. It's called the navigator palette (shown in Figure 2-28). If you are viewing an image that is too big to fit your monitor, the navigator palette will help you move to other portions of the image quickly. An entire view of the image is shown inside the navigator palette with a red outline box that represents how much of the image is actually being viewed on the monitor. Simply clicking any portion of the image will move you instantly to the new area. As we mentioned earlier, a slider is provided; you can make changes to viewing size by moving the slider back and forth. You can also select the number at the bottom-left corner and type in a new percentage. This box works just like the box at the bottom-left corner of the image box.

Figure 2-28
The navigator palette helps you move to other areas of a large image quickly.

The Actions Palette

The actions palette is also new to Photoshop 4 (see Figure 2-29). An *action* is like an extremely powerful macro-like function. Actions will allow you to program Photoshop to perform a single command or a series of commands, with or without your interaction. Photoshop shipped with a set of actions already for you to use with some others that can be found on the install CD. We are confident, as time goes by, that there will be actions-o-plenty floating around the Internet when users start thinking up creative ways to use this new feature. Keep your eyes open for fun and functional actions.

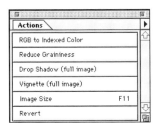

Figure 2-29
The actions palette in the List mode shows what macro-like functions are available.

Button and List modes

The actions palette has two modes: Button mode and List mode. In Button mode (Figure 2-30), Photoshop performs the action when one is selected. In List mode (Figure 2-31), clicking an action allows you to change many attributes of the action.

Figure 2-30
The actions palette appears in Button mode with the submenu open.

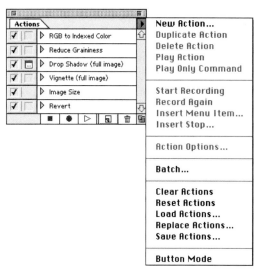

Figure 2-31
The actions palette appears in List mode with the submenu open.

To determine which mode you are currently in, look at the actions palette itself. When the actions palette is in the Button mode, all you will see are the action names in the palette with their function key shortcuts if any.

When the actions palette is in the List mode, you will see small boxes to the left of the action names. The palette will look similar to the layers and channels palettes. Instead of having eyeballs and chain links in the boxes, however, the actions palette sports check marks and tiny dialog boxes.

To switch between modes, select the Button Mode menu item in the submenu of the actions palette. It is the last entry in the submenu. When the menu has a check mark beside it, you are in Button mode. No check mark indicates you are in List mode.

Recording an action

Let's look at how this feature works. To record an action, first make certain you are in List mode. Select New Action under the actions palette submenu to display the dialog box shown in Figure 2-32. Give the action a name and click Record. Now everything you do will be part of the action. If one of the commands you perform produces a dialog box, clicking OK will include the command in the action, whereas clicking Cancel will not include the command in the action. When you have finished all the commands, select Stop Recording in the submenu of the actions palette, or click the Stop Recording button at the bottom of the actions palette.

TIP Colors are useful for organizing actions. Use one color for all actions pertaining to a certain type of modification or project.

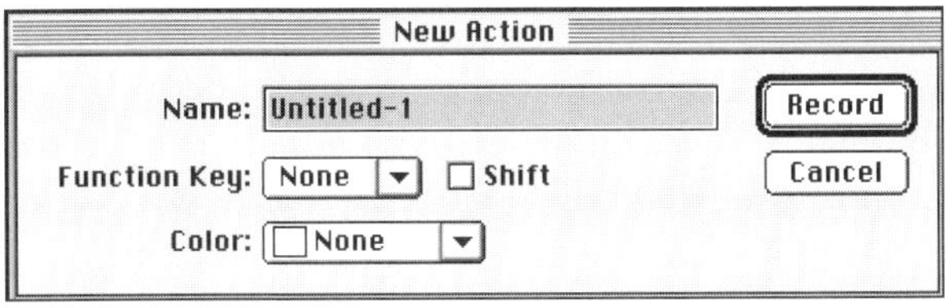

New Action

Name: `Untitled-1`

Function Key: `None` ▼ ☐ Shift

Color: `☐ None` ▼

[Record]
[Cancel]

Figure 2-32
In the New Action dialog box, along with naming an Action,
you assign a function key and a color to it.

Playing an action

To play an action, you can view the actions palette in either mode. In Button mode, click the action name to play it. In List mode, click the Play button at the bottom of the actions palette. The Play button appears as a triangle pointing to the right. If there are any *break points* (we'll talk about them next), make any adjustments in the dialog boxes and click Continue or OK.

Break points occur whenever an action brings up a dialog box that requires you to either make adjustments or OK the current settings in the dialog box. (Figure 2-33 shows a command in which this occurs.) For example, if the Gaussian Blur Filter dialog box is brought up by the action, the settings will be the same as they were when the action was recorded. You can leave them alone or change them to another number. When you click OK, the action will continue performing the other commands.

Dialog box icon

Figure 2-33
Whenever you see the dialog box icon alongside
a command, a dialog box will appear when Photoshop
comes to that command during playback, giving you
the opportunity to change any settings.

You can use any of the existing actions to see how the break points work. Open any file and choose an action. Select something like Reduce Graininess. Click the small triangle appearing adjacent to the action name to expand the sequence. You'll notice Gaussian Blur is the first action to be performed. Observe the palette, and you will see a column with check marks and another column with embossed squares. Click the square adjacent to Gaussian Blur in the sequence. An icon will appear representing a tiny dialog box. Now play the action. The Gaussian Blur dialog will appear so that you can make user-defined adjustments to the blur amount. By checking the break point box in the palette, you can control any action that permits user-defined settings.

Editing an action

After an action has been recorded, you still have the option to fine-tune it. In List mode, actions can be viewed by command. Each command is visible and can be edited. To show the commands, click the white triangle to the right of the action name. Individual commands can be turned on or off by clicking the check mark on the left.

You can change the settings that are currently in any command by double-clicking the name of the command. Let's say a Feather command of 10 pixels is in an action that you wish to change to 15 pixels. Double-click the Feather command. A dialog box will come up with the 10-pixel setting. Change it to 15 pixels and click OK. Now whenever the action is performed, the dialog box will be set to 15 pixels.

Inserting a nonrecordable menu

Some menu items are not recordable in an action. You still can insert these items into an action. Select the command in an action that you want the new command to follow. In the submenu of the actions palette select Insert Menu Item. In the dialog box (Figure 2-34) you can either type the command or partially type it in and click the Find button. You can also just select the menu item and click OK. The new command will be added to the list of commands after the currently selected command.

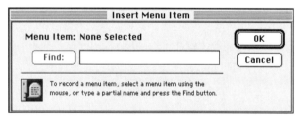

Figure 2-34
When you cannot record a menu item in an action, you have to insert it manually.

Adding a Layer Mask

Two options are now available for creating a layer mask: Reveal All or Hide All. Reveal All will create an all-white mask that will allow the entire layer to be visible. Then it is up to you to add black to hide portions of the layer. Hide All will create an all-black mask that will hide the entire layer. As you add white to the mask, portions of the layer will be revealed.

If a selection is made, then two other options become available: Reveal Selection and Hide Selection. You may also click the Layer Mask icon at the bottom of the layers palette. By default it will Reveal All or Reveal Selection. Option/Alt-clicking it will Hide All or Hide Selection.

The Enhanced Gradient Tool

The gradient tool has been thoroughly overhauled in Photoshop 4. You are no longer limited to a start color and an ending color. Any number of colors can be added to a gradient. You can change how much area any two colors occupy in the overall gradient area and where the midpoint falls for the two colors. Transparency is also available for each gradient. This means you can determine where a gradient can be blended in and out of the background image.

Photoshop 4 ships with 16 different gradients, all ready for use. Since you can save any gradients you create, you will be able to use them for other projects as well. You may want to start developing a standard set of gradients that you commonly use. To fully understand how this new editor works, let's take a brief look at creating a few simple gradients.

Gradient presets

Adobe makes a series of gradients available when you select the gradient options palette (see Figure 2-35). To activate this palette, click the gradient tool in the Photoshop toolbox and press Enter.

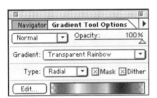

Figure 2-35
The gradient options palette comes with preset gradients.

You can select any of the gradient presets from this palette, or you can create custom gradients complete with your own color, percentage of value, and degree of transparency.

Creating custom gradients

Photoshop's Gradient Editor is new to Photoshop 4 but closely resembles gradient editors found in other programs such as Adobe Illustrator and Macromedia Freehand. To activate the Gradient Editor dialog, select the gradient tool and press Enter to reveal the gradient options palette. Click the Edit button in the palette, and the Gradient Editor will appear, as shown in Figure 2-36.

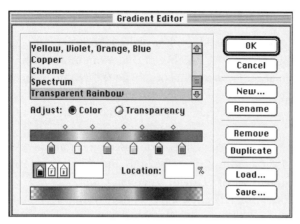

Figure 2-36
The Gradient Editor is shown in the Adjust Color mode.

In this dialog box, you have a choice of changing an existing gradient or creating a new gradient. To create a new gradient, simply click the New button. A dialog will prompt you to name the gradient. Photoshop will automatically name the gradient as Gradient 1 if you choose not to supply a name.

When you accept the new gradient name, the Gradient Editor will display two radio buttons for the type of adjustment to be made. The first is Color, and the second is Transparency. When Color is selected, you can choose a color for the foreground and the background. Color sampling can be made by moving the cursor over an open document window, by selecting from the color or swatches palette, or by clicking the swatch to the right of the three small icons in the editor to reveal the Photoshop Color Picker. You must have either the color or swatches palette open before addressing the Gradient Editor as Photoshop will not permit you to select the palette tabs while the Editor dialog is open.

Avoiding problems when creating color gradients

When you first try to create a gradient, the process may not appear entirely intuitive. Before you specify a color, you need to first identify where that color will be applied. As you observe the Gradient Editor, note that two small icons shaped like houses appear on the left and right sides of a slider bar. When identifying a foreground color for your new gradient, click the house icon on the left side of the slider bar and then sample the color you wish to have applied. Next, click the right house icon and sample the color to appear as your background color. You can add more colors by clicking below the slider bar; more house icons will appear, enabling you to specify further colors in the same manner. Each of these icons can be repositioned by dragging it to the left or right. To eliminate an established color, drag the icon down below the slider bar and it will be eliminated.

Avoiding problems when creating transparent gradients

Blending a color to transparency is a great feature, and Photoshop 4 provides you with many opportunities to blend to transparency, then to a color, again to transparency, and so on. You can create, move, and adjust transparent opacities in the Gradient Editor. Unfortunately, this process is even less intuitive than creating color gradients.

Note the Transparency radio button in the Gradient Editor. To create a simple gradient that blends from a color to transparency, you first identify the color as we described previously. Next, click the Transparency button and you will notice another set of house icons below the slider bar (see Figure 2-37). Click the icon on the right to select it and set the Opacity box to the degree of opacity desired. You should try to think of the color adjustment and the transparency adjustment as two separate sets of controls. The color is identified with the Color radio button, and the opacity is adjusted with the Transparency radio button. In essence, you add all the color points on the gradient bar to establish the color values, and then you move to the Transparency button to establish all of the levels of opacity. Just keep in mind that color and transparency can be positioned independently. Your final result will appear in the gradient bar at the bottom of the Gradient Editor, which is dynamically updated according to your adjustments.

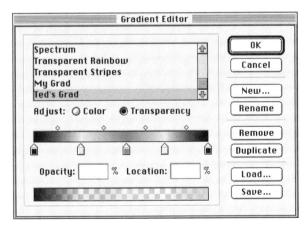

Figure 2-37
A new gradient is created with multiple colors and multiple transparency.

Every tool in Photoshop's toolbar can be activated by a keyboard equivalent. Without having it visible, each and every tool (including the nontool functions at the bottom of the toolbar, such as Quickmask and foreground/background color definition) can be accessed with a touch of a single key. And when we say a single key, we mean that literally. These keyboard equivalents are not like your standard Command/Ctrl+*keystroke* combinations, the ones that require you to hold down two or more keys simultaneously. These keyboard equivalents require you to type only the single letter associated with its tool, as you can see in Figure 2-38. This makes them very easy to use.

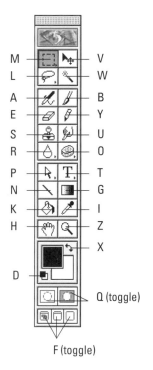

Figure 2-38
These are the keyboard shortcuts you can use for each tool or function.

USING
KEYBOARD
SHORTCUTS
FOR THE
TOOL
PALETTE

At first, using these keyboard shortcuts can be a little awkward, even frustrating, if you accidentally type a letter and don't realize you're now using a tool that may be different than the one you were expecting to use. (Finding yourself airbrushing black paint when you thought you were going to start drawing a box can be a bit unnerving.) But this will soon pass, and before long you'll love this wonderful feature.

CHAPTER THREE

AVOIDING MEMORY
PROBLEMS

Photoshop is the one program for which you need as much RAM as possible. One of the most commonly asked questions concerning Photoshop is how much memory does it really take to work efficiently? The short answer to that question is, "How much money do you have to spend on RAM?" In other words, purchase and install as much RAM as you can afford. Photoshop will use, and benefit from, as much as you can give it, and you can't have too much. Regardless of the amount of installed RAM in your computer, Photoshop will always want more. This chapter will demonstrate how to avoid memory problems and provide some solutions when memory for a given job is limited.

Understanding Memory Requirements

The more RAM you have available to Photoshop, the faster and more efficiently it will run. The reason: when Photoshop opens an image, it reads the entire image into RAM. If the image is larger than available RAM, Photoshop uses disk space, that is, the scratch disk, in lieu of actual RAM. And of course, the scratch disk is considerably slower than real RAM. If you open a 30MB file, for instance, but only have 15MB of RAM available to Photoshop, the remainder of the image data is dumped into virtual memory, again, using the hard disk as if it were memory. Since RAM is considerably faster than a hard disk (at least 10 times faster), whenever Photoshop uses the scratch disk, program performance suffers. And it only gets worse from there. Every time you perform a filter function, use the copy and paste commands, and so on, Photoshop performs these duties using the hard disk instead of RAM.

Adobe's basic rule of thumb for the ratio of RAM to image size is you should have 3–5 times the amount of RAM available to Photoshop as you have image size. So if you have a 10MB image, you should have 30–50MB of physical RAM allocated to Photoshop using the Finder's Get Info command. As you can see, the RAM requirements can get pretty steep. An image that fills a standard $8\frac{1}{2} \times 11$–inch ad at 300 dpi using the CMYK color mode with a $\frac{1}{8}$-inch bleed on all sides will produce a 33.8MB file. And this is only for a single-layer Photoshop file at that. If you start adding layers and channels to the image, it only gets larger. If you then open multiple images to copy and paste portions back and forth, you again push up the RAM requirements.

Performing other functions within Photoshop also adds to your need for more RAM. Even though Photoshop has only one level of Undo, that one level can mean significant RAM requirements. If you perform a Gaussian Blur on a 30MB file, for example, and then choose Undo from the Edit menu, Photoshop remembers both the Gaussian-Blurred version of the 30MB file and the original version of the 30MB file. That's a total of 60MB of image information that Photoshop has to put somewhere, either in RAM or in virtual memory.

Now let's say you copy the entire image to the clipboard, perform the same Guassian blur again, and again Undo it. You now have an original copy, a blurred copy, and a copy on the clipboard. That's three full copies of the 30MB image floating around in RAM or virtual memory. Having multiple versions of your image available makes Photoshop quite versatile, but you pay a price for this versatility. And that price is performance if you don't have enough RAM installed.

Yet another function copies your entire image into a buffer area for future retrieval. This is called "taking a snapshot" of an image's current condition. This is a great feature, but again it adds another full copy of the image to RAM or virtual memory.

To illustrate how memory requirements grow in a Photoshop session, we took a 10.7MB file and performed a filter operation with a Gaussian Blur. Then we used the Edit ➪ Undo command, which placed the entire 10.7MB image in a memory buffer. We next performed the Edit ➪ Take Snapshot command, which required another 10.7MB of memory since this operation is placed in a separate memory buffer. The final edit was a pattern created from a 500K image, which added yet more memory requirements. The final image is shown in Figure 3-1.

Analyzing Your Memory Efficiency

Photoshop performance can be assessed with tools right in the program. Several of these tools can help us determine memory requirements and also provide us with feedback on how well Photoshop is performing. All of these tools are located in a pop-up menu at the lower left of every document you open in Photoshop (see Figure 3-2).

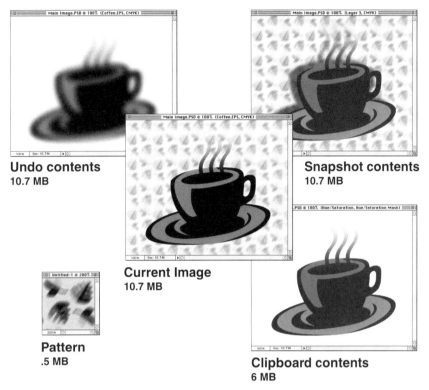

Undo contents
10.7 MB

Snapshot contents
10.7 MB

Current Image
10.7 MB

Pattern
.5 MB

Clipboard contents
6 MB

Figure 3-1
Here is a 10.7MB file that has had a filter, snapshot, and pattern applied.

Figure 3-2
This pop-up menu is your road map to memory efficiency.

Experimenting with Document Sizes

The first item available in the pop-up menu shown in Figure 3-2 is Document Sizes; the information displayed provides feedback on the amount of memory consumed to work on your image (see Figure 3-3). Note the two numbers divided by a slash character. The number appearing before the slash indicates the amount of memory required to open your image. When you first open a single-layer image, both numbers will appear identical.

Figure 3-3
Document Sizes displays original image data memory requirements and additional layer memory requirements.

The second number reveals memory requirements as new layers are added to your document. If you duplicate a layer, the second number will grow to reflect the addition of the new layer. Memory requirements grow according to the amount of pixel information on the new layer. Transparent areas add nothing to these requirements. Let's perform a simple experiment:

1. Choose Select ⇨ Select All (Command+A/Ctrl+A) and then choose Layer ⇨ Layer via Copy (Command+J/Ctrl+J). The entire layer is copied to a new layer. Note the increase of the value appearing after the slash character at the lower left of your document window. The value has doubled.

2. Invoke the Undo command by choosing Edit ⇨ Undo (Command+Z/Ctrl+Z). The value is decreased and appears identical to the first value appearing before the slash character.

3. Marquee a small square in the document window.

4. Choose Layer ⇨ Layer via Copy (Command+J/Ctrl+J). Notice that the value is smaller than the value we were provided in the previous step. Since only a portion of the layer was copied to a new layer, the memory requirements were less.

TIP Here's how you can avoid document size problems. Since the document size grows with each new layer created in your image, you can avoid memory problems by merging layers when the independent layers are no longer needed. As you work on a Photoshop file, you can use the Merge Down, Merge Visible, or Flatten Image options available under the Layer menu or the flyout menu in the Layers palette.

To keep a document available with all independent layers intact, choose File ⎡ Save a Copy. When you save a file in the native Photoshop format, a copy of the file is stored on your hard drive. If you then merge layers or flatten the image and then decide to edit an independent layer, you can open the copied image with the independent layers. Next, perform your edits, save another copy, and merge the layers.

Using Scratch Sizes

Your second feedback source is the next item appearing from the pop-up menu in the lower left of the document window shown in Figure 3-2. The Scratch Sizes display (see Figure 3-4) contains two important values. The first figure represents the amount of RAM required to work on all open documents. This figure constantly updates as you open additional images and perform various edits in a document window.

The second value remains constant. It won't change during any Photoshop session. The value represents the amount of total RAM available to Photoshop minus the amount Photoshop needs to run. When you change the Preferred and Minimum sizes in the Info dialog box, those size changes will be reflected in the scratch sizes when you reopen Photoshop.

Scratch Sizes

Figure 3-4
Scratch Sizes displays image data memory
requirements and total memory allocated
to Photoshop.

TIP Here's how you can avoid scratch size problems. When the number preceding the slash for the scratch sizes exceeds the number appearing after the slash character, Photoshop is using virtual memory. If this becomes the case in a Photoshop session, try to close all document windows except the one being edited. If you have unnecessary layers, delete them and purge all memory buffers. If the problem persists, you need to upgrade your machine's RAM or accept slower performance.

Using Efficiency

You can check to see how efficiently Photoshop is managing image data at any given point. Click the arrow icon in the lower-left of the window and choose Efficiency (checked in Figure 3-2) to display a value indicating the percentage of Photoshop operations currently performed using RAM. A value below 100 percent means Photoshop has run out of real RAM and is using the scratch disk. Expect progressively decreased performance as this value dips further below 100 percent. Adopt the suggestions in the previous Tip to maintain performance as much as possible.

Diagnosing problems with Timing

Photoshop 4 has a new feature known as Timing; like the other features we have described, it can be accessed from the lower-left pop-up menu of the document window shown in Figure 3-2. If you believe your system has lost performance and appears to run slower than it should, the problem may or may not be the amount of RAM you have installed. The Timing display can help you diagnose problems with your system without a technical background or expensive testing equipment. Here's a test you can perform on your own equipment to compare performance with another system:

Open a large file (40MB to 50MB) and perform a math-intensive function such as Radial Blur or Polar Coordinates. Select the Timing option from the pop-up menu in the lower-left portion of the document window. Record the result. Take the same file to another computer with the same configuration and perform the same operation. Compare the timings for applying the filter on both systems (as shown in Figure 3-5).

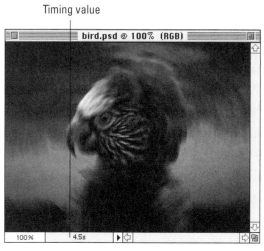

Timing value

Figure 3-5
By running a Timing test, you can diagnose problems or decide which hardware purchases are best for your system.

Timing can also help you decide what kinds of hardware purchases you should make next. If you want to know if a RAM increase will be preferable to a faster processor, you can run the same type of test, once on your system and again on a higher-performance workstation with a configuration you might desire. You can also perform similar tests on different operating systems. Make comparisons between similarly configured systems running on Macintosh, Windows 95, and Windows NT.

Freeing up memory with Purge

Once you work on a file requiring memory-intensive duties, you will often wish to flush out of memory any unnecessary data or operations. Consider what happens if you copy a large image area, for example; once it is pasted into a new document, you may not want the copied data to remain in precious RAM. In previous versions of Photoshop, you would have to select a small area in the document window and copy again. This task would replace clipboard information, flushing out the old while retaining the new. Fortunately, we have a new feature in Photoshop 4; it appears as the Purge command under the Edit menu. When you access this menu item, you can purge any of four memory-holding areas: Undo, Clipboard, Pattern, and Snapshot (see Figure 3-6). Each of these operations are held in separate memory buffers and can occupy much memory, especially when you are working on large files. When you elect to use the Purge feature, it clears the chosen memory buffer, thereby permitting you full memory access for your next Photoshop task.

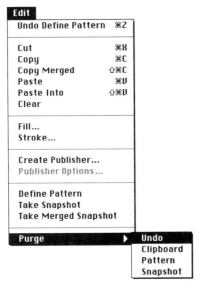

Figure 3-6
The Purge command allows you to select the memory area to empty, so you can free up extra memory.

Working Faster with Proper Memory Allocation

Notwithstanding the need for hardware upgrades, you can optimize Photoshop's performance on your system by properly configuring it within your available memory. Photoshop does require some minimums, as we discussed in Chapter 1; however, if you have at least the minimum amount of memory installed in your computer, then you still have some adjustments to make for the best performance.

Memory allocation

Allocating the proper amount of memory to Photoshop is a very important step in configuring the program to work efficiently. This really applies to all programs, so you might want to go through your most used applications and check memory allocation.

One misconception a lot of people buy into is that if you have 72MB of RAM installed in your computer, Photoshop automatically uses as much RAM as it can get its hands on. This cannot be further from the truth. Photoshop uses only memory that's specifically allocated to it.

MEMORY ALLOCATION IN THE MACINTOSH To see how much RAM is allocated to Photoshop, click its icon in the Finder and choose Get Info from the File menu to see the dialog box shown in Figure 3-7.

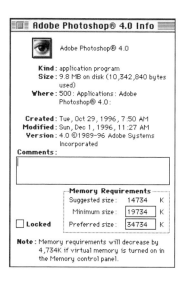

Figure 3-7
Photoshop's Info box shows its memory allocation and requirements.

In the Get Info box are three items under Memory Requirements. The Suggested Size is the size the developer of the program, in this case Adobe, has given you as a starting point. You cannot change this setting. The next is Minimum Size. Every time Photoshop is opened, your Mac will allocate at least this amount of memory to it. This is the absolute bare-bones amount of RAM that Photoshop can run with. It is highly suggested never to work with only this amount of RAM. In fact you should increase the amount as much as possible. Consider setting the Minimum Size to a value no less than the Suggested Size.

The last of the three items is Preferred Size. This is the most important setting, and it should be as large a number possible. To figure out how large this number can be, first quit any open applications, including Photoshop. From the Finder, select About This Macintosh from the Apple menu. The About This Macintosh dialog box appears. "Built-in Memory" represents how much physical RAM is installed in your computer. "Largest Unused Block" is the amount of memory left over after the System has taken what it needs to run the computer. The RAM ceiling you have for Photoshop is something less than this number.

You shouldn't just take the Largest Unused Block number and put it into the Preferred Size for Photoshop. That would basically appropriate all of your RAM for Photoshop, leaving nothing for other system functions should your system require it (and it will). The system dynamically changes all the time and needs RAM to accommodate those changes. We suggest you take whatever number is listed for Largest Unused Block, subtract 1–2MB, and use that number for the Preferred Size in Photoshop. So if you had 35MB as your Largest Unused Block, you could allocate as much as 33–34MB as Photoshop's preferred size.

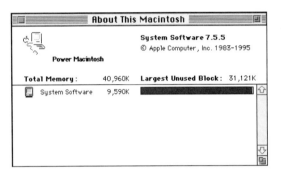

Figure 3-8
This Macintosh currently has a Largest Unused Block of 31MB RAM.

MEMORY ALLOCATION IN WINDOWS 95 As a Windows 95 user, you face many of the same general RAM requirements and potential need to purchase additional RAM as do Macintosh users, with the exception that in Windows, you can allocate up to 100 percent of available memory. What is available simply depends on how much memory Windows uses, plus how many applications you currently have open. If you use Windows 95 and run into memory problems or begin to experience problems with an out of memory error when attempting to save a Photoshop file, then you will need to increase the virtual memory in Windows. In Windows 95 go to the Control Panel and open the System file. From the tabs choose Performance and click the Virtual Memory button. As a guideline, Adobe recommends doubling the amount of RAM you have installed in your system. If, for example, you have 24MB of RAM installed, set the minimum and maximum values to 48MB. By making this change, you will enable Photoshop to control the hard disk scratch space for best performance rather than having Windows 95 manage it.

As a Windows user, you are more likely than a Mac user to have an auto-compression utility for your hard drive. Many PC users have compression utilities that compress and decompress files on the fly. If you have such a configuration on your computer, you should disable it when using Photoshop. You can avoid many problems and improve performance by not compressing either the Windows Swap File or the Photoshop scratch disk.

If you don't have tons of RAM to work with, you have an alternative. You may want to install RAM Doubler from Connectix. This program uses a virtual memory scheme that tricks the Macintosh into thinking you have more RAM than you actually have. It can double or even triple the amount of effective RAM.

Let's say your computer has 40MB of RAM installed. After you've installed RAM Doubler, your computer should report back to you that it now has 80MB of RAM or even 120MB (version 2.0 lets you *triple* your RAM), depending on how you configure RAM Doubler. The program is very inexpensive and, if needed, can be used with some good results.

There is one thing to keep in mind, though. Adobe recommends that you still not allocate more memory to Photoshop than you have physically installed in your computer. Physical RAM is what you have in your computer before RAM Doubler does its magic. Let's look at an example of what Adobe means. Say you have a 40MB system. With RAM Doubler installed you now have 80MB of RAM available. The system takes 8MB to run the computer. You now have 72MB of RAM to allocate to programs. You in fact have only 32MB of actual RAM and 40MB of virtual memory. You can allocate any amount of the 32MB of physical RAM to Photoshop, but you shouldn't dip into the other 40MB of virtual memory RAM.

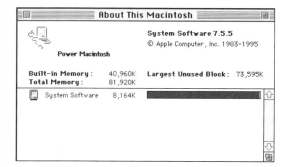

Figure 3-9
After installing RAM Doubler, this Macintosh now has a Largest Unused Block of 73MB RAM.

We suggest allocating the 32MB of RAM to Photoshop and using the other 40MB to allocate to other programs you want to run alongside Photoshop in the background. Using the previous example, you should be able to run Photoshop and a couple of other programs on a computer with only 40MB of actual RAM installed.

RAM DOUBLER

Installing your own RAM

No book offering tech support would be complete without mention of user hardware installations. The temptation is great when you think about those wonderful price reductions on RAM chips. As of this writing you can purchase RAM chips for less than

$300 for a 64MB DIMM. You may decide to call that toll-free number, order a few chips, and tackle the installation yourself. If you do, you should consider a couple of things.

RAM UPGRADES FOR THE MACINTOSH If you own one of the higher-performance Macintosh computers such as the 8500, 9500, and 9600 series, RAM chips need to be installed in the appropriate bank. On 9500 computers, for example, you have an A bank and a B bank of DIMM slots. When you install new RAM chips, you need to place them as recommended by Apple Computer. Configurations and recommendations typically change with each new computer model released.

Second, after RAM chips are installed, you need to zap the parameter RAM. You achieve this by holding down the key combination Command+Option+P+R while you start up your computer. Let the piano chord sound three times before you release the keys.

With these points in mind, we have a recommendation for you — don't try to do this yourself unless you really know what you are doing. If your livelihood depends on the documents you create on your computer, then you will always want to keep it in top running order. It is well worthwhile to pay a few extra dollars to hire someone to maintain your system and help you with the hardware upgrades. When you do hire a technician, be certain that she or he is authorized. Authorized technicians are schooled by manufacturers and receive update bulletins routinely. A lot of people are out there advertising themselves as consultants and technicians who are not qualified to perform the most routine repairs and maintenance. If you are in need of a referral, look to service bureaus and digital prepress shops for recommendations. These are the people who see more Photoshop files than anyone else, and they usually know who in town can take care of you as well as who you should avoid.

RAM UPGRADES FOR PCS As a PC user, you face some of the same questions confronting Mac users; however, you may find many more qualified technicians available locally. Still, compatible hardware and careful installations are necessary to keep your system running optimally. A word of caution to those of you who have a significant other desiring to perform surgery on your computer. You express a desire to upgrade your RAM, and one day you find this Cro-Magnon in the garage with parts scattered all over. "Don't worry honey, I'll have you up and running in a jiffy!" For piece of mind and a much better interpersonal relationship, you will be well advised to find qualified technicians to help you with your hardware upgrades. Your retort can always be, "Sweetheart, I knew you could do it, but you do so much for me and you're so busy, I thought I would take this burden off your shoulders."

Supercharging Screen Refreshes

If you are a designer who works with large image files and if you have loaded your system with RAM and high-performance drives, you still may feel the pain of waiting too long for Photoshop screen refreshes. Going out and purchasing more RAM may not be the best solution for you. Ted Padova has a computer loaded with 300MB of RAM and two 4.3GB Seagate Wide SCSI Barracuda 2 hard drives, yet he still gets impatient when he needs to do something fast. He hates the stopwatch and wants Photoshop to speed up. In his case, it would be foolish to spend more money on additional RAM when there are some other solutions available.

When you work in Photoshop, you work on the image data as they are loaded into memory. The whole file comes in and when you perform a rotation, Photoshop calculates the rotation value for the file as it pulls it in from the hard drive. Two applications are available to you, each of which has a different scheme and different approach to editing your images. Live Picture and xRes are image editing programs that work with proxies. Essentially, when you open a file in either application, you see and work on a low-res version. All your transformations, filters, and effects are applied to the low-res version. When you finish editing and save the file, the final high-res version is rendered complete with all the edits. Editing capabilities of both programs are not as extensive as you would find in Photoshop, but you can save much time in layering and applying many common operations to an image file and greatly speed up your production tasks.

Macromedia offers a bundle price for their FreeHand 7 suite, which includes Free-Hand 7, xRes, and Fontographer. It's cross-platform, so you can take advantage of it whether you use a PC or a Mac. Live Picture, which was formerly priced at just under a thousand dollars, has become much more competitive, and the price has been brought down to the average consumer level. These programs are not intended to replace Photoshop, but rather to work in tandem with it.

Avoiding File Size Hassles

The amount of storage on your hard drive that a file occupies determines the amount of RAM needed to fully load Photoshop. RAM purchases can help out when working on the file, but storage itself is a different matter. We discussed some of the issues related to file storage back in Chapter 1, and, as we pointed out, you will definitely need to acquire an external storage drive for even the most casual Photoshop use. Times may arise in your Photoshop life, however, when you just can't fit the image on the storage media you use. Since this can become a problem, let's look at some of the ways you can reduce a file's size so that you can transport it to the service bureau, to another computer, or to multiple storage cartridges.

Using file compression

In terms of the files they create, file compression schemes can be described in two basic ways: *lossy* compression schemes and *lossless* compression schemes. We won't go into the details of the file formats here, since we cover them in Chapter 5, but we will discuss a basic difference between the two.

Lossy compression actually destroys data in your file. It tosses away pixels from the image, and once lost, they cannot be regained. JPEG is an example of a lossy compression method. You can conserve a tremendous amount of space by saving your file with

JPEG compression, but you will loose information; and at the higher levels of compression, you will notice degradation of the image when printed. Therefore, it is important to know what the output requirements will be before you choose the compression method for your file. If you have a high-res image that needs to remain in a high-res form, but you don't care about the loss of data, then you can save the file with JPEG compression. This typically won't be a common practice, but it is available to you.

LZW compression, which can be used with TIFF images, is an example of a lossless compression scheme. You can save in TIFF format and select the LZW Compression option to compress the file (as shown in Figure 3-10). There is no data loss, and the file will reduce in size. If need be, you can compress the file and then copy the smaller image to your storage media for transport.

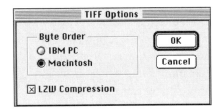

Figure 3-10
This file is being saved as a
TIFF with LZW Compression.

TIP Here's how you can avoid problems with compressed files. The two compression methods just described are discussed for the purpose of transporting your images only. These formats should never be used when outputting your file to imaging equipment. Both compression schemes would be undesirable if the results were imported into another program and sent off to the imaging center for film separations. If you need to transport a file on a storage disk to the imaging center, you can compress the file with LZW compression and then provide the imaging technicians with a note to decompress the file after it is received. To perform this decompression, the technician would open the file in Photoshop and resave it with the LZW Compression turned off. Since the JPEG compression scheme is lossy, you should avoid using it altogether when submitting files for high-resolution output.

Splitting Photoshop files

Another method for getting your file size down to fit on storage devices is to divide the Photoshop image into channels or separations. Regardless of whether your file needs to fit on a floppy or a Jaz cartridge, you can split the image without compressing it. There are actually two ways to handle splitting an image: you can split channels or you can save our file as a DCS file.

To split channels, view the Channels palette and, from the flyout menu, choose Split Channels. Depending on whether your image is RGB or CMYK, the file will be divided into either three or four separate grayscale images (as in Figure 3-11). After the channels are split, you can save these channels as separate files. The final file sizes will each be one third or one fourth of the composite image.

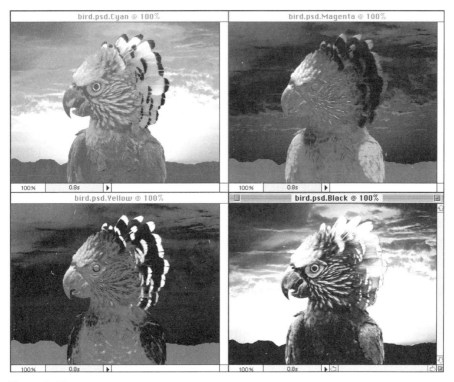

Figure 3-11
A CMYK image assumes this form after splitting the channels.

If you use Split Channels to transport a large file, you can copy all four channels to a hard drive and open all four images in Photoshop. Choose Merge Channels from the flyout menu in the Channels palette to restore the image. The result will be your original image with no data loss. A good example of using such a procedure is if you have a Zip drive with a maximum capacity of 100MB for the cartridge and a 350MB file to transport. After splitting the file into separate channels, you can copy each channel to a separate cartridge, transport the file to the imaging center, and have them restore the image prior to printing it.

Using Desktop Color Separation files

The benefits of Desktop Color Separation (DCS) files are described more thoroughly in Chapter 8, where we talk about assuring reliable output. In terms of splitting a file to fit on storage media, DCS is another method that can be used to split a Photoshop file into smaller elements. To use the DCS option, the file must be in CMYK mode and saved as EPS, as shown in Figure 3-12.

```
┌──────────────────────── EPS Format ────────────────────────┐
│                                                             │
│   Preview: │ Macintosh (8 bits/pixel) │ ▼│      ┌───────┐   │
│                                                │   OK  │   │
│      DCS: │ On (72 pixel/inch grayscale) │ ▼│    └───────┘   │
│                                                ┌────────┐   │
│   Encoding: │ Binary                  │ ▼│      │ Cancel │   │
│                                                └────────┘   │
│   ┌ Clipping Path ─────────────────────────────┐           │
│   │   Path: │ None │ ▼│                          │           │
│   │                                            │           │
│   │   Flatness: │     │  device pixels          │           │
│   └────────────────────────────────────────────┘           │
│                                                             │
│   ☐ Include Halftone Screen                                 │
│   ☐ Include Transfer Function                               │
│                                                             │
└─────────────────────────────────────────────────────────────┘
```

Figure 3-12
**Desktop Color Separation options appear in the EPS Save
dialog box.**

When you choose EPS as the format, a dialog box will appear offering you an option to turn on DCS. The default is presented with DCS turned off. When you choose On in the dialog box and save your file, Photoshop will separate the image and create *five* files. One file will be created for each of the CMYK separations, and a composite image will be created for placement in a layout or illustration program. These files can be copied separately to data storage disks and transported to the imaging center. The advantage of using this method is that the imaging staff can copy your files to a hard drive and image the document without having to restore the original Photoshop file.

As noted previously, the true benefit of DCS will be discussed later. For now, we've given you some tech support tips on how to work with memory limitations and make your file transport a little easier. If you're feeling a little lost on file format issues, don't worry—we'll look at all of Photoshop's file formats in the next chapter.

CHAPTER FOUR

DEALING WITH
COLOR MODES AND
FILE FORMATS

Photoshop affords an artist the luxury of opening and saving images in a variety of file formats, and this is undoubtedly one of its strengths. Photoshop also uses color modes to specify what kind of pixels are stored in a file, and these interact in different ways with file formats. When a program is this versatile, it usually becomes more complex, and problems inevitably arise. By understanding a few file format and color mode issues, such as what happens when you combine a file format or color mode with a particular application or output device, you can avoid time-wasting glitches. This chapter describes the different file formats and color modes found in Photoshop and shows how to avoid problems while getting predictable results.

Color Modes

There are eight unique color modes in Photoshop:

- **Bitmap:** Bitmap images are black-and-white files. Every pixel is either black or white. There is no grayscale or color information. Bitmap images have far less detail than, say, that of a grayscale image, and many of Photoshop's tools are not available when in Bitmap mode.

- **Grayscale:** Grayscale images are usually black-and-white photos. Pixels in grayscale images contain varying intensities of gray tone that when put together make up an image. Because each pixel can contain much more information than a bitmap pixel (which can only be 100 percent black or 100 percent white), these files can be considerably larger in file size.

- **Duotone:** Duotones are two-color images; however, the Duotone mode can be used to create a monotone, which is a one-color image; the duotone; a tritone, which has three colors; and a quadtone, which is a four-color image. The last of these should not be confused with process color, which is described in varying levels of cyan, magenta, yellow, and black. Duotones provide opportunities to use from one to four spot colors in an image. For those clients on limited budgets who wish to use, for example, two-color brochures, Photoshop's duotone capability is ideal for setting up two-color separations.

- **Indexed Color:** This mode creates a specific, limited color palette optimized for a particular image. This is useful for Web graphics or other media or platforms where screen views are the desired output. Indexed color contains a maximum of 256 colors that can be represented on screen at any time. File sizes will generally be approximately $1/8$ the size of RGB color images, which makes them desirable for memory-sensitive applications such as Web graphics and multimedia programs.

- **RGB Color**: Perhaps the most common mode in Photoshop, RGB is described in varying blends of red, green, and blue. On 24-bit monitors the RGB color gamut is capable of producing color drawn from a palette of 16.7 million colors. RGB color has two distinct advantages when working in Photoshop. First, it is the desirable mode when output requirements are for Web graphics, screen presentations, and RGB printing devices, such as film recorders. Second, RGB files are smaller than their CMYK counterparts and thus takes less disk space to edit an image. For many Photoshop sessions, you can work in the smaller RGB mode prior to converting your image to CMYK for output.

- **CMYK Color:** CMYK color is process color and the mode of choice for all digital prepress output devices. Whether you choose to output your documents on low-end desktop color printers or use imagesetting services for film separations, your files will need to be converted to this mode. CMYK color has a much narrower color gamut than the RGB color mode.

- **Lab Color:** Lab Color was originally developed by an international commission to mathematically describe all color perceptible to the human eye. You don't really need to know as much about the theory behind Lab Color as what you can actually do with it in Photoshop. The Lab mode is a three-channel image with the first channel, known as the Lightness channel, representing all the brightness. The other two channels, the A channel and the B channel, represent all the color in an image. The advantage of converting an image to Lab mode is that it provides you a means to view and edit all the brightness values without affecting the color in your image. For example, you could apply a filter to the Lightness channel or perform some other Photoshop editing task on it without affecting the a or b channels, which hold the color information.

■ **Multichannel:** Multichannel images contain two or more individual channels viewed in grayscale. Any of the previously described modes with two or more channels can be converted to multichannel, which provides you an opportunity to work on grayscale channels independently. If you convert an RGB image to multichannel, you'll see three grayscale channels. Conversion back to RGB will reestablish the RGB image without color loss. Multichannel images can be used to create some interesting special effects by swapping or replacing color channels. For example you could swap the red and blue channels and convert back to RGB for a totally different view of your image.

Modes and Formats

Photoshop provides many different formats in which you can save or export your file for placement in other programs or output to a variety of printing devices. In this section we'll look at the various formats supported by each mode and identify any problems that can potentially be encountered. Rather than mention all the formats for a given mode, we provided a table at the end of the chapter as a guide for all possible combinations of mode and format. We will discuss in this section some of the advantages of one format over another for a given mode and any problems associated with other options. Before we begin, familiarize yourself with the various choices for color modes by choosing Image ➪ Mode (see Figure 4-1).

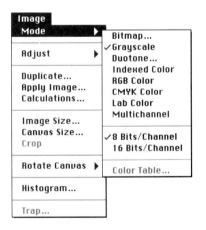

Figure 4-1
These are the color mode options available in Photoshop.

Bitmaps and File Formats

Bitmap images have far less detail than, say, that of a grayscale image, and many of Photoshop's tools are not available when in Bitmap mode. So why would you want to work with an image that has these types of limitations?

Perhaps the most common use of bitmap images is for line art scans. Line art has two color values — black and white. With the absence of gray values, the images in bitmap mode are approximately $1/8$ the size of the same file in grayscale mode. If handled properly, bitmap images can be a good friend. If handled improperly, they can result in some of your worst printing nightmares. When you know a bitmap is the mode of choice for your design work, you have many choices for choosing the right format for the job. Each format depends on the kind of output device you intend to print to or the kind of application that may receive the Photoshop image. Here's a list of some of the more common formats associated with bitmaps:

- **Photoshop:** Photoshop's native format may be desirable if you intend to return to the image and further edit it in Photoshop at a later time or transfer it between Windows and Mac platforms.

- **BMP:** This format is a bitmap format more common to PC users than Mac users. BMPs can be transported between platforms. A Mac user may wish to export a file as a BMP for a Windows user to edit in Windows Paint.

- **CompuServe GIF:** Bitmaps can be exported to GIF files for Web graphics by choosing the Save command or using the Export GIF89a format available by choosing File ➪ Export ➪ GIF89a.

- **Photoshop EPS:** Bitmaps saved in EPS format have a distinct advantage in creating a mask without the aid of a clipping path. When you choose EPS as your file format, a dialog box will appear enabling you to make all the white information in the image transparent (see Figure 4-2). By checking Transparent Whites, you will render the image with only the black visible when the image is placed in another program.

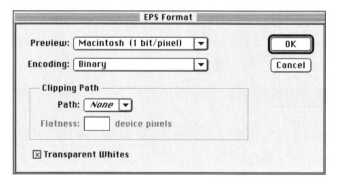

Figure 4-2
The EPS Format dialog box shows Transparent Whites selected.

- **PCX:** Another format common to Windows users, this format can be used to transport files between platforms. Common uses for PCX are importing graphic images in software not capable of importing EPS or TIFF images.

- **PICT:** This is the Mac counterpart to PCX and is usually preferred for either screen graphics or output to devices supporting Apple's QuickDraw file structure.

- **PNG:** Portable Network Graphics (PNG) is a new format designed for Web graphics. Unfortunately, most Web browsers either don't currently support this format or require special plug-ins to view files in it. As the Web evolves and PNG becomes more popular, you have the capability of exporting a bitmap in this format.

- **TIFF:** Tiff is one of the most common file formats chosen for bitmap images. Unlike EPS formats, TIFF provides you an opportunity to colorize your Photoshop file after it has been imported into layout or illustration programs.

Avoiding bitmap jaggies

Since a bitmap image holds less detail than a grayscale image, you need more resolution for it to print without jagged edges. More resolution means a larger file size. Therefore, the critical issue is how much resolution to give the bitmap without overdoing it. Too much resolution will create problems with image editing and the demands placed on memory as well as potential printing problems. To avoid problems, you need to know what to target as the resolution for the bitmap to achieve smooth edges without jaggies and how much resolution will be too much. Knowing the exact resolution is a very simple task; you need only commit this simple rule to memory: image resolution = device resolution. In most instances, if your image resolution matches the output resolution of the device, your files will print with optimal results. Therefore, if you intend to print a bitmap image on a 600 dpi laser printer, the bitmap should be 600 dpi. Conversely, if you print to a high-end imagesetter, your device resolution will be 1200, 2400, or even 3600 dpi. In these instances, we recommend you use 1200 dpi for all imagesetting. Like anything else in Photoshop, no rule is absolute without an exception. Trust us, though; you'll be fine and eliminate all jagged edges with 1200 dpi for high-end devices (see Figure 4-3).

Figure 4-3
A bitmap image has been printed at 2400 dpi with image resolutions of 150 dpi (left) and 1200 dpi (right).

Using "unavailable" tools on bitmap images

A drawback when manipulating bitmap images is that you cannot use all the tools you would normally work with. The tools that are unavailable are the ones that need grayscale information to work properly, such as the blur tool, the gradient tool, and the magic wand. But this is usually just fine because you probably don't want to use such tools on a bitmap image anyway. If by chance you do need to use one of these tools, convert your image to grayscale mode (Image ➪ Mode ➪ Grayscale). Keep the Size Ratio set to 1, and then manipulate the image as needed. When you're done, convert the image back to Bitmap mode. When converting it back to a bitmap, maintain the current resolution setting, and be sure to select 50% Threshold under Method.

Avoiding antialiasing edges

When you scan an image in bitmap mode as line art, even with high-resolution scans, the edges may still be a bit jagged. To overcome jagged edges, Photoshop uses a method of rendering a smooth appearance known as *antialiasing*. The antialiasing process involves placing intermediate gray values (that is, values averaging the foreground and background pixel values) around the image to give us the illusion of smoothness. When we view such an image, our visual perception views it as smoother around the edges. Unfortunately, bitmaps hold only two values: black and white. As a result, we can not antialias edges with various gray pixels, since the grays are unavailable in Bitmap mode. To overcome the problem, we need to perform a mode conversion. To do so, choose Image ➪ Mode ➪ Grayscale. Now in the Grayscale mode we can soften the edges around an image.

If you have similar images and need to improve them with Photoshop, follow these steps:

1. Scan your image at the highest resolution provided by your scanner software.

2. Convert the line art scan from its bitmap form to grayscale.

3. Choose Filter ➪ Blur ➪ Gaussian Blur. The amount will vary according to how much fill is needed on the edges to render them smooth.

4. Choose Image ➪ Adjust ➪ Levels. Click on the Preview box and move the sliders from either edge of the input values to eliminate all grays.

Figure 4-4 shows an image on the left that's scanned from a poor-quality original and in need of severe antialiasing. On the right, the Gaussian Blur amount applied was set to 25.

Figure 4-4
An image is shown before (left) and after (right) applying a Gaussian Blur of 25 and Levels Adjustment.

Grayscales Images and File Formats

Grayscale images are among the most common modes in Photoshop. We print grayscale images to laser printers, and we use grayscale images to create halftones for offset printing. Most often, grayscale is not used for screen views, since almost all computers and projection systems are commonly supporting color. Grayscale file formats, therefore, are almost always used to get the grayscale image from your computer to a printing device. The more common file formats supporting grayscale include these:

- **Photoshop:** Since grayscale images support layers, you will often find it appropriate to save your file as a native Photoshop format in order to preserve the layers. Layers cannot be exported to other programs, so the final image will need to be exported in a different format.

- **CompuServe GIF:** If for some reason you want grayscale images to appear on a Web page, then the GIF format is available to you from the Grayscale mode. As with the bitmaps mentioned earlier, the GIF89a Export option would be the best choice for saving a GIF image for the World Wide Web.

- **EPS:** One of the two most common formats for printing, EPS offers the advantage of allowing you to save a grayscale image together with a clipping path to mask a portion of that image. Figure 4-5 shows the results of using a clipping path.

- **PDF:** Adobe's Portable Document Format (PDF) is available directly from Photoshop 4 and supported in the Grayscale mode. Use this format to import images in Adobe Acrobat. One great advantage of PDF is that the file can be used on many platforms and that the Adobe Acrobat Reader software is available free from Adobe Systems. If you have clients who don't use Photoshop but want to see the images on their computer, save in PDF and point your client to `http://www.adobe.com`, where Acrobat Reader can be downloaded free from Adobe's Web site.

Figure 4-5
An image has been saved as EPS without (left) and with (right) a clipping path and then placed in Adobe PageMaker and printed.

- **Scitex CT:** the Scitex Continuous Tone (CT) format is proprietary to Scitex imaging equipment. If you want to output a Photoshop file to an IRIS printer or a Scitex Workstation, the service center may request a Scitex CT file. Grayscale images support Scitex CT.

- **TIFF:** The TIFF format is probably the most common for all Photoshop grayscale images and can be printed on almost any output device. TIFF has one distinct advantage over EPS: the image size and storage requirements are less than for EPS files.

Grayscale images present another set of rules differing substantially from those for bitmap images. In contrast to the previous examples, grayscale images contain much more information and color data. As a result, we will always be concerned with preserving as much information on the printed document as we see appear on screen.

Grayscale resolution requirements

In describing bitmap images, we discussed the need to match the image resolution to the device resolution. That's fine for the bitmap image; however, the rules change with grayscale and color images. In order for you to understand what resolution is required for any given grayscale image, a few fundamental rules need to be tucked away in your imaging belt. With this in mind, let's take a look at the fundamentals.

One thing to always keep in mind is the magic number 256. When you look at various dialog boxes in Photoshop, you'll see many references to scales measuring from 0 to 255. Dialog boxes such as Levels and Curves have such references. These scales demonstrate a total of 256 gray levels capable of being displayed in an image other than a Bitmap. Two hundred fifty-six is also the magic number used in PostScript. The Post-Script page description language is capable of rendering only 256 levels of gray on any given device. Therefore, your objective is to try to capture all 256 levels every time you send a file to an imaging device.

To capture all these levels of gray, you need to image your files at sufficient image resolution and have sufficient resolution in the Photoshop image. If you know something about halftone frequency, you know that the image resolution doesn't need any more than twice the screen frequency. In many cases resolution can be 1.25 to 1.5 times the frequency. Device resolution is not controlled on desktop machines but can be controlled on high-end imagesetting equipment. Imagesetters typically provide resolutions of 1200, 2400, or 3600 dpi. Therefore, which resolution to request is something you need to know. A simple rule to follow is called the Rule of 16. Just take the line screen you require and multiply that times 16 to determine what resolution you need to have from the service bureau's imagesetter. A 100-line screen requires 1600 dpi to produce all 256 levels of gray ($16 \times 100 = 1600$). Your Photoshop image would not require any more resolution than 200 dpi ($100 \text{ lpi} \times 2$).

 TIP Lowering the screen frequency or increasing the output resolution is a good way to solve any problems you might have with banding, covered in Chapter 6.

The important point for you to remember is that grayscale images require certain criteria for proper imaging. If you don't understand frequencies or device resolutions, ask the people at your service center, and then plug in the values in the formulas.

Proper scanning for grayscales

Since we know what the output resolution requirements are, we can determine what resolution our scanned image needs. This will always be your approach to any Photoshop task requiring scanning. First, assess the output needs, and then scan the image with sufficient resolution. To avoid any problems with scanning, we need to briefly look at some differences in resolution. Way back in our discussion on bitmap images, we suggested you scan your image at the highest resolution. For most of today's desktop flatbed scanners, you will find interpolated resolutions equaling 600, 1200, or maybe 2400 ppi (pixels per inch). These scanners, however, have optical, or true, resolutions of lesser values ranging between one half to one fourth the interpolated resolution.

Interpolated resolutions are a form of mathematical guesswork by which pixels are created by the software scanning the image. In addition to scanning software, Photoshop is also capable of interpolating resolution. To examine Photoshop's interpolation capabilities, choose Image ⇨ Image Size and look at the Image Size dialog box.

Notice the Resample Image check box in Figure 4-6. When this box is checked and a new size or resolution is supplied, the image will be interpolated as Photoshop eliminates pixels to size your document down or creates additional pixels when upsizing the image. Interpolation should be avoided whenever possible. Interpolating images will always create some degree of deterioration. As good as Photoshop is, it can't do as well in manufacturing pixels as an original scan. To avoid problems with interpolation, you should always scan images at no greater than the highest optical (or true) resolution of your scanner when scanning for grayscale or color. As we mentioned earlier, bitmaps are the exception to this rule. When the resolution needs exceed the capabilities of your desktop scanner, look to service centers for drum scans. The prices will be higher, but the results will be much better.

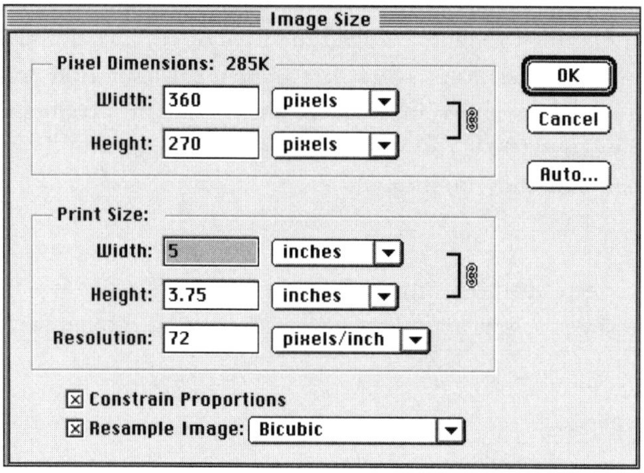

Figure 4-6
The Image Size dialog box has Resample Image (bicubic) selected.

Duotones and File Formats

Duotones can include one, two, three, or four spot colors. With monotones, duotones, and tritones, the designer has the capability to provide your clients with more affordable color documents. Four-color or more process separations will be more costly than two-color jobs.

When you save a duotone, you have only two formats of any value available to you. They are these:

- **Photoshop:** The native Photoshop format is available for duotone images and should be used to save a file when you have layers and/or channels. Since Photoshop files most likely won't become the final printed image, consider this format your working image before the final form is exported to a layout program.

- **Photoshop EPS:** EPS is the end product of all duotone images, whether they include one, two, three, or four spot colors. Those with four spot colors can be converted to CMYK for process printing, in which case you could have other formats available to you. For most circumstances, however, consider only the EPS format available for duotones.

Perhaps more problems are associated with duotone images than any other color mode. These problems usually involve identifying the spot color, getting all spot values to print on the same separated plate, and having the colors print at the right angles in the final film separation. The first two of these are up to you to make right, while the last one is the responsibility of your service center.

The most common means of avoiding problems with any type of file that will eventually be printed is to first print separations to your laser printer. When you print a separation, you will immediately know whether all your elements are printing on the right plate. If you have an image and text, for example, that are identified with the same colors, and one prints while the other doesn't, you know you have to go back to work before the image is shipped off to the service center.

Getting duotone colors right

One item in Photoshop's Preferences is particularly important to those who create duotones. If you choose File ⇨ Preferences ⇨ General, the dialog box appearing (Figure 4-7) will display an item for the naming convention used for Pantone colors. If you check Short PANTONE Names, colors will be identified with the "CVC" suffix. If the check box is selected, the colors will include the shorter "CV" suffix. Therefore, a long Pantone name will appear something like PANTONE 145 CVC, whereas the short name for this color will appear as PANTONE 145 CV. Proper naming conventions will always assist you in producing files that image properly.

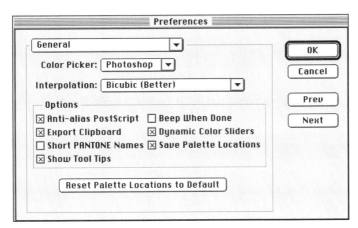

Figure 4-7
In this Preferences dialog box, Short PANTONE Names has
been deselected.

If you decide to import your Photoshop file into Adobe Illustrator or QuarkXPress, the default Pantone Coated libraries are identified in those programs with short names. If, on the other hand, you elect to import files into Adobe PageMaker or Macromedia FreeHand, the default Pantone Coated libraries are identified with long names.

You can run into many problems when using the short names in one program and the long names in another. In many cases you will get separate plates although your desire was to print all Pantone inks of a given name on the same plate. To avoid this kind of problem, it's wise to either edit the names in the respective program or set your Photoshop preferences to be consistent with the program to which you intend to export your files.

Getting the angles right

The other problem with a duotone or any type of spot color separation is printing angles. For process separations, each color is printed at a different angle. The standard printing angles are 15 degrees for cyan, 75 degrees for magenta, 45 degrees for black, and 0 degrees for yellow. If all the colors on a film separation printed at the same angle, your final print would be produced with a severe moiré pattern. To avoid a moiré, the colors need to be adjusted to different angles. The problem with duotone and spot color images is that all the colors will default to 45-degree angles.

As we suggested earlier, this type of problem is the responsibility of the service center. A good service center with knowledgeable staff will usually set the angles of their imaging device for appropriate output before imaging your file. What happens, though, when you are backed up against a deadline and they make a mistake or you use a service center with less qualified staff? You could be out some time and money, and you could potentially lose a client. If you want to avoid problems of this nature, then we suggest you take charge of your work and control as many variables as you can. Doing so may save you some precious time on those rush jobs. Here's a tip that will guarantee correct separations of duotone images every time.

TIP When printing spot color, identify all your colors in Process Inks. On a two-color separation, set one ink to black and the other to either cyan or magenta. Almost every imaging center by default prints process separations with the correct angles noted earlier. When the film is printed, put a piece of masking tape on the film to tell your commercial printer what ink you want to print. For example, let's say you want to use black and Pantone 141 for a two-color job. Identify your Photoshop duotone as black and cyan. Set the type in your layout program to black and cyan colors only. On the separated film, put some masking tape on the cyan plate and label it "Pantone 141." When your job goes to press, the printer will know what ink to print on each plate.

Refer to Adobe FaxYI document #173309 (written by Don Day, this book's technical reviewer) to learn how to create documents containing one to four spot colors in Photoshop for printing from page layout applications. You can view it by going on the Web to http://www.adobe.com, clicking on the Support Databases link, and searching for the document number. (You can also call the FaxYI phone list at (206) 628-5737 and enter the document number.) The process is also referred to (in less detail) in the *User Guide*.

Indexed Color and File Formats

We like to think of indexed color images as falling into two categories. The first category is the intentional, which involves converting your Photoshop file to indexed color when this format is appropriate, that is, for screen graphics, including images to be viewed on the World Wide Web, multimedia presentations, and screen displays. The second category is the unintentional. You may receive an image from someone who created a graphic in a low-end paint program and saved the file as indexed color, or you may find an image on a CD of clip art that you wish to include in a printed piece. If this file is to be printed, then the Indexed Color mode should not be used. If your desire is to use this image for a screen graphic, you have many different formats to choose from for indexed color. The more popular formats for screen images include these:

- **BMP:** The BMP format is available in indexed color and might be used to export to a low-end paint program or a cross-platform user who wishes to place the image in a program not supporting EPS or TIFF.

- **CompuServe GIF:** We noted earlier that GIF is usually used for Web graphics. You can export in GIF format from the File ⇨ Save As menu option, which will include the CompuServe GIF87 and GIF89a formats, or you can select File ⇨ Export ⇨ GIF89a Export. When you choose the latter, you can include Transparency and Interlacing. Figure 4-8 displays the dialog box that appears when you choose the GIF89a Export option.

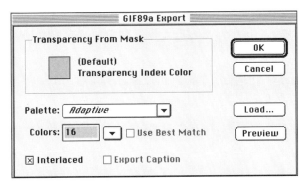

Figure 4-8
The GIF89a Export dialog box includes the Transparency and Interlacing options unavailable elsewhere.

- **PCX:** This is the Windows counterpart to the Mac's PICT format. PCX can be used effectively with screen presentation programs such as Microsoft PowerPoint and Adobe Persuasion. When you first convert your image to indexed color and then save it as PCX, the file size will be smaller than in formats such as EPS or TIFF.

- **PICT:** PICT (Picture) is the standard Macintosh native format. PICT is ideal for screen graphics for multimedia purposes. Web users, however, should look to the JPEG or GIF format for inclusion of graphic images in Web pages. PICT can be used with screen presentation programs such as Microsoft PowerPoint, Adobe Persuasion, and Macromedia Director.

- **TIFF:** TIFF files fall into the same category as the EPS files described earlier. Since we wouldn't consider using an indexed color image for printing purposes, TIFF files saved from the Indexed Color mode would rarely be used.

WARNING Although indexed color images can be exported with the Photoshop EPS option, the EPS format does not support indexed color. When you open the file in Photoshop, it'll be listed as RGB.

Avoiding problems with indexed color for the Web

When you intentionally wish to use indexed color images for something like Web graphics, you can handle the conversion from such modes as RGB to indexed color in either of two ways: you can convert the image yourself by choosing Image ⇨ Mode ⇨ Indexed Color, or you can have Photoshop automatically convert to indexed color when you choose the File ⇨ Export ⇨ GIF89a export function. When you perform a conversion by choosing Image ⇨ Mode ⇨ Indexed Color, Photoshop will display a dialog box prompting you to describe the attributes for the conversion. Figure 4-9 shows which attributes should be used with a Photoshop image for your Web browser.

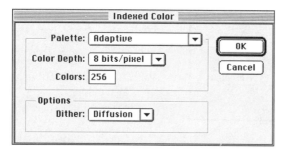

Figure 4-9
This Indexed Color mode conversion dialog box
shows the settings you want for Web images.

Remember, when converting to indexed color for Web graphics, use the adaptive palette and use diffusion for the dithering. These attributes should be set for images that don't require transparency. If you need transparency or if you have text that requires transparency so that all the area outside the text will display the Web browser background, then the dithering can present some problems. The most obvious problem is a halo effect appearing around your type. This problem occurs because the text is antialiased. A way to avoid this problem is to create a channel for the areas you wish to render transparent and use the channel instead of a color for the transparency. Let's look at an example to make this clear.

Figure 4-10 illustrates a line of type that was converted to indexed color. The sampled color, white in this case, was selected for the transparency.

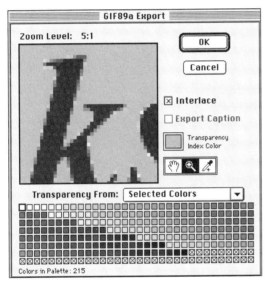

Figure 4-10
The white background is selected for the transparency.

The sampled white value will be rendered transparent when this image is imported in a Web browser. When you zoom into the image in the thumbnail preview offered from the dialog box, you will notice individual pixels of varying percentages of gray. This effect was created from the antialiased type. When you import the image into Netscape Navigator or Microsoft Internet Explorer, the text will appear with bits of white around the edges. This result is created because the sampled color is only one of the values within the range of 256 colors. Therefore, any value less than 100 percent white was not included in the sample.

The alternative to sampling color for transparency is to first load the type as a selection and then choose Select ⇨ Save Selection. The saved selection creates an alpha channel. To avoid problems, create the alpha channel and then convert your image to indexed color. When you choose File ⇨ Export ⇨ GIF89a Export, the dialog box offers you several choices for how the transparency is created. In this case we would choose Transparency From Channel #2 instead of a selected color, as illustrated in Figure 4-11. With this choice, the antialiased edges will be excluded from the transparency mask, thereby producing a much preferable display of your type when imported into the Web browser.

TIP You'll get the same results, without going through Indexed Color mode with an alpha channel, if the text is on a layer and you have only that layer visible when you select Export Í Gif89a and choose Export as RGB. Choose Adaptive and 255 Colors, and then initiate a Preview. The result will look the same as in Figure 4-11.

Figure 4-11
Create Transparency from an Alpha channel through this dialog box.

Avoiding problems with indexed color and printed graphics

Regardless of whether you intend to print to CMYK printing devices or to RGB devices, the mode should be converted respectively to CMYK or RGB. This is a simple matter, but many designers often overlook this simple rule. We would also recommend that you use an indexed color image only when absolutely necessary. When a file is converted to indexed color, the colors are reduced to a maximum of 256 values. The illusion that the image is displayed in a wider range of color is created by the dithering process, which is fine for screen views but terrible for printed documents. Once these colors are reduced to 256, they cannot be regained when you convert back to RGB or CMYK. They're gone forever. Indexed color images will always reproduce as inferior to original RGB or CMYK images.

To avoid reproduction problems when printing images that have been converted to indexed color, try to obtain the original RGB image. You can perform an RGB to CMYK conversion for separations or print the RGB image to devices such as film recorders. If you can't obtain an original RGB version, you would be better off with another image when going to high-end digital prepress.

RGB and File Formats

We have addressed RGB throughout this chapter. We can't talk about color in Photoshop except by reference to the RGB mode. RGB is the mode you will find all desktop color scans producing and the mode most commonly used for editing purposes. From RGB, we have a choice of many different file formats, all depending on our output requirements. Regardless of whether we wish to use our images for screen views or printed results, RGB offers many opportunities. The more common ones include these:

- **Photoshop:** The native Photoshop format is used as discussed with the previous formats for preserving layers and continuing editing operations.

- **Photoshop EPS:** The EPS format can be used when exporting RGB images to slide output applications such as Microsoft PowerPoint or Adobe Persuasion. The EPS format may be preferred by service centers that have Postscript RIPs attached to film recorders instead of QuickDraw devices. On rare occasions, some CMYK printing devices actually produce better results with RGB files. One example is the LaserMaster DisplayMaker. Although this is an oversized inkjet printer producing CMYK inks, the LaserMaster ColorMark software handles RGB better while ripping the image and creating the dithering to produce high-quality prints from low-resolution files. This example is the exception rather than the rule. You should always check with your service center before offering them a file and let the service technicians dictate which mode they prefer.

- **JPEG:** JPEG files are similar to those we discussed in the section "Indexed Color and File Formats" and may be appropriate where screen views are desired. JPEG is an excellent format for Web images, in which transparency is not needed. In Photoshop 4 we now have an opportunity to export JPEG files as progressive JPEGs. A progressive JPEG file appears in the Web browser much like an Interlaced GIF image, in increasing resolutions as the file is downloaded from a server. JPEG images for the Web are best created from RGB files, since they retain a wider color gamut than CMYK images. When you choose the JPEG option, you will be provided with a dialog box offering some choices for setting the quality and the number of scans to fully load the image, as illustrated in Figure 4-16. Photoshop offers 11 levels of image quality and three levels of scans. What to choose is a matter of personal choice. Since the final image will be produced on screen, you can start with higher levels of compression, which result in lower image quality but smaller file sizes. Then preview the results and make changes by resaving the original with different values until you arrive at the desired look.

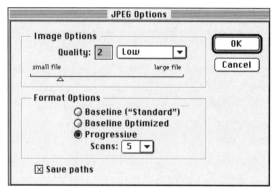

Figure 4-12
The JPEG Options dialog box is shown with a Quality of 2 selected.

WARNING Avoid saving a JPEG file over itself. It can cause artifacts and image degradation if done too much. Always resave from the original RGB or save it as a JPEG under a different name.

- **PDF:** Another screen mode is the Adobe Acrobat PDF. Acrobat files can be used for document transport and a form of multimedia presentation. The latter use is a most respectable alternative to other, more expensive applications that enable importing video and creating hypertext references. Acrobat Exchange offers it all, and you may wish to experiment with Acrobat when the need for multimedia arises. To give you an idea of some things you can do in Acrobat, we've included a sample on the CD-ROM accompanying the book, as well as the Acrobat Reader software. (It's called VCAdClub.pdf.)

- **PICT:** RGB files saved in PICT format are most commonly used for slides and screen viewing. Multimedia programs such as Macromedia Director make use of PICT formats. When you use programs supporting EPS, PICT, and TIFF for screen output, choose PICT over the others. The file sizes will be smaller and the results, identical. As stated earlier, never use PICT formats for PostScript printing devices.

- ■ **Scitex CT:** When you think of Scitex CT, think of many uses similar to those for formats such as EPS and TIFF. Since the files will surely be used for output to high-end printing systems, you would not use the RGB mode. If you save a file in Scitex CT from an RGB image and print to an IRIS printer, you'll notice very different color results than from files converted to CMYK and then exported in Scitex CT format.

- ■ **TIFF:** Although you would not use RGB TIFF images for print, you can make use of RGB TIFFs while editing your images. Saving in TIFF format provides the capability of using Photoshop's Quick Edit mode. Files need to be saved in TIFF before the File ➪ Import ➪ Quick Edit function can be used. After editing, convert to CMYK to print the final image.

When working with RGB images for screen presentations and Web graphics, you have a great advantage over those who wish to print their Photoshop files. What you see on screen is what you get. If you don't like the results, keep working with the image until it displays properly on your monitor. Unfortunately, when you set up a Photoshop file to be printed, what you see on your monitor will often not print properly.

Since RGB can be used effectively as an editing mode in Photoshop before you export the final image for print, you need to consider a safeguard during the editing process. The best safeguard available to you is to view CMYK colors while working in RGB. To create a CMYK view, choose the View ➪ CMYK Preview menu option. When CMYK Preview is active, your file size will be smaller as you edit your image, yet the colors will be displayed on your monitor within the CMYK gamut, which will ultimately be more true to the final printed piece.

RGB files should always be converted to CMYK as your last step in the editing process. For proper printing results, always be certain to convert to this mode before importing your images in layout or illustration programs.

CMYK and File Formats

We have spoken of CMYK throughout this chapter. By now, you should realize that almost all files to be output for color composite prints or color separations should be converted to CMYK. After you convert your images to this mode, you have several choices available for the file format. The more common formats for printed pieces include these:

- ■ **Photoshop:** The native Photoshop format is available for CMYK images. Once you convert to CMYK, you should not reconvert your images to RGB for editing. Since Photoshop will preserve all layers and channels, you can save a duplicate copy or your image in the Photoshop format to make any changes in the final document.

- ■ **Photoshop EPS:** We recommend CMYK images saved as EPS for color separations. EPS offers some capabilities the other formats will not provide. You can, for example, save your files with JPEG compression, which will provide a smaller file size yet not visibly deteriorate the image. When you choose File ➪ Save ➪ Photoshop EPS, a dialog box will appear enabling you to choose the compression amount as illustrated in Figure 4-13.

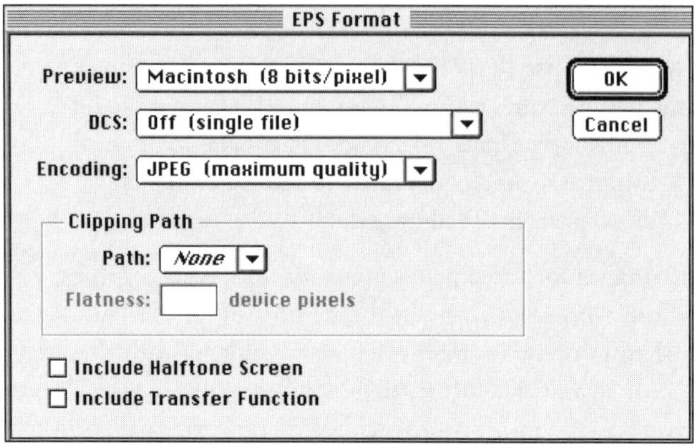

Figure 4-13
You can include JPEG compression when exporting an EPS file.

Another option available for EPS formats once converted to CMYK is to create a Desktop Color Separation (DCS) file. When printing color separations, you can use the DCS option, which enables Photoshop to create the separation before your file is imported into another program. If a layout program such as QuarkXPress or Adobe PageMaker prints the final separation, your Photoshop files saved as DCS will relieve the layout application of the burden of having to separate the Photoshop images.

■ **JPEG:** CMYK files saved as JPEG should not be confused with the JPEG option available with EPS export. Although Photoshop provides you with the option of going directly to a compressed JPEG, the files will definitely not print properly when creating color separations. In almost all cases, you would not use CMYK JPEG formats.

■ **Scitex CT:** This format will typically be dictated by your service center. If you print to IRIS Inkjet printers or Scitex Dolev devices, the service center may offer a discount if you provide them with Scitex CT files. Different service bureaus and print shops have many different ways of preparing files for printing to their devices. You should always speak to service technicians before supplying the final document to be printed.

■ **TIFF:** The temptation to save CMYK TIFF is forever present, since the file sizes are smaller than for Photoshop EPS images. Although you can print and separate files equally as well from TIFF format as from EPS, the latter may provide more suitability for the imaging center. You will always be faced with the question of whether to save CMYK files as TIFF or EPS. Here again, you should ask the imaging center for guidelines. What saves you a bit of time and hard disk space may cost the imaging center much more time when your files are printed. If they charge additional money for overtime printing, you may face greater expense for your film separations, not to mention time delays.

Whether your imaging center prefers Photoshop EPS, Scitex CT, or TIFF formats, one problem to always avoid is using multiple formats for the same document. You can be faced with potential imaging problems if you save one Photoshop file as TIFF and another as EPS and then import both images into a layout program. The most important point here is just to be consistent. If you have some files saved as TIFF and others as EPS, use Photoshop's Actions commands to batch-process a mode conversion. You can open a folder of TIFF images and set up an Action command to convert them all to EPS. This feature can be used to process a number of files while you walk away from your computer. After completing the conversions, update your links in the layout program.

Another problem common to imaging centers pertains to files saved as JPEG. If you save a CMYK file as JPEG, import the file into a layout program, and try to separate it, only the black plate will print. If you find this problem occurring, you have already lost data in the image through the JPEG compression. To correct the problem, go back to the original scan, reedit the image, and save it in either EPS or TIFF.

For film recorders and RGB printing devices, CMYK images will often print in grayscale only. If you have a file that you wish to print on a film recorder, you can convert the CMYK image back to RGB for printing. Doing so, however, will not regain the color lost when the image was converted to CMYK. You would be better off going back to the original scan in RGB mode and exporting that file for printing to such devices.

Lab Color and File Formats

Lab Color represents documents in three color channels. The L channel holds all the brightness values, whereas the A channel holds color values ranging from green to red, and the B channel holds color values ranging from blue to yellow. Files saved in Lab Color can be printed directly to Postscript Level 2 devices, and they can be color separated. In most cases, you would not save files in the Lab mode, but you can make great use of Lab Color while editing an image. Since the color is separated from the brightness while in Lab mode, you can apply brightness adjustments, editing, filter operations, and more to the L channel only and not affect the color in your image. Native Photoshop, Photoshop EPS, and TIFF formats are available to Lab Color and follow the same rules we discussed earlier with CMYK images.

Multichannel and File Formats

Multichannel images are perhaps the least understood and therefore the least used mode in Photoshop. When you convert an image to Multichannel, the file will be divided into separate grayscale images for each of the channels that was present in the original image. Grayscale, RGB, CMYK, and Lab Color images can all be converted to Multichannel. If you delete a channel from the RGB, CMYK, or Lab mode, a Multichannel image will automatically be created by Photoshop. Once you create that Multichannel image, the only formats available to you are Photoshop's native format and the Raw format. Since you can't do much with the Raw format, at first glance, you may feel Multichannel images are worthless. Multichannel, however, is most advantageous when you wish to print spot color, use varnishes, or carry out other specialized color separations.

With all the enhancements and new additions to Photoshop in version 4, we still don't have an internal capability of separating spot color. Unless you wish to use a duotone, you can't pull out individual spot colors for screen printers or create separations from individual color assignments. Some third-party utilities (discussed in Chapter 8) can help us out, but they are costly. If you have an immediate need to create a spot color separation from a Photoshop image and don't have the time or money to acquire another software utility, you can create a workaround by using Photoshop's Multichannel mode.

Let's assume for a moment that you wish to create a duotone image with a varnish. Your commercial printer will want three pieces of film: one for each of the duotone colors and one for the varnish. The two colors will have various levels of gray where each spot color will be applied, and the varnish will require a solid color to be applied evenly in the desired area. If you ask Photoshop for a tritone image, the third color will be unevenly spread over the entire image. In this case, the varnish could not be used as the third value in the tritone. To solve our problem, we'll use the Multichannel mode to separate the colors. Figure 4-14 illustrates a duotone image and a selection that was saved to an Alpha channel. Channel 2 will be our varnish, and the duotone has been identified with black and a spot color.

Figure 4-14
A duotone has been given an Alpha channel.

When you choose Multichannel from the Mode menu, the file will be split into three channels. Next choose Split Channels from the Channels flyaway menu. The result will be three separate, grayscale documents. These separate files can now be exported in the format you desire for placement in a layout program. Since the duotone will separate into two plates, you can import the duotone and have it printed. Then place the Alpha channel image and run the third plate. With PageMaker's Replace Existing Image command or QuarkXPress' Get Picture command you can replace the duotone with the Alpha channel in precise location for pin registration.

Handy File Format Guide

The previous sections covered the most common formats for various color modes. The complete range of all existing formats for each color mode can be viewed at a glance in Table 4-1.

TABLE 4-1 FORMATS FOR COLOR MODES

FILE FORMAT	BITMAP	GRAYSCALE	DUOTONE	INDEXED	RGB	CMYK	LAB	MULTI CHANNEL
Photoshop	X	X	X	X	X	X	X	X
Photoshop 2.0	X	X	X	X	X	X		X
Amiga IFF	X	X		X	X			
BMP	X	X		X	X			
CompuServe GIF	X	X		X				
Photoshop EPS	X	X	X		X	X	X	
JPEG		X			X	X		
PCX	X	X		X	X			
PDF		X			X	X		
PICT	X	X		X	X			
PICT Resource	X	X		X	X			
Pixar		X			X			
PNG	X	X		X	X			
Raw		X	X	X	X	X	X	X
Scitex CT		X			X	X		
Targa		X		X	X			
TIFF	X	X		X	X	X	X	

CHAPTER FIVE

ACHIEVING GOOD
COLOR CORRECTION

Color-correcting photographs has always been a part of the graphic process. Usually it has been performed by skilled personnel who have made a career in photo color correction, but for the past several years, Photoshop has given the rest of us more control than earlier color correction artisans could have ever imagined. Along with these wonderful new tools we also have many problems to consider. Issues such as discrepancies between what we see on our computer monitors and what appears on our printed documents have long been major concerns to the discriminating artist.

This chapter covers some basics we've picked up using Photoshop as a color correction tool. These examples do not cover all the possibilities but will hopefully get you started down the right path. In addition, we'll look at some of the problems to avoid and issues to be considered when our final output is the printed document. The following are more than just step-by-step techniques — they represent some key concepts in modifying color images that you can apply to your own images and circumstances.

Color Correction Concepts

Before attempting to color-correct an image, you must understand what's wrong with it in the first place. Anyone can look at an image and say whether she or he likes the color or not. It's another thing to look at a bad image and articulate exactly what is wrong with it. The following sections address a few of the most common color problems.

Muddy colors

The term *muddy color* is associated with colors that have a dirty or muddy appearance. An example would be an image of green grass. In order to make grass look green, cyan and yellow are mixed in varying amounts. When magenta is introduced, the grass starts to become darker and less defined, looking more like mud than green. In this case magenta is considered a *muddying* color. To color-correct this example, magenta is removed from the grass areas. Removing muddying colors normally gives the image an overall brighter look.

Memory colors

When looking at any photo of the sky, you expect it to be blue. Grass should be green, dirt should be brown, and so on. These colors are termed *memory colors*. When you look at an image of some foreign land that you have never seen before, you still expect the sky to be blue. If it's green, you may think you're looking at a photo of Venus (or some landscape created in KPT Bryce), not Earth. When color-correcting an image that has memory colors involved, you must pay particularly close attention to them. Otherwise the image will look as if someone has changed the colors, and the image will lose validity. The job of a color correction artist is somewhat like a special-effects artist in movies. If people don't notice the work you do, you've done the job right.

The other side of the coin is represented by images in which nobody really knows the exact color of the subject (Figure 5-1 shows some such colors). These types of images allow the artist more latitude to change colors if needed. With a well-designed mask and some imagination, you can create some interesting images.

Figure 5-1
**The original image (left) has both memory and non-memory colors.
The sky, water, and sand are memory colors. The swimsuit and fan are
non-memory colors, which you can change without losing the validity
of the image (right). No one has any preconceived notions of what
color the fan should be.**

Color casts

Color casts in images produce photos that seem to be dominated by a single color. Normally photos color-cast in the primary colors of cyan, magenta, yellow, red, green, or blue. The highlight areas of an image are more susceptible to color-casting than the shadow areas. Shifting colors a few percentage points in the lighter areas of an image can drastically change the look of it (see Figure 5-2). When correcting these areas, make small shifts or color moves of no more than five percent at a time.

Remember, as you correct for color casts in, say, the highlights, you change the rest of the image too. As you make changes to one portion of the image, keep an eye on the other portions of the image as well. You may want to use the tools in Photoshop that correct only the highlights, midtones, or shadows independently of the others.

Figure 5-2
The colors in the piece of wood on the left are accurate. The colors in the piece of wood on the right are shifted to the yellow, giving it more of a golden color than a reddish color. (Too bad this part of the book isn't in color!)

Bad contrast

Bad contrast refers to when an image lacks enough dark pixels in the shadow areas and light pixels in the highlight areas (see Figure 5-3). A good example of images that look flat are photos in a newspaper. Because of the high volume and fast turnaround requirements typical newspaper publishers work under, the photos tend to have poor contrast. Due to advances in technology and equipment, the quality of photos in newspapers has improved considerably over the last few years. Still, newspaper photos usually have less contrast, especially in the shadow areas.

Figure 5-3
The image on the left shows good contrast between the shadow and highlight areas of a photograph. The image on the right looks flat in comparison because the shadow areas are not dark enough and the highlight areas are not light enough.

Photoshop Color Correction Tools

Now that we have a few color concepts to chew on, let's look at some of the tools available in Photoshop that can correct these problems.

Correcting poor color and contrast with Curves

The Curves command is probably the most common way to color-correct an image. Curves can handle most of the color correction tasks you'll encounter:

1. Select Image ⇨ Adjust ⇨ Curves to open the Curves dialog box.

2. From the Curves dialog box (Figure 5-4), make adjustments to the diagonal line to change the color and contrast of the image. Colors can be manipulated all at once or individually.

3. In the Channel pop-up menu, select the composite of all the colors or any of the individual color channels. Notice that each color has a Command/Ctrl-key equivalent. Get in the habit of using these shortcuts. They are very handy when moving from one color to next without having to pop the menu up every time you need to change the target color.

Correcting specific colors only

Occasions may arise when you need to adjust two of the colors at the same time while leaving the others intact. In the pop-up menu, you can select all the colors or each one individually. Although you cannot select two or more colors in combination with each other, there is a way to accomplish this:

1. Before you open the Curves dialog box, go to the channels palette and select one of the color channels you wish to change.

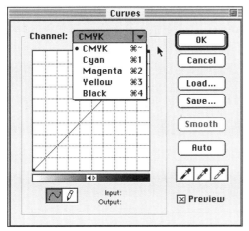

Figure 5-4
The Curves dialog box pop-up menu allows
you to alter the contrast of a specific channel.

2. Shift-select the other color(s) you want to change (Figure 5-5, left).

3. After all the colors are selected, open the Curves dialog box and make your adjustments (Figure 5-5, right).

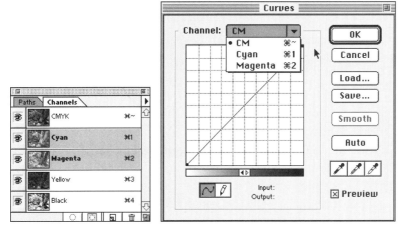

Figure 5-5
Before opening the Curves dialog box, first target the channels you want to
manipulate (left). In this example, the Cyan and Magenta channels are
targeted (right).

The Curves dialog box uses abbreviations for channel designations. For example, if you have selected the Cyan and Magenta channels, the channel designation is listed as "CM." At the bottom of the Curves dialog box are two very important numbers that are constantly updated as you make adjustments. If you are familiar with the info palette, you have noticed that there are two numbers side by side when you are making changes. These numbers represent before and after readouts of the changed pixels. The Input and Output numbers represent the same concept (see Figure 5-6). The Input number represents the Before number, and the Output number is the After. As you make adjustments, keep your eye on these numbers. By watching how these numbers change and periodically sampling actual pixels in the image while viewing the info palette readout, you should have complete control over how much color is being changed.

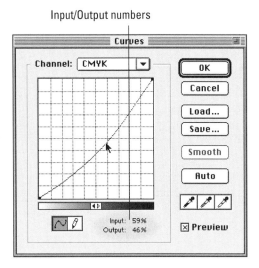

Figure 5-6
The Input and Output numbers show you how much of a change you are making when dragging the lines up and down.

Making the Curves command more accurate

If you Option/Alt-click on the curve area, a 10 percent grid will replace the 25 percent grid. Using the 10 percent grid places lines at intervals of 10 instead of 25. This aids you in making more accurate moves with the curves (see Figure 5-7).

Saving time with Curves settings

If you have a series of images that require the same Curves modification, you can save the settings and apply them to the other images:

1. After you have made all the proper settings, click on the Save button at the right.

2. Give the settings file a name and click Save.

3. Open the other files needing the same modification and select Curves.

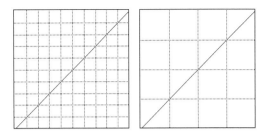

Figure 5-7
The Curves dialog box set to a 10 percent (left)
and 25 percent (right) grid.

4. In the Curves dialog box click Load, find the file you saved earlier, and then click OK. The original settings will be imported into the Curves dialog box and then applied to the image.

Improving contrast with Levels

Many photos don't necessarily need color corrections but simply need better contrast. The Levels dialog box is the best tool to address this problem.

The Levels dialog box consists of a channel designation pop-up menu and five areas in which you can make adjustments (see Figure 5-8). You can use the sliders or make changes numerically. As with Curves, after you have made the adjustments, you can save the settings for use on other images.

The graphic in the middle that usually resembles a mountain range is called a *histogram*. It basically gives you a graphic representation of what color pixels fall where in the image. If there are higher mountains of lines in the lighter portions of the histogram (on the right), the image is probably lighter overall. The histogram is a good reference point for an image. Sometimes just looking at the image itself may not give you an accurate idea of the overall image.

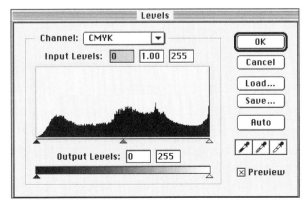

Figure 5-8
A sample histogram appears in the Levels dialog box.

To see whether your problem involves contrast, look at the image's histogram and see whether there are few pixels on the extreme left or the extreme right edges (see Figure 5-9). This means that the image is lacking dark and light areas.

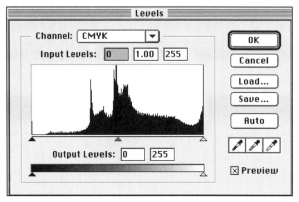

Figure 5-9
Few vertical lines appear on the left side of this histogram, indicating that the image has little in the shadow areas. By moving the left slider on top to the right where the vertical lines start, you can make shadow pixels in the image darker, improving the overall contrast.

To correct this problem, make some adjustments with the top bar of sliders in the Levels dialog box. Move the slider on the left to the right. Then move the slider on the right to the left. (It's starting to sound as if a square dance may break out at any time.) When you move the left slider (the one that represents the darker portions of the image) to the right, you make the image darker. When you move the right slider (the one that represents the lighter portions of the image) to the left, you make the image lighter. In essence, you create more contrast by making the dark parts darker and the light parts lighter.

The middle slider represents the midtones of an image. If after you make the contrast adjustments you notice that the midtones have darkened slightly, move the middle slider to the left. This will make the midtones of your image lighter.

NOTE When making any kind of color or contrast adjustment to any image, make certain the info palette is visible. This will allow you to take readings at any point of the modification. As you make changes and print them out, you will gradually learn how much to change an image to make it look better than the original. When performing any kind of adjustments, note that the numbers actually consist of two sets of numbers that are split with a diagonal line (/). The set of numbers on the left are the Before readings, and the numbers on the right are the After readings (shown in Figure 5-10). This gives you an idea of how much of a change you are making to the image.

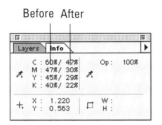

Figure 5-10
The Info palette shows Before and After readings when you make color and contrast changes.

Getting contrast adjustments right the first time

Where do we set the Levels sliders for precise adjustments? Wouldn't it be nice if we had some means of targeting adjustments and getting them right the first time? Hold on, there *is* a way!

1. Open the Preferences dialog box and view Display and Cursors.

2. In this dialog box, check the box for Video LUT Animation. As a Windows user, you need to test this setting against your monitor card. Some display systems on PCs may not work properly with Video LUT Animation turned on.

TIP You can also try lowering the color bit depth to 256 colors. Some Windows video cards support this capability only in 8-bit mode.

3. Open a file with low contrast. For grayscale images, make only one adjustment on the Input Levels sliders. On RGB and indexed color images, adjust the channels independently.

4. In the Levels dialog box, be certain the Preview box is unchecked and hold down the Option/Alt key while moving the black slider. You should see a dynamic preview in the background. It will first appear all white, but as you move the slider, you will begin to see black pixels, as shown in Figure 5-11. At the first appearance of black in the image, release the mouse and keys. (For CMYK files, you must first target a single channel before entering the Levels dialog box. It won't work if the composite CMYK channel is selected or if multiple channels are Shift-selected.)

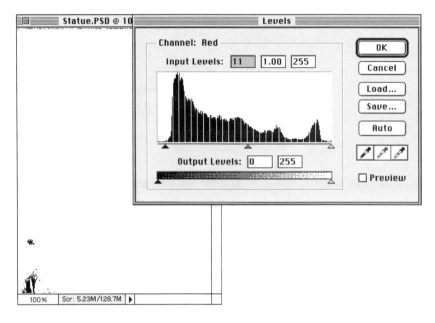

Figure 5-11
Adjust levels with Video LUT Animation and the Option/Alt key depressed.

5. Repeat the procedure for the white input slider and release the mouse button upon the first appearance of white pixels. Be certain you don't go too far with either slider. If you do, performing this operation will remap the black and white points in the image. (Notice that the histogram displays the redistributed pixels.) When you print to film for prepress, 100 percent black will print solid black, and all white areas will not receive any ink. You don't want solid black or the absence of dots where solid white appears, so be certain you release the adjustment slider at the first appearance of either value.

Colorizing with Hue/Saturation

Hue/Saturation is great for colorizing an image. You can start with either a grayscale or a color image. Here's how you colorize an image:

1. Open the image in Photoshop.
2. Select Image ➪ Adjust ➪ Hue/Saturation to open the Hue/Saturation dialog box (see Figure 5-12).
3. Click on the Colorize button at the bottom right.
4. Slide the Hue slider back and forth until you like the results. Adjusting the Saturation slider changes the overall intensity of the color hue. When the slider is all the way to the right, the full intensity of the color is used. As the

slider is moved to the left, less color is visible in the image until it becomes completely grayscale when the slider is all the way to the left. Lightness controls overall brightness of the image.

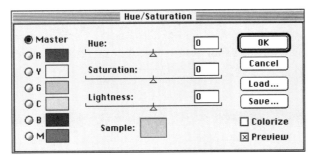

Figure 5-12
The Hue/Saturation dialog box is great for colorizing an image.

Changing color mixtures with Color Balance

Color Balance is not as precise a color correction tool as Curves or Levels (see Figure 5-13). It does allow you to change the mixture of colors, for example, shifting the cyans more into the reds. With the Preserve Luminosity button on, you can also keep the overall brightness of the image intact as you make corrections. In other words, some color correction tools tend to oversaturate an image. But this feature will keep the overall intensity of the image basically the same as you shift Color Balance settings.

What's nice about this control is that you can target just the shadows, the midtones, or the highlights of an image. As we mentioned earlier, at times you will want to affect just the highlights, the midtones, or the shadows of an image and leave the other portions alone. Color Balance is one tool that allows you to do just that.

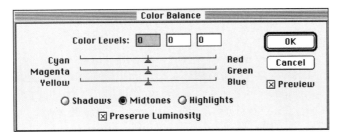

Figure 5-13
The Color Balance dialog box allows you to pinpoint the shadows, the midtones, or the highlights of an image.

Fixing muddy colors with Selective Color

Muddy colors are a common problem. Selective Color gives you the ability to search the entire image for a certain color hue and adjust the colors accordingly without manually masking off those areas (see Figure 5-14). You can set the pop-up menu to any one of nine different color hues and then change the color sliders to add or remove color percentage of your choice.

To color-correct a sky that has too much magenta or yellow, target Cyan from the Colors pop-up menu and move the Magenta slider to the left. As you move the slider, you will be removing magenta from the cyan portions of the image.

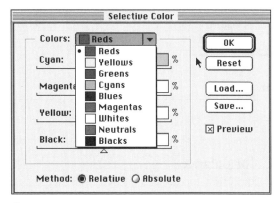

Figure 5-14
You can fix muddy colors using the Colors pop-up menu in the Selective Color dialog box.

At the bottom of the Selective Color dialog box are two buttons marked Method. Relative means that if you start with a 50 percent dot and add 10 percent to it, you will end up with 55 percent, in that 10 percent of 50 percent is 5 percent, so 50 percent plus 5 percent equals 55 percent. Absolute means that if you start with a 50 percent dot and add 10 percent to it, you will end up with 60 percent, since 50 percent plus 10 percent equals 60 percent.

Improving dull images

An image is considered flat if the colors are unsaturated and dull. This is a common problem with originals that may have been shot under poor lighting conditions. Location shooting is an example of a circumstance in which you may not be able to light the subject properly. Photo-CD images can also be somewhat dull and undersaturated.

Fortunately a very simple and quick fix exists for undersaturated images:

1. Open the image in Photoshop.

2. In the layers palette, make a duplicate of the layer that holds the image. In the sample shown here of the flowers, the layer that holds the sample image is named, appropriately enough, Flowers (see Figure 5-15).

Figure 5-15
After you've made a copy of the original layer, the layers palette should look like this.

3. Click the layer name and drag it onto the middle icon at the bottom of the layers palette. An exact copy of the Flowers layer should appear above the original layer in the layers palette.

4. With the duplicate layer targeted, set the Blending pop-up menu to Overlay. (The Blending pop-up menu is located in the upper-left portion of the layers palette. You should find it set to the default setting of Normal.) When you select Overlay, you should see an immediate improvement in the image (see Figure 5-16).

Figure 5-16.
Compare the original Flowers image (left) with the Flowers image after both layers have been composited to create a fully saturated color image (right).

Look at the before and after samples of the Flowers image. There is quite a bit of difference between the two images, and all we did was make a copy of the original image and set the Blending mode to Overlay. This example shows a very simple solution to what otherwise could be an unusable photograph. The Blending mode is sometimes overlooked and underutilized.

Another aspect of this technique centers on the Opacity setting on the overlay layer. In this example, the opacity of the overlay layer was left at 100 percent, the default setting. But leaving the opacity at 100 percent may overcorrect the image. In these cases, simply reduce the Opacity setting. As you move the slider, less of the overlay layer is visible and more of the original layer is revealed. This slowly returns the image to its original condition if the slider is moved all the way to the left. But there should be a happy medium somewhere between 100 percent and 0 percent.

Color Correction with Adjustment Layers

Adjustment layers are a very welcome addition to Photoshop 4, especially when it comes to color correction. The main reason adjustment layers are perfect for color correction is that they use a nondestructive method to correct the image. This means the original image is never modified. Nondestructive modifications are applied in such a way that the original pixels are never really modified and can, at any time, be restored to their original condition. Obvious advantages exist to using a nondestructive modification whenever possible. And we suggest that, as you perform color corrections from any of the five procedures mentioned earlier, you use them in conjunction with adjustment layers (discussed in detail in Chapter 2).

Here's how you do it:

1. In the Adjustment Layer dialog box, select which type of modification you wish to make. Photoshop even gives you a chance to name the layer. This is helpful when using several adjustment layers.

2. Click OK, and the appropriate dialog box will appear for you to make the required adjustments.

3. Click OK to apply the changes to the adjustment layer.

Nondestructive modification gives you the ability to change your mind when you're performing color corrections. Since the modification is applied to a separate layer and not to the pixels of the image, the modification can be further changed or removed at any time.

If you wish to change the modification settings, double-click the layer name. (If you want to change the layer options such as the name of the layer, double-click the layer thumbnail.) After you've double-clicked the name, the appropriate dialog box will appear. The settings will be exactly as you left them the last time they were changed. You will never need to write down all the settings in the dialog boxes.

A default adjustment layer is pure white. This means that the entire canvas area of the image will be modified by the adjustment layer. You can change the adjustment layer as you can any grayscale channel. If you create a black box in an adjustment layer, the space that the black box occupies will no longer be affected by the adjustment layer. Where there are white pixels, the adjustment layer will modify the image. Where there are black pixels, the adjustment layer will not modify the image.

Grayscale will also affect the image in different ways. If you put a box in the adjustment layer that is 50 percent black or gray, the image will be modified accordingly. For example, if the adjustment layer is set to Invert, all the white pixels in the adjustment layer will allow the image to be inverted at an intensity of 100 percent. Where the pixels are black, the image will be unaffected; where the pixels are 50 percent gray, the image will be inverted at 50 percent. You have the ability to change the adjustment layer with any tool you can use in any other channel, but note that it can handle grayscale pixels only.

TIP When you use the method described earlier related to levels adjustments and using Video LUT Animation, you can't get the same feedback from the Levels dialog box while working on an adjustment layer. When working with adjustment layers, first perform the same operation we described by accessing the Levels dialog box and deselecting the Preview button. Next, hold down the Option/Alt key and move the input sliders. Record the values displayed for the new Input Levels sliders. Click on the Cancel button, then create a new adjustment layer, and enter the recorded values.

Third-Party Color Correction Tools

With all the wonderful capabilities of Photoshop, the newest upgrade still falls short in providing sophisticated tools for color adjusting. We discussed how Curves, Levels, Hue/Saturation, and Color Balance can aid us in making color adjustments, but if you feel like we do, you will find that the real-world applications of these controls are less than intuitive and complex to use.

Let's face it, Color Balance has been around since day one and hasn't given us a whole lot more than was first introduced in Photoshop. If you want to find some better tools, you need to look to third-party vendors. There are two plug-ins for the Macintosh that we particularly like and that make all of what we've covered in this chapter much more automated and easier to use than Photoshop's tools. Similar plug-ins for the PC are harder to find. We're told that they may be available sometime in the future.

Improving scans with ScanPrepPro

ScanPrepPro by Flamingo Bay/ImageXpress, Inc., is more than a color-correction application. The plug-in can improve the brightness and color of your images, and you can use it as a scanning plug-in to acquire scans. If your scanning software is crude and unsophisticated, then ScanPrepPro may be a worthwhile addition to your Photoshop accessories. If your scanning software is satisfactory, then ScanPrepPro can act as an image processor to help you fine-tune your scanned images. In either case, the toggles you set for Curves, Levels, Hue/Saturation, and Color Balance are all handled automatically by ScanPrepPro.

When you first run the program (shown in Figure 5-17), notice the number of attributes you can change for your desired output. You can process a previously scanned image with ScanPrepPro and tell it your desired output, halftone frequency, size, paper stock to be printed on, and type of printing process to be used. When you click the Import button, ScanPrepPro processes the image to attain the best possible results.

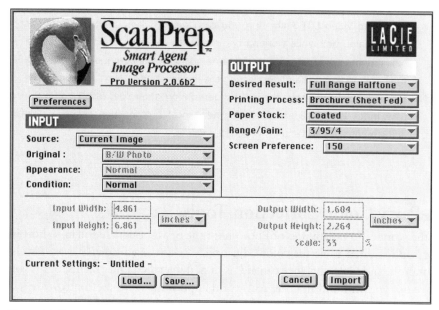

Figure 5-17
ScanPrepPro is a powerful color-correction application.

Watching ScanPrepPro fly through the menus is like watching a magic show: with the passage of each dialog box, you see improvement in the original image. Processing halts momentarily at the Variations dialog box for user-controlled adjustments. If you like the default view, just click the OK button and ScanPrepPro will continue processing the image, stopping at a Save dialog box.

Getting better color adjustments with TestStrip

TestStrip by Vivid Details is a software plug-in suited to the specifics of color correction. Kirk Lyford of Vivid Details calls his creation "[the] Variations [command] on steroids." TestStrip functions in an intuitive manner, and the correction results offer what photo labs have used for years — a test strip with individual color adjustments on the same image. You can make color correction adjustments, print the test strip file, and compare the various adjustments. Figure 5-18 shows how a file can be divided into different strips.

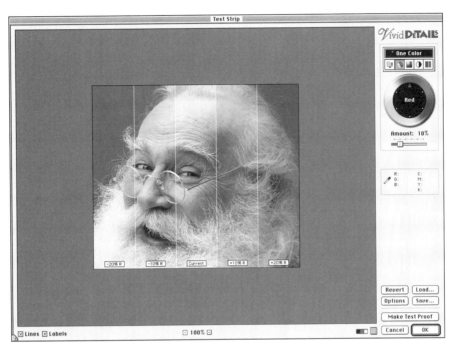

Figure 5-18
TestStrip divides a file into strips for making color corrections.

Notice the color wheel in Figure 5-18 with a slider to alter the amount of color adjustment to be made. TestStrip also handles the color adjustment more intuitively. Rather than adding or subtracting opposite colors for correction, you use TestStrip's control to add red when you need more red, blue when you need more blue, and so on. After making the adjustments, you can print the file as it is displayed in Figure 5-18, complete with various adjustments and the labels indicating the variances. The file can be separated to film, and you can have a Matchprint made or print to a dye-sub or IRIS printer for proofing. In either case, you wind up with a file showing several color controls, which most assuredly reduce costs for the discriminating artist.

CHAPTER SIX

AVOIDING COMMON
IMAGE EDITING
PROBLEMS

Photoshop provides us with tools and methods to create and manipulate images suited to the most discriminating artists. As you work more with Photoshop, you may find new methods of approaching a task or invent techniques to suit your own needs. The beauty of Photoshop is that it provides you with many opportunities to explore, invent, and develop on your own. To elaborate on all the possible techniques available to you in Photoshop would be well beyond the scope of a single publication. For this chapter we've decided to select a few techniques recommended for working with Photoshop images and to describe some of the problems you need to avoid.

Smooth Gradients

Gradients have been a standard among designers ever since computers entered into design. Prior to Photoshop (and similar software) with its gradient tool, graduated screens had to be produced by traditional means — a laborious task that yielded uncertain results.

Now it's easy to create gradients. Just select a tool and click the mouse a few times and there you have it. But this ease doesn't mean gradients are without their problems.

Avoiding gradient banding

Banding is a term associated with gradients that have visible steps or bands. When a gradient is banded, it no longer provides the illusion of a smooth blend from one color to another. A smooth gradient can make a design look great. A banded gradient can destroy an otherwise decent design. Figure 6-1 shows a severely banded gradient and a smooth gradient.

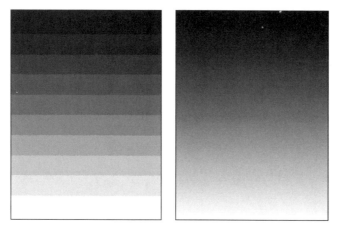

Figure 6-1
A banded gradient (left) is contrasted with a smooth
gradient (right).

What causes banding? To fully understand what causes banding, you need to understand gray levels. The term *gray levels* refers to how many different shades of gray are present in a gradient. The maximum number of gray levels possible in any given gradient is 256. For now, keep this number in mind — 256 grays is your target and what you will always hope to reproduce from Photoshop files. Figure 6-2 illustrates a full range of 256 grays compared to a narrower range of 128 grays.

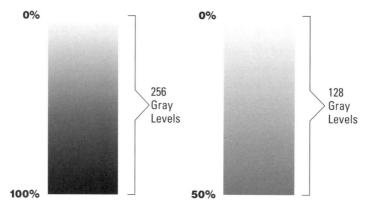

Figure 6-2
Contrast a gradient with 256 grays (left) and one with 128 grays (right).

Another factor to consider is the length of the gradient. If the gradient is short, then each shade that makes up the gradient will likewise be short and have little chance of creating a banding effect. If the gradient is long, however, each shade that makes up the gradient will likewise be long and be more likely to create a banding effect.

To avoid banding problems with gradients, you can use one of the following solutions:

- If the two colors used for the beginning and end of a gradient are too close together in percentage, not enough gray levels will appear to differentiate the colors over the blended area. Suppose, for instance, you graduate between 40 percent cyan and 50 percent cyan. The solution here is to increase the gap between the percentages of cyan. Try using 30 percent to 60 percent, for instance.

- If the gradient is too long, you may well see banding. Consider, for instance, a gradient that extends for 10 inches or more. The solution is to decrease this span. If this is not acceptable, try increasing the percentage gap between the two colors.

- If the resolution of the printing device is not high enough to produce an acceptable number of gray levels, you will definitely experience banding. (Note that the two factors that determine the number of gray levels for a gradient are the line screen frequency and the imagesetter resolution.) The solution for this problem is to print your file with sufficient resolution to capture all grays. The formula and further tricks for capturing grays with high-end output systems are detailed in Chapter 8.

Another solution to banding problems is to build gradients first in CMYK mode. If you work in RGB and convert to CMYK later, you can sometimes get banding as a result of the mode change.

Photoshop's solution for banding

The previous solutions were all related either to controls you perform in recalculating the gradient or to controls you implement outside Photoshop. Using Photoshop as a tool, you could choose one other solution instead: add the *noise filter* to the gradient in Photoshop. To add noise to a gradient, select Filter ⇨ Noise ⇨ Add Noise, as shown in Figure 6-3. In the dialog box that appears set the Amount to 5 or less and watch the gradient on screen. You should see a difference in the look of the gradient. Save the file and print it again. It should show some improvement or eliminate the banding altogether.

TIP Even better, avoid adding noise to the composite CMYK channel altogether. View the individual channels and add noise to only those channels in which the banding is most pronounced. You can also invert the image to Lab mode and work only in the L (Luminance) channel, converting back to CMYK when done.

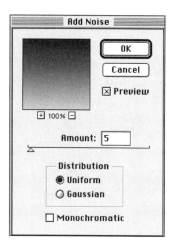

Figure 6-3
The Add Noise filter dialog box
allows you to fix banding.

Sometimes you will be able to see the banding effect in Photoshop. But at times the gradient will look fine in Photoshop yet print with banding. These situations are tough to deal with since it's difficult to correct a problem you can't see. In these cases, carry out the solutions as you would normally and reprint the job. More often than not the problem will be solved.

If you have gradient banding that was created in a program other than Photoshop, you may want to try recreating the gradient in Photoshop and replacing the original gradient with the new one. If you still have problems, then you can carry out the Photoshop solutions described in this section.

Outlining Techniques

Creating outlines around objects is a very common task in Photoshop. On a daily basis, we find that we must select an object from one image and add it to another to form a composite. Here are some suggestions as to how to approach any outlining project you may come across.

Creating efficient paths with the pen tool

The pen tool is a very underrated tool in Photoshop. Many people shy away from it because they don't have experience working with Bézier lines. We're the first to admit that Bézier anchor points and direction lines can be confusing to the uninitiated, but we feel that in many cases the Pen tool is the first tool to try when outlining an object.

You can utilize a path created with the pen tool in either of two ways:

- Use it as a clipping path. To read more on clipping paths, see the section titled "Transparency Problems" later in this chapter; see Chapter 8 for advice on avoiding problems with clipping paths.
- Use it as a method to make selections.

Using a path as a selection is very powerful, accurate, and efficient. Its power comes from its versatility. Almost any kind of object can be outlined with a path, as illustrated in Figure 6-4. After the paths are created, you can use any combination of paths to create selections. Or you can add or subtract a path from any selection.

Figure 6-4
Use the pen tool to create a path.

The pen tool's accuracy stems from the fact you can infinitely readjust a path until it is exactly what you need. Using the lasso tool to make selections is clumsy in most situations. Even though you can add and subtract from a selection using the lasso tool, we find it to be less accurate than using the pen tool. And since paths are stored as vector information, even the most complex path requires very little disk space. Paths are stored inside the Photoshop document but add little to the file size of the image. Thus several paths can be stored with an image very efficiently.

When paths are used in conjunction with density masks, a very complex selection can be made quickly and accurately. (See the section "Density Masks in Photoshop" later in this chapter for step-by-step instructions on creating these unique masks.) Images with smooth outlines and organic, flowing curves are best suited to a combination of density masks and paths. An example of such an image is the outline of a person. Hair, for instance, is organic and flowing. Hair on a person's head, or even hair on a close-up of a person's arm, can be very hard to outline using the pen tool, which can nonetheless outline the rest of the image. As a final step, the density mask and the pen tool path can be combined to create one single mask.

Using the marquee and oval tools efficiently

The marquee and oval tools are pretty much self-explanatory. The marquee selection tool makes box and rectangular selections, and the oval selection tool makes oval and circular selections. Not much surprise here.

Using the lasso tool efficiently

As mentioned before, the lasso tool should be used less often than the pen tool. That doesn't mean we don't use the lasso tool. It can be very useful at times. In fact, the lasso tool is really two tools in one. It's most commonly used as a freehand selection tool. With the tool selected, you can draw freely with it. When you let go of the mouse button, the lasso tool automatically connects your beginning point and ending point to complete the selection.

The lasso tool is also a polygon selection tool. This means that a selection is made up of a series of straight lines leading from one point to the next. You define the different points, and the lasso tool does the rest. To turn the lasso tool into a polygon selection tool, first select it. Then hold down the Option/Alt key and click the mouse once at the first point. Let go of the mouse button, move to the next point, and click again to define the second point. Do this for all of the definition points, making sure not to release the Option key. Once you do let go of the Option key, Photoshop connects the beginning point with the last defined point and creates a selection for you.

You can change back and forth from a freehand tool to a polygon tool simply by holding the mouse button down for the freehand tool and clicking the mouse button for the polygon tool. For example, select the lasso tool and hold the Option key. Click once at the starting point and let go of the mouse button. Move the mouse to a new location and click the mouse again to define a polygon. At the next point click and hold the mouse button down and start drawing a freehand selection. Then let go of the mouse button to start drawing a polygon selection again. Remember, while all this is going on, you must be holding down the Option key. If you let it go, the selection will automatically be connected.

Avoiding magic wand problems with Color Range

The novice Photoshop user tends to migrate to two tools at once. These tools are the magic wand and the rubber stamp tool. Both tools tend to be overused, and other methods deserve to be explored. With the magic wand tool, you can run into problems when using higher-resolution images. You may have no problem editing your image but will find that it takes too long to create a selection. We recommend using the magic wand tool as your last resort for creating selections. If you need magic wand-style selections, try instead choosing Select ➪ Color Range to bring up the dialog box illustrated in Figure 6-5.

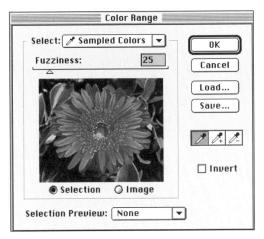

Figure 6-5
The Color Range Dialog Box expedites making selections.

The advantage of using the Color Range command rather than the magic wand is that the time to complete your selection will be greatly reduced. With the Color Range option you can add to or delete from a selection in the thumbnail preview box. (The actual sampling occurs only when you click the OK button.) When you use the magic wand, the high-res image is sampled with each addition or deletion from the selected area.

Using selection tools together

The information in this section pertains to all the selection tools. The techniques work for the marquee, oval, lasso, and magic wand selection tools.

As with all selection tools, you can add or subtract from the selection with the Shift and Option/Alt keys, respectively. To add to a current selection, hold down the Shift key. Notice that a small plus sign (+) appears with the current selection tool cursor. Draw the selection you want added to the current selection. The two selections should now be visible. To subtract from a current selection, hold down the Option/Alt key. Notice that a minus sign (–) appears with the current selection tool cursor. Draw the selection you want subtracted from the current selection. The original selection should be visible with the other selection subtracted from it.

If you hold down the Option/Alt *and* Shift keys, a little "×" is added to the current selection tool cursor, indicating that you are in intersection selection mode. With these keys down, select any portion of a current selection. Where the new and old selections intersect, that portion becomes the new selection.

Moving selections around the drawing area has also changed in Photoshop 4. As a default, you can move a selection without moving the contents inside the selection just by clicking anywhere inside the selected area and moving it. This was accomplished in Photoshop 3 by holding down the Option and Command keys. In Photoshop 4, however, this is the default setting. You don't have to hold down any keys in order to move the selection. If you want to move the contents inside the selected area as you move the selection, you have to hold down the Command key. When you hold down the Command key, notice that a scissors icon is added to the cursor. This tells you that you are about to move the contents of the selection and not just the selection itself. Holding down the Command and Option keys as you move the selection makes a copy of the selected area contents.

Transparency Problems

A common misconception about working with Photoshop is that if you have a white background, it must be transparent. Many artists believe, at least until the first time they print a job, that nothing exists in the white areas of an image, and that if you place the image into another program, you should be able to see any items behind the white areas in the image. Not so. After they print the job, they find out they were quite wrong. White pixels are not transparent. They block whatever is behind them just as black (or any other color) pixels do. The only difference is, you expect that colored pixels won't be transparent.

Transparency is a Photoshop concept used to view images through multiple layers. It's been around only since version 3 because, well, layers have been around only since 3. With two exceptions — clipping paths and GIF89a export — transparency exists only in native Photoshop files, one-bit TIFF images, or bitmaps saved as EPS with Transparent Whites. You can't export PICT files, for example, that contain transparent areas.

Photoshop lets you view transparent areas in an image by representing them with a checkerboard pattern, as illustrated in Figure 6-6 (the File ➪ Preferences command controls transparency options), but just because you can *see* the transparency doesn't mean you can print with it intact.

Avoiding transparency-related problems with other programs

The main reason you cannot print a Photoshop file with transparent backgrounds (without using clipping paths, that is, and we will talk about them later) is that when you save a Photoshop file for output, all white areas in the image are opaque. It doesn't matter if a pixel is black, white, blue, red, or any other color — *all* pixels in the image are opaque and will not let anything behind them show through. In Figure 6-7, both images are the same, yet when the image on the left is moved on top of the blue background, the white pixels move with it.

Figure 6-6
Transparency can be viewed with a checkerboard pattern.

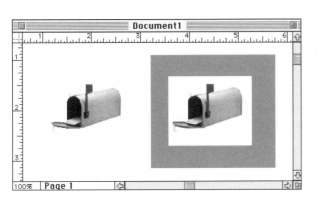

Figure 6-7
Both figures have a white background.

So why can't you retain the transparency that exists in the Photoshop file when you place it into another program such as PageMaker, Illustrator, or QuarkXPress?

The answer is, Photoshop transparency is native to Photoshop only. When you save Photoshop files, you can save them in a number of different file formats. (For more information about file formats, see Chapter 4.) These different file formats allow you to do certain things with your images.

The Photoshop file format is the only format that will save a multilayered image, and to use transparency in a Photoshop file, you must have a layered file. But you cannot place a layered Photoshop file into any other program. So you're stuck. You can save transparency only in a layered Photoshop file, and you can't use the transparency anywhere but in Photoshop.

You must first change the file format to one that can be placed into other programs, EPS or TIFF, for example. Both of these formats, as well as any format other than the native Photoshop format, require that you first *flatten* a layered image before saving it. When you flatten an image, all layers are merged into one, and all transparency is replaced with the background color. Most often, this background color will be the default white. You can save Bitmap images, on the other hand, while preserving transparent whites by choosing either the TIFF format or EPS with Transparent Whites.

Avoiding problems with transparency masks

Two possible solutions exist for creating transparent backgrounds for an image. As mentioned before, you can create clipping paths using Photoshop's pen tool, which creates Bézier lines very similar to those in Illustrator. Clipping paths can be a very efficient way to create and save outline information because they are saved as vector data as opposed to raster data. Vector information is saved as mathematical or numerical representations of the outline. This type of information is very compact by comparison with the data needed to save the same outline in raster form.

Another advantage vector information has over raster information is that it is very easily modified. If you have experience creating and manipulating Bézier curves in drawing programs such as Illustrator or FreeHand, you will be able to draw and manipulate paths in Photoshop very easily. They work and react very much like the paths in Illustrator or FreeHand. They have anchor points and direction lines, and they can be pulled and stretched to create almost any outline. They also create a very smooth selection — considerably smoother than any selection that can be made using the lasso tool. For creating certain types of outline selections, the pen tool is the tool of choice. Objects like golf clubs that have smooth curved edges are perfect candidates for using the pen tool.

After creating an outline for use as a clipping path, you must do a few things in order to use it properly:

1. Choose Save Path from the paths palette flyaway menu.

2. Choose the Clipping Path command from the paths palette menu (see Figure 6-8). A dialog box appears.

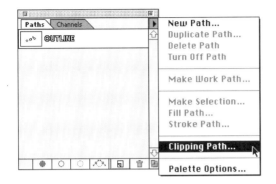

Figure 6-8
The paths palette displays the saved path name.

3. Pull down the Path pop-up menu. The path you want to use for the outline should be listed here.

4. Select it.

5. Save the file as an EPS file to maintain compatibility with most applications. Although the TIFF format can retain clipping path information, only programs like Adobe PageMaker 6.0 and 6.5 support TIFFs with clipping paths. If you use QuarkXPress, save your files as EPS.

6. Remember that in order to save an image as a EPS file, you must first flatten it. So select Layer ⇨ Flatten Image if you have not already done so. This merges all the layers into one layer, if you have more than one layer, and converts any transparent areas in the image to white pixels.

7. Select File ⇨ Save As and change the filename to keep the original intact. We suggest adding the extension .EPS to the end of the filename. After you have added the .EPS extension, click OK.

8. The EPS Format dialog box appears. (This dialog box is also covered in Chapter 4.) The one item to note here is the Clipping Path designation. Make sure that the path name you set in the path palette is listed here next to Path. Then click OK.

Now when the image is placed into another program, only the outlined object appears. It can be placed onto any background or texture without interfering with it.

Avoiding problems with clipping paths

In Chapter 8, we discuss some of the workarounds to avoid imaging problems with clipping paths, however, we do realize that times will arise where clipping paths created as we have just defined them will be necessary. Clipping paths are difficult to print on imaging devices because of the complexity inherent in the design of the path. To avoid problems, it is always best to increase tolerances whenever possible. When you first create a selection and choose the Make Work Path option from the paths palette flyaway menu, a dialog box will appear (as shown in Figure 6-9) that will enable you to enter the tolerance value for the path.

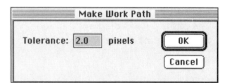

Figure 6-9
Enter a path tolerance of your choosing.

The path tolerance will establish points on the path to outline the selection. The lower the number, the tighter the path, and hence the more points used to define the path. Figure 6-10 shows a path with a tolerance factor of 0.75. Notice the number of points used to create the path.

Figure 6-10
This path was created with a 0.75 tolerance.

The same selection was used to create another path with the tolerance set to 2.0. Figure 6-11 shows the path and points along the path when this tolerance was entered in the Make Work Path dialog box. Compare the number of points on the path with the number in Figure 6-10.

Figure 6-11
This path was created with a 2.0 tolerance.

The image in Figure 6-11 would be a much lower burden to print on a PostScript device due to the fewer points on the path. Therefore, you should always try to set the tolerances of clipping paths to 2.0 or greater whenever the clipping path is needed in a Photoshop image to create a mask. Photoshop remembers the last path tolerance setting each time you bring up the dialog box. Keep this setting at a tolerance value of 2.0 for optimum results. If necessary, you can always use the pen tool to add more points and refine your path. Whenever possible, draw a path with the pen tool rather than creating a path from a selection.

Using white backgrounds

An alternative solution to the problem of creating clipping paths is to create the same background in both the Photoshop file and the page layout file. In other words, if you have a colored background in QuarkXPress onto which you want to place a Photoshop image, create exactly the same colored background in both programs.

For example, suppose you have a colored background in QuarkXPress that is made up of the following process colors: 100 percent cyan, 40 percent magenta, and 10 percent black. Now you want to place an image that was created in Photoshop with an irregular outline onto this colored background. If you were to simply place the image into QuarkXPress, the background of the image would be white, and it would knock out the colored background. Instead of creating a path in Photoshop and using it as a clipping path, you can change the background of the Photoshop image to the same color as the background in QuarkXPress. Then you can flatten the image and save it as an EPS file without defining a clipping path. When the image is placed into QuarkXPress, since both backgrounds are the same, they will look the same when printed.

A couple of things should be noted here. First, if you make any changes to one of the backgrounds, remember to change the other one accordingly. A change of only a few percent of any color will visibly change the color. Also, when you place the Photoshop file into QuarkXPress, you may see a slight difference in the colors that the two programs display. Even though the images are numerically identical, the EPS preview of the placed image may vary somewhat in color from the Quark display. Don't let this confuse you, as the images will print just fine.

Avoiding problems with common color backgrounds

On occasion, you may see some variations in background colors when using spot color values or the default definitions of color components as you switch from one program to another. If this becomes a problem, you can either spec the entire color in Photoshop or save a layout page to be opened in Photoshop to be used as your background color. If you are not certain how to import a page from a layout program, we address EPS exports and distilling files with Adobe Acrobat Distiller in Chapter 7.

If you choose to import, for example, a QuarkXPress page into Photoshop, you will be ensured of having the background color — and any color identified with the same values in Photoshop — print and separate precisely the same.

Density Masks in Photoshop

Creating masks in Adobe Photoshop can be a laborious task that can send chills up and down the spine of even the most experienced artist. A variety of reasons exist to create a mask, but probably the most common one is to knock out the background of a photo to white, in other words, to arrange that the main person or object print at its normal intensity and that the background around the subject be pure white (or the color of the paper it's being printed on).

Avoiding masking problems with hair

If we wish to knock out a background and mask it as illustrated in Figure 6-12, the hair poses an interesting problem. If you want all the strands of hair to display in the final image, and yet knock out the background color, it would be a monumental task to create a pen selection around each strand of hair.

Figure 6-12
A density mask must be created to mask the background.

When people are to be masked, you usually have to contend with hair. And as you can see in the example, some people's hair can be virtually impossible to cut around using a brush or pen tool. The mask that was used to knock out the background around the example subject's hair was nonetheless created in only a few minutes. And the beauty of this technique is that little or no artistic flair is required to create the mask.

One thing is required for this technique to work efficiently: some contrast must exist between the subject and the background. This means that you need a difference in color at the edge where the subject ends and the background begins. A dark-haired women against a white background, for example, gives plenty of contrast between the hair and the background. If the same woman were shot on a black background, this technique would not work, or not work nearly as well as it could. A well-planned photo shoot can save literally hours of production later at the computer.

Our recommended masking technique

Our technique generally works better with color images than with grayscale, because, to get the mask to work properly, you manipulate the channel information that exists in the photo. You'll see what we mean as you follow the steps we have outlined below. Since a color image has more channels than a grayscale image, you have more information to work with. We're not saying that you can't use this technique with a grayscale image, only that you may have more success with color images. To illustrate the sequence, we'll provide a series of steps to walk you through the technique.

STEP 1 Open the image in Photoshop. First, look at the individual channels to see if you have contrast between the subject and the background. Open the channels palette. Click the individual channels one by one, assuming you are working on a color image. Pick the channel that has the most contrast. Figure 6-13 shows the individual channels in the example.

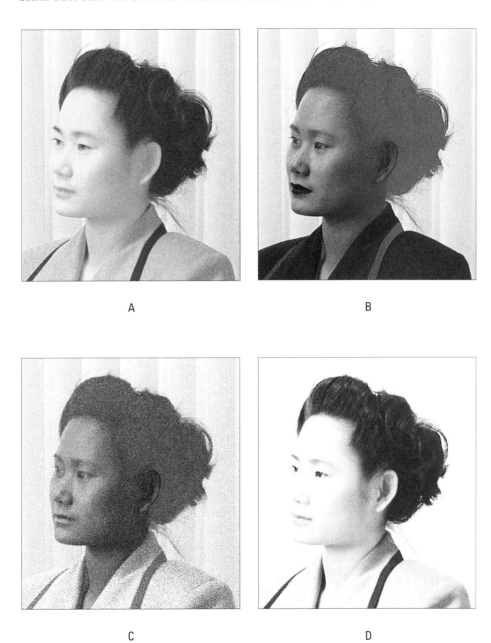

A

B

C

D

Figure 6-13
The example's (a) cyan, (b) magenta, (c) yellow, and (d) black channels are shown
side by side.

Once you've decided which channel is the most appropriate one to use, duplicate it by dragging its name to the middle icon at the bottom of the channels palette as illustrated in Figure 6-14. This will copy the entire channel into a new channel that you can manipulate while leaving the original intact.

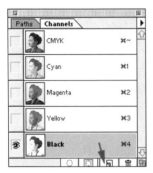

Figure 6-14
Drag the channel name to the middle icon to duplicate it.

How do you decide which channel is most appropriate for the mask? Look at the four images in Figure 6-13. These are the individual channels that make up the four-color image. The different colors are listed below the photo. Again the objective is to get the most contrast between the subject and background. In this case the subject is the hair. So we want to select the channel that offers the most contrast between the woman's hair and the background. Since the woman's black hair is on a white background, all four channels show good contrast between the hair and background, and so we can start looking at detail. Considering both contrast and detail, we picked the black channel as the one to duplicate.

STEP 2 In the channels palette, select the new channel you've just created. Make sure that you are manipulating the new channel and not any of the original four channels that make up the image. The new channel should be the only one highlighted. Also make sure that the info palette is visible. Select Image ⇨ Adjust ⇨ Levels. The Levels dialog box will come up as shown in Figure 6-15. The controls here allow you to change the overall contrast of an image or an individual channel with great precision.

The objective for Step 2 is to create a channel that has the subject pure black and the background pure white. The info palette must be visible so that you can take density readings of the subject and background while you are adjusting the Levels controls.

The Levels dialog box has four main parts. The first is the Channel list box, where you can set which channels are to be adjusted. You can either adjust all channels at once or set any individual channel. The box should already be set to the new channel you've created for the mask because you should have only that channel selected in the channels palette. Keep it set to the new channel. (In fact, you won't be able to select any other channel.)

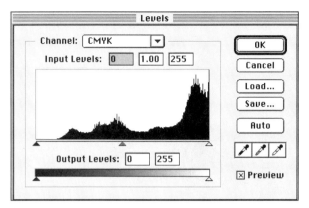

Figure 6-15
The Levels dialog box allows you to adjust an image's contrast by moving the input level sliders beneath the histogram.

The next part is Input Levels, which consists of three numbers that correspond to the three small triangles below the histogram of the channel. Notice that the triangles are different shadows of gray. The leftmost triangle is black, the one in the middle is gray, and the one at the right is white. They represent the shadow, midtones, and highlights of the channel, respectively. To make the shadow portions of the channel darker, move the black triangle right and to the middle of the histogram. To make the highlights lighter, move the white triangle left and to the middle. As you make these adjustments, take density readings of the dark and light areas by simply moving your cursor over these areas and watching the readout in the info palette. You do not have to click the mouse to get the readings.

The third important part appears at the bottom of the Levels dialog box. Named Output Levels, it allows you to flatten the contrast of the image, basically, to do the opposite of what the Input Levels controls do. For this technique you probably will not use these triangle sliders. The fourth and final important part consists of the buttons on the right. After you have made your adjustments, click OK.

Again, the objective of Step 2 is to create a high-contrast graphic (as shown in Figure 6-16) that separates the subject and the background. You should have pure black in the subject area and pure white in the background area. To accomplish this for the example image, we moved the black triangle slider to the right to darken the shadow portions of the image, and we moved the white triangle slider to the left to lighten the highlight portions of the image. Carrying out these two changes to the contrast was a good enough start, but we still have work to do.

Figure 6-16
The high-contrast channel has been adjusted with Levels.

STEP 3 In some cases, just performing Step 2 on your image is enough to create a working mask to knock out the background. But in most cases you will need to do some extra work to get the appropriate final results.

Take a look at the mask in combination with the rest of the image. First select the CMYK channel in the channels palette. Then click the eye icon of the new channel. You should see the image with the new channel laid over it in another color. Usually red is used to represent the new channel, but you can change the color by double-clicking the channel name and choosing a new color in the dialog box. With both the CMYK channel and the new channel visible, you can inspect the mask and determine if any more work is needed. If adjustments are needed, use the brush or any other tool you need to make the changes in the new channel.

In the example image we needed to brush out some pixels that remained in the hair detail. We also removed the face and shoulders portion of the image. We used the pen tool to select these portions illustrated in Figure 6-17. Remember that we need a pure black and pure white mask separating the hairline and the background.

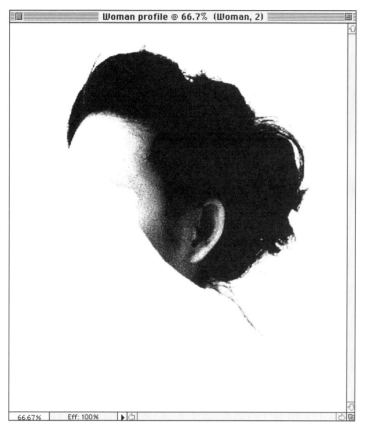

Figure 6-17
A mask has been created to isolate the hair from the rest of the image.

STEP 4 To finish the mask for the face and shoulders, we are going to use the pen tool. Density masks are great for free flowing, organic subjects such as hair, but they are not the best choice for everything. The face and shoulders of the woman are better suited for the pen tool. Not all masks require using both density mask and pen tool paths. But in this case, we need the pen tool to finish the job.

Since the hair is already done, you can bypass it and just draw a path around the rest of the woman as illustrated in Figure 6-18.

Figure 6-18
A pen tool path has been created around the rest of the image.

After the path is complete, turn it into a selection by dragging the path name to the third icon from the left. (If no brush or paint tools are selected, you can also just press Enter to convert the path into a selection.) Make sure that the mask channel is the target and fill the selected area with black. Figure 6-19 shows the results of adding the pen tool path fill.

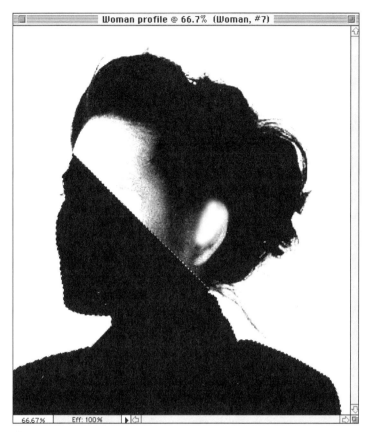

Figure 6-19
The path fill appears in black.

After both the density mask and the pen tool path are combined into one channel, you may have to do some more touch-up brushing to put the finishing touches on the mask.

In the example the selection is white and the unselected area is black. For the mask to work properly, however, it has to be inverted. To do this, target the mask channel and select Image ⇨ Adjust ⇨ Invert. The mask should now be black on the inside with a white background, as shown in Figure 6-20.

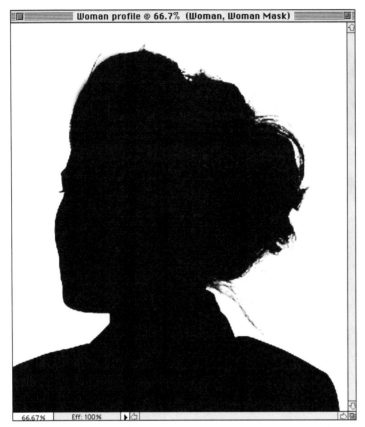

Figure 6-20
The final mask has been inverted from the combined channel.

STEP 5 After the mask has been completed, you can do any of several things with your image. You can cut and paste the image into another document after first loading the new channel as a selection. Click and hold the name of the mask channel and drag it to the leftmost icon at the bottom of the channels palette. You can also hold down the Command/Ctrl key and click the channel name once. Either method loads the channel as a selection. Then select Edit ➪ Copy. This will make a copy of the image and place it into the clipboard. Open the file into which you wish to paste your masked image and select Edit ➪ Paste. Photoshop will make a new layer and paste your image on that layer (see Figure 6-21).

Figure 6-21
The sample image appears on a new background.

You may want to keep your image in its own file and start building graphics around it. To simply knock out or delete the background around your subject, first load the new channel as a selection by Command/Ctrl-clicking the channel name. Then select Edit ➪ Cut. This will delete everything inside the selection. You should now see just the subject. This is a simple technique but it permanently deletes the background. You can never bring it back. If you think you may want to use some of the background later, use the next technique.

Adding layer masks instead of deleting the background

This time instead of just deleting the background, we're going to use the new channel as a layer mask. The advantage to using a layer mask as opposed to simply deleting the background is that the background is preserved; you just can't see it because the layer mask is masking it out. If you need to use the background later for any reason, you can always adjust the layer mask to reveal or remove any portion of the background.

To use this technique, you need to add a layer mask to the layer that holds the image. If this layer is called Background (and the name "Background" is in italics), you will not be able to add a layer mask. You first need to change this Background layer to a layer that will accept a layer mask.

STEP 1 Change the Background to a layer that will accept a mask by double-clicking the Background layer name. In the dialog box, you are given the chance to rename the channel. Changing the name is not important, except that it may aid you in identifying it later. Click OK after you have renamed the layer.

STEP 2 Add the layer mask by selecting Layers ⇨ Add Layer Mask ⇨ Reveal All. Notice that, in the layer palette, the layer now has two thumbnails for the image instead of just one. (The thumbnails are the two little images to the left of the layer name.) The left thumbnail represents the image, and the right thumbnail represents the layer mask, as shown in Figure 6-22. (It's important to know that a layer mask will also be added to the channels palette with its name *italicized*. This reflects the layer mask you just created.)

Image   Layer mask

Figure 6-22
The image is represented with its layer mask.

STEP 3 In the channels palette, select the mask channel you created earlier and choose Select ⇨ All. This will select the entire channel. Then select Edit ⇨ Copy to copy it to the clipboard. Carefully click the thumbnail of the layer mask (the thumbnail on the left) that you just created and then select Edit ⇨ Paste. Be certain that the *italicized layer mask* is selected in the channels palette and activated with the eyeball icon on. If it's not selected properly, you will paste the mask to a new layer. If this occurs, undo and recheck your selection.

This sequence will paste the new channel into the layer mask. Note what happens to your image. If the background turns white, leaving the subject visible, then all is well. If the subject turns white, leaving the background visible, all is not well. What's wrong is that the layer mask is just inverted or opposite of what it should be. What's black should be white, and what's white should be black. With the layer mask still targeted, choose Select ⇨ Inverse. The layer should now look correct.

CHAPTER SEVEN

USING PHOTOSHOP
WITH OTHER
PROGRAMS

Adobe has made great strides in making its products work with one another more seamlessly. Taken alone, Adobe Photoshop and Adobe Illustrator are powerful programs providing a multitude of useful features. In tandem they become even better, even more powerful. Using two or more programs together can also create unexpected problems. In this chapter we examine some of the ways in which you can combine Photoshop and other applications with optimal efficiency and minimal hassle.

Photoshop and Illustrator

Photoshop and Illustrator are significantly different programs that are capable of performing roughly the same tasks, albeit in very different ways. Sure, Illustrator might not be your first choice for retouching a photograph, for example, but you'd be surprised at the types of tasks Illustrator can perform on just such an image. With certain Illustrator filters, you can even create blurry drop shadows on text. Similarly, you probably wouldn't consider Photoshop for creating technical illustrations or drawings, but its pen tool lets you edit Bézier curves just as you can in Illustrator.

Photoshop is a raster image program that manipulates pixels and transparency to produce photographs and artwork. Illustrator, on the other hand, is a vector program using lines, anchor points, and mathematical equations to draw graphics. But these two programs have some common ground too. One area in particular is *pen tool paths*. Both programs produce basically the same type of path using anchor points, direction lines, and path lines themselves.

The information that can be moved between Illustrator and Photoshop can be put into two categories. The first category is information that's transferred from one program to the other and is still fully editable. This means that the information is still in a form that can be manipulated, changed, or otherwise altered from its original state. The second category is information that is simply placed from one program into the other. The placed information can't be edited but can be output by the receiving program. When you start planning a strategy of moving information back and forth, determine which category of information is needed to complete the task.

Avoiding Photoshop-to-Illustrator glitches

Let's first look at moving information from Photoshop to Illustrator. To do this, you need to know what types of Photoshop information can be used in Illustrator. As we mentioned earlier, pen paths are common to both programs and can be edited in both.

TRANSFERRING DATA In working with Adobe Photoshop and Adobe Illustrator, you will typically need to transfer paths between the two programs frequently. Even though Photoshop provides an excellent tool for creating Béziers and paths, complex illustrations are always best done in Illustrator. On the other hand, although Illustrator can create some dazzling shadows and gradients, the application of choice for this type of work is usually Photoshop. Therefore, you may wish to create a component in one program and then transfer the data to the other program to complete the project.

From the first release of Illustrator, the program was designed to provide a drawing tablet that makes use of templates for tracing illustrations. In the old days (circa 1986) we needed to save our files as PICTs and create a new file in Illustrator using the PICT image as our template. The result was a blob of gray pixels with little detail in the low-contrast areas of the image. Fortunately Adobe Systems has made some great progress in using templates in Illustrator, and we now have much better opportunities to use a Photoshop image as a template.

If you haven't upgraded to the newest and greatest version of Adobe Illustrator, version 7, you may be used to seeing templates from PICT files as this blob of gray pixels. Whether you work with a Mac or Windows, with Illustrator 7 you can now place a variety of formats and use them as templates with much more detail visible in the placed image. Figure 7-1 shows a PICT file placed in Illustrator 6 and the same file placed in Illustrator 7.

On the left, the Photoshop image was saved in PICT format and opened in Illustrator 6 as a template. Using Illustrator 7, you will find that a dialog box will no longer appear prompting you for a template. When you open a Photoshop file in Illustrator 7, you can choose to use it as a template or as artwork contained in the document. Earlier versions of Illustrator permitted *dimming* a placed EPS image, which provided a clear distinction between the template and the drawing.

Figure 7-1
**A PICT template has been placed in Illustrator 6 on the Mac (left) and in
Illustrator 7 (right).**

The placed EPS file appeared dimmed but preserved much more detail than the
older template view. Now with Illustrator 7, you can dim other file formats as well. To
further simplify the characteristics of a template versus artwork created in Illustrator,
you can lock the template in the Layers menu. With Illustrator 7, the procedure for
locking a Layer is simplified in the new layers palette. Figure 7-2 shows a dimmed
PICT file placed in Illustrator with the layer locked.

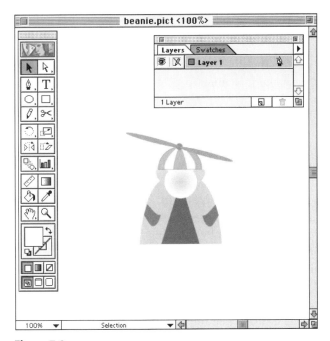

Figure 7-2
**Here is a placed PICT image locked in the layers palette
in Illustrator 7.**

When you view the image, the detail will be retained and the image will appear slightly ghosted as if viewed through tracing paper. With this method, you preserve all detail so your tracing task will be much easier. To eliminate possible movement of the placed image, you can disable Illustration on the Current Layer and create a new layer for your drawing (Figure 7-3). The many changes to Illustrator 7 are now consistent with the architecture of Photoshop, which makes working in both programs much easier. The operations of creating, selecting, and viewing layers, for example, are handled identically in the two programs.

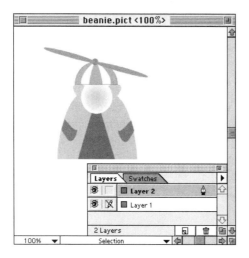

Figure 7-3
A dimmed PICT has this appearance with layer editing disabled.

Regardless of whether you choose the PICT format, EPS, or TIFF, you can use Photoshop images as templates in the same manner. If you are using older versions of Adobe Illustrator, on the other hand, you will be restricted to the EPS format if you want to dim the image.

USING DRAG AND DROP One of the best methods of transferring data between programs on Macintosh systems is via drag and drop. Adobe is making great strides in all their new software releases toward employing drag and drop to move data between programs, and the Photoshop/Illustrator duo employs this opportunity very well. If you create selections in Photoshop and convert those selections to paths, you have the choice of either exporting the paths to Illustrator by choosing File ⇨ Export or simply dragging and dropping the paths.

When working with paths in Photoshop, you may feel inclined to use the selection arrow from the paths tools and drag it to the Illustrator document. If you've tried this method, you know it won't work. Keep in mind that you need to use the Photoshop move tool to select the path and drag it to an open Illustrator window.

If your computer doesn't have enough RAM, then the Export Paths option mentioned previously will be needed, or else you can use the Copy/Paste combination to import paths to Illustrator. The latter alternative is handled by selecting the path in Photoshop and choosing Edit ⇨ Copy. Quit Photoshop and open Illustrator. In a new document window, choose Edit ⇨ Paste.

Regardless of whether you choose drag and drop, Export Paths, or Copy and Paste, the paths, if not stroked in Photoshop, will not appear in the Illustrator window if the path is not selected. This is a common problem among users. You know the darn thing came in, but where the heck is it? Choose View ⇨ Artwork (Command/Ctrl+Y) to see it. Since the path has no stroke and no fill, you can't see it in Preview mode.

When working with type, we used to have to convert our type to outlines before importing the type on a path from Illustrator to Photoshop. Now with improved compatibility between the newest versions of the programs, we can easily drag and drop or copy and paste Illustrator 7 type on a path to Photoshop. Figure 7-4 shows type created on a path in Illustrator 7 (right), copied to the clipboard, and pasted as pixels into a new Photoshop document (left).

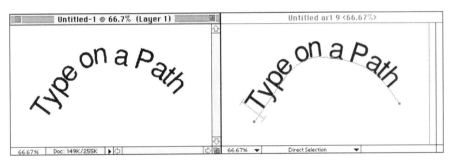

Figure 7-4
Type on a path in Illustrator 7 (right) has been copied and pasted as pixels in a Photoshop document (left).

Dealing with pen tool limitations

One disadvantage with using Photoshop paths is that the pen tool in Photoshop is not as robust as the pen tool in Illustrator. In other words you can do more with Illustrator's pen tool than Photoshop's. After you have drawn a path in Illustrator, you can use the transform tools to modify the path. In Photoshop, you can't transform (rotate, scale, reflect, and shear) pen paths without modifying the entire image. Cutting segments, moving them around, and joining lines back up again are also examples of Illustrator's drawing strengths over Photoshop. Such new additions to Illustrator 7 as the Transform Each command offer you greater flexibility in transforming objects and type, as shown in Figure 7-5. All other functions are basically the same. If you believe you will need to perform any of these tasks, you may want to do the outlining in Illustrator. You can also start the outline in Photoshop and then copy it to Illustrator to finish it there.

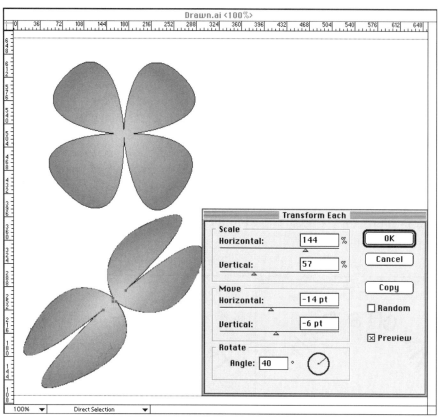

Figure 7-5
With the Illustrator 7 Transform Each command, you can preview multiple transformations before applying them.

Transferring raster image information

Another type of information that can be moved from Photoshop to Illustrator is raster information. This means you can move photos from Photoshop into Illustrator. Photoshop 4 offers several ways to move raster information. Probably the easiest way is the drag-and-drop method:

1. Open the Photoshop file and then open the Illustrator file. Make sure both documents are visible on the desktop.

2. In Photoshop, select the move tool. Click and hold the mouse on any part of the image and drag it onto the Illustrator document (Figure 7-6). After the computer thinks about it for a few seconds (larger files may make the computer think a bit longer), the file will appear in the Illustrator document.

If your computer's RAM is limited, then save your file in either a native Photoshop or EPS format. Quit Photoshop and open Illustrator. From the File menu choose Open, and the same effect will occur as with the drag-and-drop method.

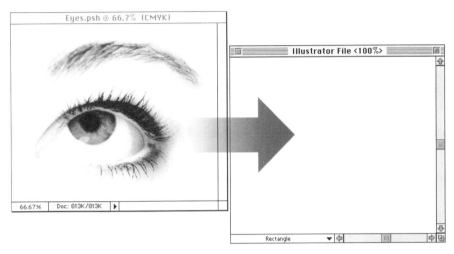

Figure 7-6
The Photoshop file is dragged and dropped into Illustrator.

TO PLACE OR TO PARSE: THAT IS THE QUESTION You can place an image from Photoshop into Illustrator using Illustrator's Place command. In Illustrator select File ⇨ Place. The standard Open dialog box appears, asking which file to place. In Illustrator 7 the dialog box offers a new selection item, denoted as Link, as you can see at the bottom of Figure 7-7.

Link option

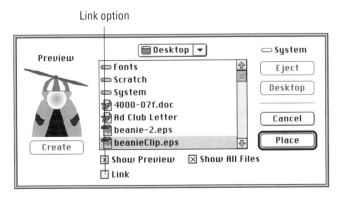

Figure 7-7
The Illustrator 7 Place dialog box has a new Link option.

When Link is checked, any Photoshop file with a clipping path will be imported as a placed image. Earlier versions of Illustrator offered a choice between *placing* or *parsing* the data. You cannot edit the path of a placed image. By contrast, a parsed data file can have the path edited where points on the path can be readjusted. In our new Illustrator, checking the Link option in the dialog box is equivalent to placing an image, and deselecting the check box results in parsing the data. The results of each choice appear in Figure 7-8, where the Link option was checked (left) when placed and not checked (right) when placed. Notice the editable points on the right image.

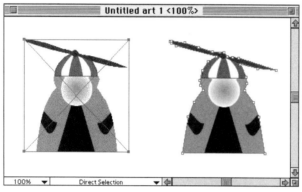

Figure 7-8
This file was placed two ways in Illustrator 7, with the
Link option checked (left) and unchecked (right).

So what, you may say! I can use the other methods just described, and I can apply all my filters in Photoshop before bringing the image into Illustrator. Why would I want to use this place method anyway? We have a super reason for you to place the image as parsed data in Illustrator. Remember that file we dropped into Illustrator and used as our template? We needed to grab Illustrator's pen tool and trace the image, right? Well, take a look at the right side of Figure 7-8. See those points on the path? This image was placed in Illustrator as a parsed data file, and the image is completely editable in Illustrator. The path was imported along with the image data.

If you choose to place an image in such a fashion, problems can occur if the file is not prepared properly in Photoshop. First you need to create a path and save the path from Photoshop's paths palette. Then export the file as EPS with a *clipping path*. A clipping path will create a mask from the path. When you place the image in Illustrator with Link unchecked, it reads the clipping path and keeps it intact. If you choose to place the image with Link checked, the path cannot be edited.

DISADVANTAGES WITH PLACING OR PARSING Now let's talk about some disadvantages. A big disadvantage is that the entire image is saved into the Illustrator file. This means that if you place a 20MB image with the Link option unchecked, your Illustrator file is going to be 20MB plus the size of the Illustrator elements. If you place the same 20MB file with the Link option checked, the file will grow only a few hundred kilobytes, not several megabytes, presuming you do not save the file with placed images. Larger files take considerably longer to import if they are not linked. This may not make much difference when importing just a few images, but if you're importing several, those extra minutes add up quickly.

TIP You cannot use the clipboard to copy image information from Photoshop to Illustrator, as you can do to copy path information.

Avoiding Illustrator-to-Photoshop glitches

When copying and pasting image data from Illustrator to Photoshop, you have a choice of pasting the paths or pasting pixels. The former option results in only the path being imported into the Photoshop document. When you paste as pixels, on the other hand, fills, gradients, and strokes will appear in the Photoshop document. A dialog box offers you the options of pasting as pixels or as paths. When you copy Illustrator paths to the clipboard and choose Edit ⇨ Paste in Photoshop, the dialog box shown in Figure 7-9 will appear.

Figure 7-9
When pasting Illustrator images in Photoshop, you have a choice of pasting them as pixels or as paths.

RETAINING VERSUS RASTERIZING Retaining paths as path information in transfers from Illustrator to Photoshop seems to be more usual than rasterizing the paths. But both techniques are very useful. Still, you need to adapt a few rules-of-thumb in order to avoid problems.

To copy a path from Illustrator to Photoshop and *retain* it as path information, use either of the two procedures. First the drag-and-drop method. This is similar to the drag-and-drop method described earlier with images. Draw the path in Illustrator and keep the window visible. In Photoshop, make a new document and make sure that window is visible. In Illustrator, hold down the Command/Ctrl key and drag the path from the Illustrator window to the Photoshop window. The path is copied to Photoshop and given the default name "Working Path." We suggest renaming the new path at this time.

If you don't hold the Command key down when dragging the path from Illustrator to Photoshop, the path is rasterized in Photoshop. The new element in Photoshop takes on any attributes that were applied in Illustrator prior to dragging it into Photoshop. These attributes include fill and stroke color, line designations, gradients, and patterns.

Photoshop provides a great opportunity to import patterns on a path directly from Illustrator. If you create a pattern fill in Illustrator and drag and drop the fill into Photoshop, most often the pattern won't appear as a seamless fill. If this is the case, marquee a section of the pattern after it's imported into Photoshop (as shown in Figure 7-10) and choose Edit ⇨ Define Pattern. Create a new layer and fill the layer with a pattern fill. If the fill is not seamless, you may need to reposition the marquee and redefine the pattern.

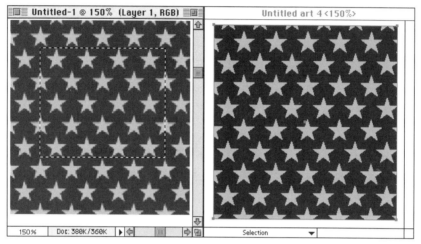

Figure 7-10
After dragging the pattern to Photoshop, marquee the area for the pattern to be defined.

The second method is to simply copy and paste between the two programs. In Illustrator, select the path and copy it. This places the path into what Adobe calls the PostScript clipboard. Click in the Photoshop window to activate it and choose Edit ⇨ Paste. Choose Pixels if you want the path to be rasterized, or Paths if you want path information. When you paste the path in Photoshop, the path will appear on the current active layer, as shown in Figure 7-11.

NOTE When you paste paths from Illustrator to Photoshop as strictly path information, all paint attributes are stripped out. You can redefine attributes by stroking the path, or by creating selections from the paths and modifying the strokes and fills.

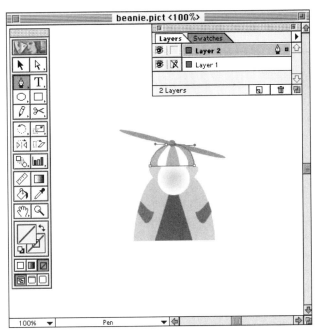

Figure 7-11
Pasting a path into Photoshop brings the path into the current active layer.

RASTERIZING VECTOR IMAGES One of the great dangers in creating complex vector drawings in such programs as Adobe Illustrator, Macromedia FreeHand, and Corel-DRAW is the burden they place on PostScript imaging devices. All those points on a path should be viewed as enemies to the PostScript RIP. Files that have extraordinary numbers of points on a path can bring the most sophisticated imaging devices to their knees.

To illustrate this point, let us share a case study with you. Not too long ago Ted Padova received a file from a designer who informed him that another service bureau had tried to print film separations and left the file to print overnight. The service center stopped the RIPing process after eight hours without a single plate imaged. The file was created in FreeHand and occupied two and a half megabytes, all of which was vector art with no placed images.

When the designer brought the file to him, Ted knew there would be problems if he went down the same road and tried to separate the file from FreeHand. His solution was to open the file in Illustrator, save it as an EPS, and then go to Photoshop, where he would open it and rasterize the data at 300 dpi. One thing to keep in mind is that Adobe Illustrator is the absolute best PostScript engine on the planet. If you have problems with EPS files that were not created in Illustrator, open and save from Illustrator. Doing so will preserve the integrity of the PostScript code. This example was saved from Illustrator so that the rasterizing in Photoshop would be flawless.

The final result was a Photoshop file that occupied over 70MB of disk space. It took over an hour and a half to save the file in Illustrator format on an 8100 Mac with a 2GB array drive. When the file was separated, however, it imaged at eight minutes a plate.

You may be called upon to solve various imaging problems. One important point to remember is that file sizes can be misleading. In the previous example, a 2.5MB vector image couldn't be printed after eight hours of RIPing, yet the 70MB file printed in 32 minutes (four plates at eight minutes per plate). It's not the size of files but the complexity and mathematical intensity of files that can create many printing problems. You can often use Photoshop's rasterizing engine to solve many of these problems.

AVOIDING COLOR PROBLEMS In Chapter 5 we discussed some of the differences in color gamuts. In one respect, digital prepress people have an advantage over Web designers and screen presentation people in matching color between Illustrator and Photoshop. Since the mode for prepress is CMYK, the prepress people can take advantage of the fact that Illustrator CMYK colors are very similar to Photoshop CMYK colors. Web designers, however, use RGB color models to bring their Web pages to life, and a great disparity exists between Illustrator and Photoshop RGB colors.

Have you ever created a bright handsome design in Illustrator and imported your proud illustration in Photoshop? What you get is what our friend Luanne Seymour Cohen from Adobe Systems calls "baby poop green." Those nice bright Illustrator colors go flat when you rasterize the image in Photoshop. The solution to the problem we learned from Luanne is to set up custom colors in Photoshop that more closely resemble the Illustrator palette.

Figure 7-12 shows the dialog box that appears when you choose File ⇨ Color Settings ⇨ Printing Inks Setup. The most common ink system designers use is SWOP (standard web offset printing) inks. Although you can choose from a variety of printing inks from this dialog box, no system provided by Adobe supports colors close to the RGB values identified in Illustrator.

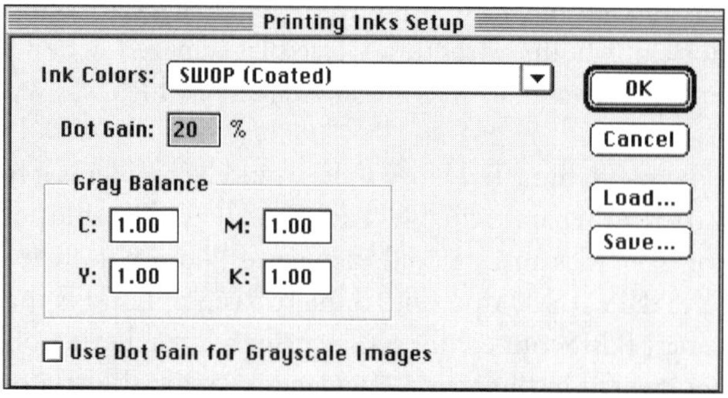

Figure 7-12
The Printing Inks Setup dialog box allows for custom color setup.

To create a new color palette, select the pop-up menu for Ink Colors and choose Custom. Another dialog box will appear enabling you to identify chromacity coordinates for various ink combinations. Figure 7-13 shows the inks that resemble the RGB values you get in Illustrator.

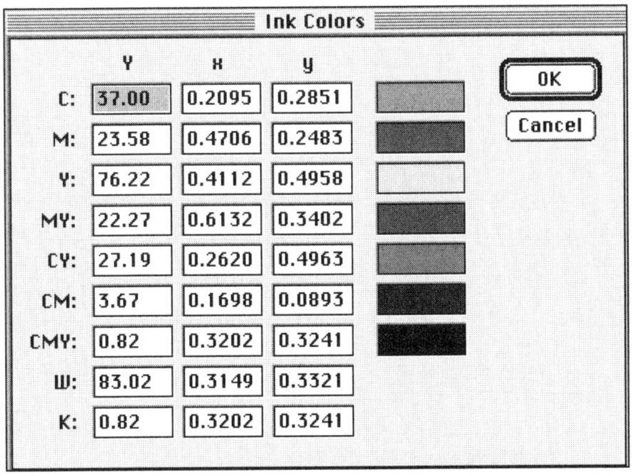

	Y	x	y		
C:	37.00	0.2095	0.2851		**OK**
M:	23.58	0.4706	0.2483		Cancel
Y:	76.22	0.4112	0.4958		
MY:	22.27	0.6132	0.3402		
CY:	27.19	0.2620	0.4963		
CM:	3.67	0.1698	0.0893		
CMY:	0.82	0.3202	0.3241		
W:	83.02	0.3149	0.3321		
K:	0.82	0.3202	0.3241		

Figure 7-13
These Custom color settings provide Illustrator-compatible colors.

You can plug in the values shown in Figure 7-13 and save your new library from the Printing Inks Setup dialog box, but we've made it easier for you. Simply follow these steps:

1. Go to the CD-ROM accompanying this book, where you will find a file called Illustrator Colors (on the Mac) or Illcolor.api (on the PC).

2. Copy the file to your Photoshop folder and place it in the Goodies ⇨ Color Palettes folder.

3. When you reopen Photoshop, choose Color Settings ⇨ Printing Inks to regain the dialog box. Select the Load button and load these colors before rasterizing your Illustrator artwork. You can run a test by opening an Illustrator file with the SWOP coated library and then opening a second file with the Illustrator colors identified. Compare the two and you will see a distinct difference between the colors.

4. To avoid printing problems, revert to the SWOP coated library when you intend to print film separations or output to color printing devices.

TIP For another technique see the section headed "Ensuring Consistent Color On-Screen" in the Photoshop 4 User Guide. Our friend Luanne Seymour Cohen has also described the same technique in the Tips & Techniques page of the Adobe Web page, `www.adobe.com/studio/tipstechniques/`.

AVOIDING PROBLEMS WITH WEB GRAPHICS Color is not the only problem the Web designer can face when working between Illustrator and Photoshop. Sizing raster images in Photoshop can also present some problems. If you decide to rasterize some Illustrator artwork and then resize the image in Photoshop, you will have to interpolate the image up in size. Figure 7-14 shows, on the left, an Illustrator file that was opened in Photoshop and then sized up. The interpolation severely degraded the image.

 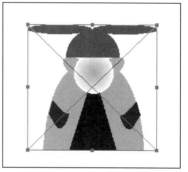

Figure 7-14
An Illustrator file was opened in Photoshop, sized up (left), and placed in Photoshop (right).

To avoid problems with images appearing like this one, you have two choices. You can open the file and choose the final size in the Open dialog box — Photoshop will rasterize the image at that size, thereby avoiding any interpolated effects. Your second choice is to place the Illustrator image in Photoshop, which will offer you control over sizing before the image is rasterized (as on the right side of Figure 7-14). When the file is placed, the transformation handles appear, enabling you to transform the image. If you size the image up, the file will be rasterized only when you press Enter.

Photoshop and Layout Programs

At times you may experience or be called upon to deal with all kinds of bizarre digital circumstances resulting from a variety of problems. You can always count on one axiom in the computer art world: designers do the craziest things in software applications! For the life of us, we don't know why software manufacturers offer their beta testing to the tech people. They could simply throw out a few copies to some graphic designers and get the greatest conglomeration of workarounds found in the universe. These workarounds and shortcuts are quite often used in layout programs — and often not as the program designers intended.

Programs like Adobe PageMaker and QuarkXPress are designed as layout programs. However, the people who use these programs, and the software manufacturers who respond to user requests, use and provide opportunities to do more than a layout. Find someone married to QuarkXPress and we'll show you someone who uses it as an illustration program, creating logos, icons, and various forms of illustrated artwork.

Most of the problems arising from improper printing in layout programs could be avoided if people would use a program to do only what it was designed for. Unfortunately, this will never happen. The need will always arise to fix problems so that the output will be properly imaged. We should jump with glee, for this means we will always be employed!

 NOTE Avoiding transparency problems with other programs is covered in Chapter 6.

Saving time when rotating and scaling images

Rotating an image requires a fairly large amount of computer power. Rotating what are essentially square pixels to a new angle will take time, even on small files.

We strongly suggest rotating images in Photoshop before placing them in your page layout program, rather than rotating them in the page layout program itself. There are a few reasons for this. If you place an image into a page layout program and then rotate the image, the processing power it takes to recalculate the new angle is called upon every time you print the file. Every time you print a laser proof (we tend to have a good number of black-and-white proofs made of any project before it goes to final printing), the computer has to perform the rotation on the image. But if the image is rotated in Photoshop before it is placed, the image is output at the standard angle and no recalculation of pixels is needed.

Another reason for rotating the image in Photoshop is that when an image is rotated, the quality of the image is degraded slightly. How much the image is changed is determined by the original quality of the image and the amount of rotation performed. If the image is rotated in a page layout program, the image quality is degraded with no chance to improve it with sharpening tools. If the rotation is performed in Photoshop, you can apply sharpening filters before saving the file. You should be able to produce a rotated image as sharp as the original.

At times, you won't know how much to rotate an image until you place it into a page layout program, because you need to see how it interacts with other graphic elements. In these cases, go ahead and place it and rotate it to the desired angle in the page layout program. When you have determined what the angle should be, go back into Photoshop and rotate the image to the new angle. Then place it again and set the angle back to zero.

Likewise, scaling an image involves the same problems as rotating an image. If an image is placed into a page layout program and then scaled, the scaling calculation is performed every time the page is printed. So we recommend scaling images in Photoshop prior to placing them in your page layout program.

Avoiding problems with cropped images

Most programs that allow you to place images from other programs also give you the ability to crop out unwanted portions. This is a very helpful feature, but when abused it can create problems. If you are using most of the placed image and cropping out only small portions, then it makes sense to crop the image in your page layout program. But when you place an image that is 10″ × 10″ and plan to use only a 1″ × 1″ area, you may be asking for trouble. As with rotation and scaling, cropped portions of an image are processed with the visible portions every time the page is printed.

For example, let's say you have built an elaborate initial-cap font with all 26 letters. Each letter is ornate and very complex, and so even one letter takes up a lot of memory, let alone all 26 letters. You save all 26 letters in one large EPS file. In the page layout program you place this file wherever you need an initial cap. Then you crop out the other 25 letters, leaving just the one needed. You carry out this same procedure every time you need an initial cap. Every time you print this document (odds are it never will print), wherever an initial cap is placed, all 26 letters of the alphabet will be processed, where only one is needed.

When you copy and paste images from Illustrator to Photoshop, the pasted image will appear in the center of the Photoshop document on a new layer. Let's assume you export a path from Photoshop to Illustrator, edit the path with a stroke or fill, and wish to return the data to Photoshop at the precise position at which it originated. Let's further assume the image is not at the center of the Photoshop document. To ensure precise placement, follow these steps:

1. First choose Select ➪ Select All (Command/Ctrl+A).

2. Choose Make Work Path from the paths palette with a tolerance of 2.0 and include the boundary with the text path or document data you are exporting.

3. When you paste into Illustrator, the boundary path will appear. Do not edit this path; it will simply be the definition of your canvas size when you return to Photoshop.

4. When finished editing in Illustrator, choose Select All Copy and paste the data back to Photoshop. The boundary will ensure precise placement and pin registration.

A great problem-solver in your tech support arsenal is Acrobat Distiller, included with Adobe Acrobat. If you have Adobe PageMaker, then you already have Acrobat Distiller, since it ships on the CD with PageMaker. If for some reason you don't have Acrobat Distiller, we suggest you run out and purchase it right away. This is the Swiss army knife for the tech support person. What we're about to tell you is not documented in most computer books, so you can feel delighted in having purchased *Photoshop Tech Support*.

Figure 7-15 shows an example of a file that won't print properly. The logo was created in QuarkXPress for a color separation. The fill used to knock out the ellipse shape won't create a knockout when separated on an imagesetter. Interestingly enough, we've found cases where laser printers can separate such a file properly, but it chokes when going to high-end imagesetting equipment. You can export the QuarkXPress page as EPS, but unfortunately, not all exported pages from QuarkXPress can be opened in Illustrator — at least not consistently. If this is the case, you need to find another method to get the file into Illustrator.

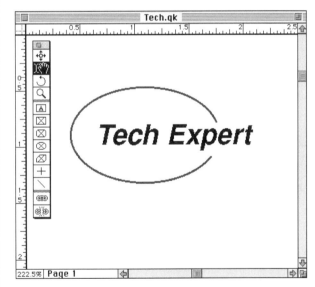

Figure 7-15
This two-color logo, created in QuarkXPress, won't
print properly.

Let's assume your task is to modify the logo, add a drop shadow to the type, and prepare the file to separate properly. You need to preserve the text integrity, and you know that the text will print best as a PostScript font and not rasterized in Adobe Photoshop. On the other hand, the drop shadow would be best suited for a Photoshop job.

(continued)

USING
ACROBAT AS
A FIX WHEN
YOU CAN'T
PRINT

Here's how we go about accomplishing our task:

1. To distill the file in Acrobat Distiller, create a PostScript file. PostScript files are readily created in the Print dialog box for most programs.

2. When you view the Print dialog box in QuarkXPress (Figure 7-16), you'll notice the radio button for File below the radio button designating Printer in the Destination area. Choose File as your option and click Save.

3. Another dialog box appears. For the format, choose PostScript Job (see Figure 7-17). Then click Binary and Level 2 Only. For Font Inclusion, choose All.

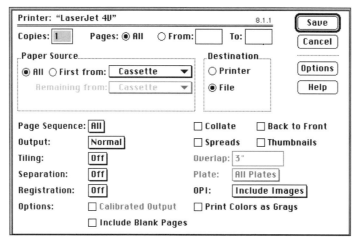

Figure 7-16
Choose to print to file in the QuarkXPress Print dialog box.

4. The file will be printed to disk as a PostScript file. (You must have a PostScript printer driver targeted in order to print a file to PostScript.) This file needs to be distilled with the Acrobat Distiller with Acrobat 2.1 compatibility.

5. When you launch Distiller, you simply open the file and let it do its thing. The resulting file will be a PDF document.

Even though Photoshop 4 now supports PDF exports, it won't open PDF documents except those created by Photoshop. This is of no concern in our example, since we still need to do some work in Illustrator.

When PDF files are opened in Illustrator, all the paths are available for editing. In the example, we follow this further sequence of steps:

1. Open the file in Illustrator, delete the text, and save the file under a new name.

USING ACROBAT AS A FIX WHEN YOU CAN'T PRINT

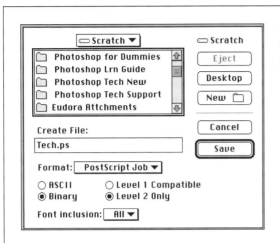

Figure 7-17
Choose these Save options
when creating a PostScript file
for Acrobat Distiller.

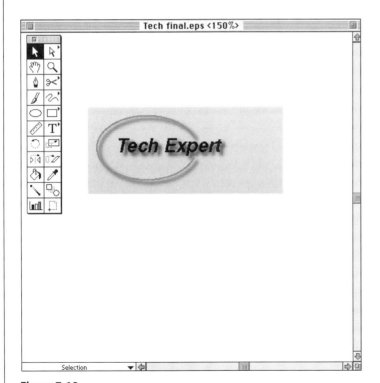

Figure 7-18.
The logo has been imported back to Illustrator after
the shadow and the gradient were created in Photoshop.

USING
ACROBAT AS
A FIX WHEN
YOU CAN'T
PRINT

(continued)

2. Reopen the original PDF file, delete the gradient, and save the result as a second file. Fortunately, the bounding box will be the same for both files, giving us an opportunity to rasterize both images in Photoshop at the same size.

3. Next launch Photoshop and rasterize both files. The text and ellipse are used to fill black, apply a Gaussian blur, and add a slight offset, which creates the shadow.

4. Drag and drop the final shadow image onto the gradient while holding the Shift key down. The Shift key provides us with pin registration for precise placement.

5. Finally, export the composite image as EPS and bring it into Illustrator to reset the type on the logo, as shown in Figure 7-18.

USING ACROBAT AS A FIX WHEN YOU CAN'T PRINT

The final Illustrator file is a composite image saved with Placed EPS art and imported back into QuarkXPress. The file will now separate properly. Imagine, if you will, trying to create a clipping path around the shadow? By compositing images in Photoshop, you'll gain much success in design and avoid many potential printing problems. Additionally, by using Acrobat Distiller you can open files from many computer systems and a variety of application software to import and edit in Illustrator.

Photoshop and Adobe Dimensions

Both Illustrator and Photoshop provide some nice transformation controls; however, neither program is designed as a 3-D application, and they both fall short of controlling any Z-axis rotations. Creating simple 3-D artwork and working with perspective control and rotation are much better handled in a program like Adobe Dimensions.

The best way to begin a Dimensions session is to first create your line art in Adobe Illustrator. Figure 7-19 shows a simple box to which we want to add some perspective, a good candidate for Dimensions. The figure was first created in Illustrator.

The line art is exported from Illustrator as an EPS file and imported into Adobe Dimensions. In Dimensions, we rotate and scale the image to create the perspective desired, as viewed in Figure 7-20.

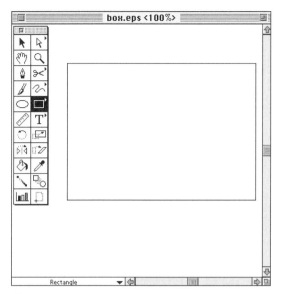

Figure 7-19
A simple box is first created in Illustrator.

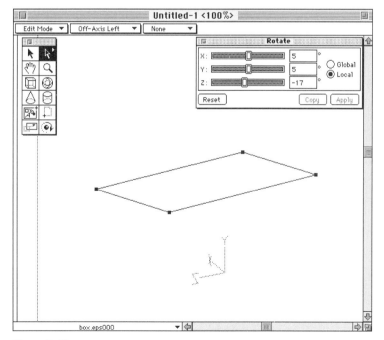

Figure 7-20
The box is then transformed with the Z-axis control in Adobe Dimensions.

From Dimensions, export the file as an Adobe Illustrator file. If any problems occur when you attempt to open the file in Photoshop, open it first in Adobe Illustrator and resave it from Illustrator as an EPS file. The document can then be opened easily in Photoshop. This process works well with other PostScript modeling applications as well.

Figure 7-21 shows a book cover design that first used Illustrator line art brought into Dimensions to create the perspective and placement locations of the images. A design like this one would be much more difficult without the aid of Dimensions to first create the guides.

Figure 7-21
This book cover design first used Dimensions to set up the perspective guides.

CHAPTER EIGHT

ASSURING RELIABLE
OUTPUT

After creating your magic in Photoshop, you probably will need to output the file in some manner. "Outputting" can refer to many things. You may need a version of the Photoshop file that is compatible with digital presentations. Or you simply may need a copy of the file on a disk to give to someone else. But the most common way of outputting a Photoshop file is to actually print it to an output device. These devices will normally use either composite color or color separations. What's more, you will often print Photoshop files from some program other than Photoshop. In this chapter you'll learn how to avoid many potential printing problems.

Printing Photoshop Files

If you are a graphic designer or layout artist, you know that your Photoshop files will ultimately be imported into a layout application such as QuarkXPress or Adobe Page-Maker. If you create display ads, posters, or small brochures, you may use such programs as Adobe Illustrator, Macromedia FreeHand, or CorelDRAW. At any rate, your Photoshop work winds up in another program before it is printed. In Chapter 4 we talked about file formats and proper modes for imaging Photoshop files. If you're not certain which mode or format to use, you may wish to turn back to Chapter 4 and review it. In this chapter we'll assume you know the proper way to set up a file for importing into other programs.

Photoshop fortunately has many capabilities that you can bring into play when preparing images for importing into the programs just mentioned. You can bring Photoshop files in many different formats into a variety of high-end applications. With this wonderful transportability, however, come many problems that can arise if you don't follow some simple rules.

Avoiding problems with transformed images

When PostScript Level 2 arrived, people falsely assumed that this new upgrade would eliminate all those long evenings watching a RIP (raster image processor) churn through complex files. Since Level 2 PostScript greatly improved printing performance, people began to deviate from some rules we learned back in the PostScript Level 1 days. Among our early lessons was a simple rule: never, never, never size, rotate, or scale placed images. For instance, if you place a Photoshop file in another program, don't size the file up or down in the application receiving the Photoshop image. You must return to Photoshop and complete all your transformations there, and then place your image in the application of choice. If you rely on a layout program to perform these transformations, you will create complex files that need to be mathematically calculated for RIPing and printing. In simple transformations and PostScript Level 2 RIPs, you may not see the problem. As files grow in size and complexity increases, however, one day it will all catch up with you. So make a habit of following this rule, and you will avoid many imaging problems.

You may claim that you already have a document laid out and don't know the transformations imposed in the application. Hold on, *Photoshop Tech Support* is here to help you!

As your firm's new creative director, you may suddenly find yourself responsible for numerous layouts assembled by someone who hasn't read *Photoshop Tech Support* and who has put together an incredibly complex document, which needs some revision and has to go off to the imaging center for new color separations. As you review the invoices for the previous jobs, you notice how expensive these files have been to image. You call the imaging center, and they tell you every file they receive is a nightmare and takes over six hours to RIP! Deciding to examine the files, you notice that every Photoshop image has been sized to one-eighth its original size, rotated, stepped, and repeated over 20 times, as well as that they're 800 ppi and all have clipping paths. You know you have some work to do.

Figure 8-1 demonstrates a problem with rotated images. Each of the Photoshop files was rotated in Adobe Illustrator and then masked to the outline of the text characters. In this case, it would be best to perform the rotations in Photoshop and then import the rotated images for masking in Illustrator.

To accurately perform the rotations in Photoshop and recreate the Illustrator document, you need to determine the degree of rotation for each image. In programs like Adobe PageMaker and QuarkXPress, the task is easy when you examine the control palettes that provide readouts of the rotation angles. In programs like Illustrator and FreeHand, you can determine rotation angles by using the info palette or info bar, as described on the next page.

Figure 8-1
These Photoshop images have been rotated in Adobe Illustrator.

1. Using the measure tool in Illustrator or the line tool in FreeHand, draw a straight line from the lower-left corner point. The readout in the info item shows zero degrees for the angle. As you move up to the lower-right corner of the image, the info readout shows the rotation angle. Figure 8-2 shows the angle of rotation in the info palette for Adobe Illustrator.

2. As you assess the angle of each rotated item, record the values.

3. Return to Photoshop, rotate each image, and resave the file.

4. Import the Photoshop documents back into your application. Each image will be rotated and the PostScript RIP won't need to calculate rotation angles when RIPing the file.

Rotation angle

Figure 8-2
The angle of rotation is indicated in the info palette in Adobe Illustrator.

In complex documents, taking the time to perform the transformations in Photoshop eases the burden on all printing devices.

Avoiding clipping path problems

A fallacy you may encounter in your migration to PostScript Level 2 is the belief that any Level 2 device will handle clipping paths just fine. Believe us on this one: if you use clipping paths to excess, you can bring a $250,000 imagesetter to its knees in a heartbeat. Excessive use of clipping paths should always be avoided. In creating your layout assemblies, keep in mind that every single point you add to an image increases the RIPing time of the printing device. Since clipping paths are expressed as a series of points, each one of these points is an enemy to the PostScript RIP. As a general rule, the fewer clipping paths used, the more easily the file will image.

"But I have this document created with all these clipping paths! How do I fix the problem?" Well, since you probably got a nice fat raise for fixing the previous little number, this one will probably get you the key to the executive washroom. As creative director, you find out that all those images you just finished rotating in Photoshop now have clipping paths and are carefully placed in the document. To fix the problem, you need to recreate the document while keeping all the images in their same positions:

1. Whenever you need to recreate a composite image in Photoshop from any application, make a template or guide to carefully position all elements in the precise location. To create a template, open the file in the application in which it was created and make a screen dump by pressing Command+Shift+3 on the Mac. Windows users can press the Print Screen key (or Alt+Print Screen), which copies the contents of the screen or the current dialog box to the clipboard for pasting into a new Photoshop file later. You can also use any of various third-party applications, such as Corel Capture. Figure 8-3 shows a screen capture of our entire layout.

Figure 8-3
Make a screen capture of the layout page.

2. Once you've captured the screen, open it in Photoshop and crop it to the edges of the document page. The screen capture is a full-sized page, and the capture resolution is 72 ppi.

3. Now you need to increase the resolution to the final output resolution you desire. Choose Image ⇨ Image Size and enter the proper resolution. Be certain to click the Resample Image check box. The resampled image will be interpolated up in resolution, but since this is just your template, you don't care about the image being interpolated.

4. On the template, draw a path around the objects you wish to mask and also include a path around the image border. The border path ensures precise placement of the paths in a new document window.

5. When you are finished creating the paths, copy them to the clipboard and paste them in a newly created document window. Figure 8-4 shows the paths pasted into a new document.

Figure 8-4
**Paths have been pasted into
a new document window.**

6. With the paths in place, you can now open the individual Photoshop images and drag and drop to the new document window. The paths, when visible, will serve as guides to assist you in proper placement and transformations.

7. After placing all the images, create a selection from the paths and invert the selection. Then press the Delete key to eliminate all the data outside the masked items. You can handle this operation in two ways, either by making individual selections on layers or by merging the layers and using a single selection. Figure 8-5 shows individual layers after removal of the excess data.

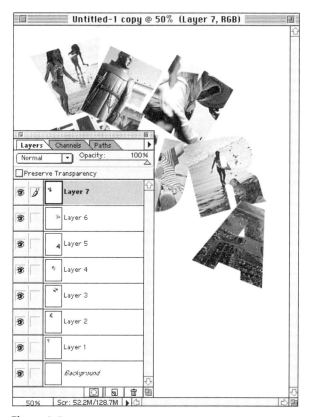

Figure 8-5
Images have been masked on individual layers.

8. Apply the background color and then merge the layers for export in Photoshop EPS format. Bring the composite image back into Illustrator, where you can now place the type.

The steps involved in compositing images are obviously more time consuming than just submitting the original file with clipping paths to the service bureau. You might think these steps unnecessary and prefer to have the service bureau deal with the file. If this is the case, you would be well-advised to rethink your position. You should always consider the time involved in producing digital output as a partnership between you and the service bureau. If you take two hours to complete a job and the service bureau takes eight hours to print the job, your total time is obviously 10 hours to obtain the product you need just for the prepress items. In cases where time crunches and demands to get the job mailed overnight to the client are forever present, all the delays you experience can cost you both time and money. If by following our recommendations, on the other hand, you can produce the same job in three hours, and the service bureau takes 45 minutes to produce your film, then you have saved a total of six and a quarter hours — maybe enough time to get the job out via courier the same day.

Avoiding file corruption problems

By now, this book has taken you through a journey of setting up your files properly and creating the necessary workarounds for efficient document output. But what happens when you do everything right and somehow the computer has goofed you up? You might get angry and send us e-mail suggesting something radical and (politely?) telling us off. Well, we can't let that happen, so we've decided to discuss how to avoid or fix some common file corruption problems.

FIXING A FILE WITH CORRUPTED DATA BITS Files can get corrupted in many ways, and you have undoubtedly experienced a few of them already. Most of what we have seen involves either of two kinds of corruption. The first is the case of a data bit getting skipped or corrupted as a Photoshop file is written to an external media cartridge. What you see in your Photoshop document is a line appearing in the image, maybe with some noise viewed along the path of the line (see Figure 8-6).

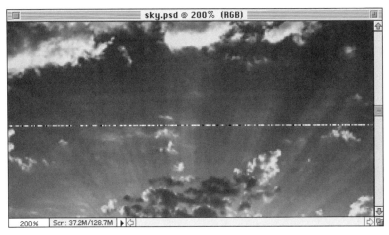

Figure 8-6
This Photoshop image was corrupted as the file was copied to external media.

Notice how difficult it would be to use the rubber stamp tool and clone the area in Figure 8-6. The fix for this kind of problem is much easier than using the rubber stamp tool:

1. Select the Single Row or Single Column option of the marquee tool from the toolbox and click directly one pixel below the corrupted line.

2. Select the move tool or depress the Command/Ctrl key and hold the Option/Alt key down while pressing Up Arrow. This action creates a floating selection of a clone positioned over the corrupted area.

3. Flatten the image and export it to your layout program.

FIXING A FILE THAT DOESN'T SEPARATE PROPERLY The second type of corruption we have seen is a little more difficult to diagnose and fix. Suppose you've prepared your file properly and you have controlled all the variables that would otherwise create a problem with imaging, but your file for some reason doesn't separate properly. It's a TIFF image and you know it is CMYK, but for some unknown reason, the final film shows the image on the black plate only. This is rare but known to happen.

Here's how you can fix this type of problem:

1. Open the file in Photoshop.
2. Choose Image ➪ Duplicate to create a duplicate image.
3. Choose File ➪ Save As and save the file in EPS format.

Most often, the new duplicate image saved in another format will solve this problem.

TIP To avoid file corruption, run Photoshop with as few system extensions as possible. Use the Extensions Manager Control Panel to create a minimal set for working in Photoshop.

Halftoning Photoshop Files

As the reader, you are certainly as enamored as we are with Photoshop and all the wonderful things it can do. Sometimes you can dazzle novices by performing what appears to be magic on your images. Yet at times you may wish there really were a magical solution to some problems. As good as Photoshop is, sometimes you need to image a file that you cannot rescan and that doesn't offer sufficient resolution for any desirable output. In such circumstances, you can treat your images with different halftone frequencies and patterns. This approach may require a little practice, but when you develop some predictable results, you will find a solution for the image that must be included in your client's document.

To fully comprehend what we are addressing, you should understand that a file imaged on RC (resin-coated) paper or film at the service bureau always carries a *halftone frequency*. This frequency is represented in dots, and the dots can carry many shapes. Photoshop provides you with a number of dot shapes when you choose File ➪ Page Setup ➪ Screen (see Figure 8-7).

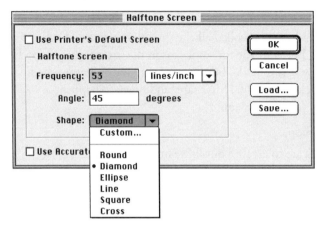

Figure 8-7
Photoshop's Halftone Screen dialog box offers control over
dot frequencies, angles, and shapes.

In this dialog box you can set the shape of the dot you desire from the available choices, or you can create a custom dot shape to suit various design needs. Additionally, you can embed the frequency within the Photoshop file by entering the desired value in the Frequency box. That poor scan we commented on a couple of paragraphs ago might be better off with a line shape at 45 lpi rather than with a diamond shape at 133 lpi. Whatever the case, you will need to decide what shape and frequency work best for your design needs.

After you choose the frequency and shape, you need to save the file appropriately so that the embedded attributes follow your Photoshop file to the layout application. To do this, save the file as Photoshop EPS and check the box for Include Halftone Screen in the EPS Format dialog box (Figure 8-8), which comes on-screen when you choose the Photoshop EPS format.

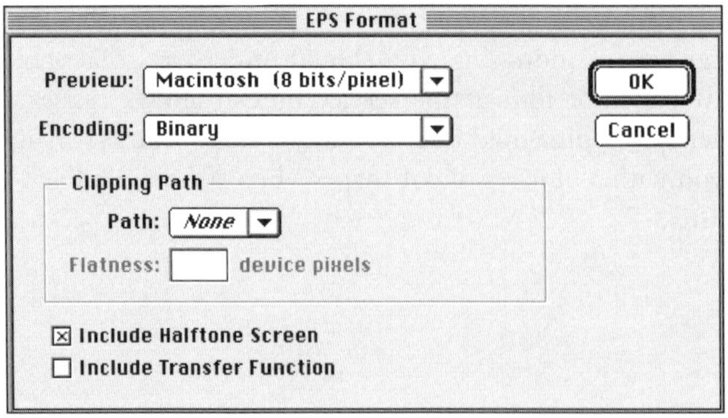

Figure 8-8
This file in EPS format will have the halftone screen included.

Creating custom dots

Sometimes you may wish to have more choices for dots available to you than those provided by Photoshop. Fortunately, Photoshop provides a means for customizing dots. If you select Custom from the list in the dialog box shown back in Figure 8-7, then another dialog box will appear. This dialog box requires you to enter PostScript code to create a custom dot shape. If you don't know how to write code in PostScript, you needn't worry; we've included several custom shapes for you on the CD — look in the folder entitled Ted's Dots. To get the dots into the dialog box, click the Load button and load one of the files. Figure 8-9 shows a loaded file to express a pinwheel dot shape.

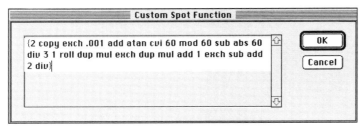

Figure 8-9
This PostScript code creates a pinwheel dot shape.

You may not know what many of the dot shapes will look like when you view them in the Load dialog box, so you may want to print a sample of each one on your laser printer. Be certain to load the dot and choose a low enough frequency so that the dot will be large enough to view — something on the order of 30 lpi. You'll also have to save the file as Photoshop EPS with Include Halftone Screen checked. The file can be printed directly from Photoshop or imported into another application for printing. Figure 8-10 shows a file with the pinwheel shape printed at 30 lpi.

Avoiding problems with embedded frequencies

Our discussion on creating custom halftone dots and frequencies should be applied only to Photoshop images for which you intentionally wish to control these attributes. One of the most common imaging problems related to frequency control is the inadvertent use of the Include Halftone Screen option when designers export Photoshop EPS files. When you select this item, the application receiving the Photoshop document cannot override the frequency embedded by Photoshop. To avoid problems of this nature, always leave the check box unchecked unless you have some definite need to embed a custom frequency.

Figure 8-10
This halftone has been printed with a pinwheel dot
shape at 30 lpi.

Color-Separating Photoshop Files

In our earlier chapters related to file formats and color correction basics, we stated several times that all process color images need to be saved as CMYK before you export your Photoshop file to a program for color separation. Once you get the hang of it, separating process color from Photoshop files is a snap. We also recommended that the most desirable format is Photoshop EPS with Desktop Color Separation (DCS) turned on. All of this is fine when dealing with process color.

Spot color, on the other hand, is a different issue. Apart from the Duotone mode, spot color cannot be separated from a Photoshop file even in version 4 — at least without the aid of some workarounds or third-party applications. If you need to create files for screen printers or if you need to create a two- or three-color job using Photoshop's Duotone mode, you'll need to examine one of the alternatives for getting the separations out properly.

Two ways exist to handle separating spot color from Photoshop documents. One alternative is to set up individual colors on separate layers and save each layer as a separate file. When you import the first separation into a layout program such as Quark-XPress or Adobe PageMaker, you can set the bounding box area to position the image in your document. If you import the image in QuarkXPress, you can print one color or separate multiple colors, choose Get Picture, and replace the previous image with a second color. Placement in QuarkXPress offers you pin registration as long as you don't size or move the placeholder. In PageMaker, you can use the Place command and select Replacing Entire Graphic. Once again you'll get pin registration when one image replaces another.

The problem becomes much more complex, however, if you have an image similar to Figure 8-11. The background and the graphic in the logo are specified as CMYK colors, whereas the text is identified as a Pantone spot color. The final separation will be a five-color job.

Figure 8-11
A CMYK logo and spot color text present a complex color separation problem in Photoshop.

If you try the procedure we just described, you need a clipping path around the text so that the shadow appears for the logo as intended. Since we've already discussed the need to eliminate clipping paths as much as possible, we should consider a second alternative. Third-party applications are available to separate spot color from Photoshop. PlateMaker is a plug-in that works with Photoshop and QuarkXPress; it enables you to save files in DCS 2.0 format. You can identify each separate color as an alpha channel; in Quark use Platecheck (PlateMaker's companion QuarkXtension) to separate the spot color. If you are a PageMaker user, Photospot is a plug-in that will perform the same operation. At any rate, you'll need a third-party utility, since Photoshop cannot pull apart spot colors.

CHAPTER NINE

MACINTOSH SYSTEM
ERRORS

The very fact that you work on a computer means you will always encounter various system errors and crashes. If these errors persist, you may need to take some corrective action or find various means of salvaging your files. This chapter discusses some of the more common system errors and how to fix them.

If you use Photoshop for any length of time, you will inevitably come across error messages. When Photoshop encounters a problem, it displays these messages to help you interpret what problem occurred. These problems range from minor nuisances to complete crashes.

This chapter describes, under each common error message, the problem and the means either to fix it or to avoid it altogether.

"Out of memory" or "Disk or scratch disk is full"

Problem

You have tried to open a Photoshop file that is too large for your current system configuration. You do not have enough RAM and/or hard disk space available on your computer to accommodate such a large file.

Solutions

First check how much memory you have allocated to Photoshop. At the Finder, find the application icon for Photoshop. It should be in the Photoshop folder somewhere on your computer. Click the icon once and select Get Info under the File menu as shown in Figure 9-1.

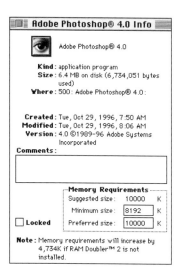

Figure 9-1
The Get Info dialog box shows basic memory requirements.

Under Memory Requirements are three settings. Look at the Preferred Size, which represents how much RAM is allocated to Photoshop. When you open the program, it will use this much RAM and no more. Even if you have more RAM available, it will stop at this point and start using much slower virtual memory off the hard drive.

If you have never changed this number from the default installation setting, more than likely it is set too low. During installation, Adobe puts in a number that should work on most machines. To do this, it must be kept as low as possible but still leave enough to run Photoshop. This ensures compatibility with as many machines as possible. But if your computer has a generous amount of RAM installed on its motherboard, you should change this setting to a higher number. See Chapter 3 for a more in-depth explanation of memory requirements and how to adjust the memory allocation for Photoshop.

Sometimes you will get this error because Photoshop does something that people don't realize it can do — and it does it automatically. Photoshop uses a compression scheme (run length encoded, or RLE, compression) when it saves a file in its native format. Basically Photoshop compresses the file with its layers and channels as much as will allow it to recover the original file intact when you reopen it. (This is called lossless compression.) You can open and save a file as many times as you like and keep image integrity. RLE compression started with version 2.5.

Since Photoshop is compressing your files, when you look at the file size on the desktop you can get a false sense of how large your image actually is. The Finder may report your file size as 20MB, but when you open the file in Photoshop, the image will prove really to be 45MB. Photoshop was able to compress 25MB of information out of your file. Again don't worry. Your image will be just fine when you reopen it.

You will see more compression of files that are less complex or that have extra channels. When we say "less complex," we are referring to images that are of similar colors throughout. An example is a photograph of a sky with few clouds. This type of image will be heavy in blues and cyans with little or no information for the other colors. Photoshop can take that information and compress it to a very small disk file.

Files that contain extra channels or "alpha" channels are similar to the files described in the previous example. Since channels carry only grayscale information, they are good candidates for compression. For example, suppose you have three channels that contain square boxes used for selections. In this case you have only pure black or pure white pixels throughout a channel. Photoshop will be able to compress these channels to a very small amount of information that will add very little size to your file. Conversely, if your channels have gradients or blends in them, they will require more file space to save them.

As an example, we created a rainbow gradient in Photoshop. The file was 5×7 inches at 300 dpi in CMYK mode. The image size in Photoshop was 12MB. After saving, the file size as reported by the Finder was 4.7MB. So Photoshop was able to take a 12MB file and compress it to 4.7MB. We then added three channels to the file. Each new channel was filled with black and had a white square box cut out; the box had a different position and size in each channel. (In theory, each channel should add 3MB of information to the file, and thus the three should add 9MB to the file size. If four channels, CMYK, equal 12MB, each channel should be 3MB.) We then saved the file with the new channels. The original 12MB file that compressed to 4.7MB with no channels added now occupied only 4.8MB, even though three 3MB channels had been added to it.

Because of this compression scheme, your file size readings at the desktop can be misleading. If, although you know that you can open a 20MB image in Photoshop, you get an "Out of memory" error while trying to open a file of that size, you may be trying to open a much larger image and, in turn, prompting the error. In most instances you need to free up space on your hard drive. Be certain at least five times the file size is free on the hard drive.

"Could not complete your request because there is not enough memory (RAM)"

Problem

This happens when you attempt to do something in Photoshop that requires more memory to complete the task. An example is applying a filter to or copying a large file. Most anything in Photoshop requires memory, but with small files you should be able to do pretty much anything. Once you start venturing into larger file sizes, above 20MB, it can very quickly become impossible to do anything with a computer configured with a small amount of RAM.

Solutions

As in the example for "Out of memory," you can try allocating more RAM to Photo-shop. See the example under "Out of memory" for a description of how to allocate more memory to Photoshop. But you may have to run out to your local RAM dealer-ship, pry open that wallet, and purchase more RAM. Believe us, if you regularly spend time in Photoshop, buying more RAM is the best thing you can do to increase your productivity. The extra memory will also help every other program you use on a daily basis. Note that the price of RAM has come down considerably over the last year or so.

Another solution, less destructive to your pocketbook, is to "downsize" your file. By decreasing your resolution, you can decrease your image size and in turn decrease your RAM requirements. Choose Image ⇨ Image Size to reveal the dialog box shown in Fig-ure 9-2. Make sure both Constrain Proportions and Resample Image are checked and set Resample Image to Bicubic. At the top of the dialog box after the words Pixel Dimensions, Photoshop will tell you the new size of your file, displaying the old file size in parenthesis. This is the version 4 dialog box; version 3 was slightly different but similar in concept.

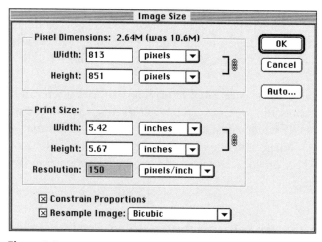

Figure 9-2
The Image Size dialog box allows you to control the
 image resolution.

Set the resolution to a smaller number. If you have it set at 300, then try 250 or 200. You have issues to consider when doing this type of change; see Chapter 8 for an in-depth look at outputting Photoshop files.

Bitmap mode and special filters, such as the Distort, Lighting Effects, and Effects filters, require memory for a scratch partition larger than the usual amount of five times the file size. The filters especially need additional RAM. If your computer does not have sufficient RAM, you may need to reduce the file size to apply the filter.

Rather than reduce image size and risk working on a lower-resolution image, reduce the file size of a document temporarily by choosing the Split Channels command from the channels palette. When you split the channels on a three-channel document, apply the filter to each individual channel and work on one third of the original file size. After completing the editing, reassemble the document by choosing the Merge Channels command in the channels palette. Try splitting channels with RGB or Lab images. If you choose Lab mode, you can apply the filter to the Lightness channel with excellent results.

Another workaround for editing smaller files is to use the Quick Edit mode to work on a smaller portion of the image.

TEMPORARILY REDUCING FILE SIZE

"Disk Error -34 while reading or writing virtual memory file. Sorry, but this error is fatal."

Problem
Photoshop 3.01, 3.02, and 3.03 running the 68K version on a Mac or Power Mac will give you this error when the primary scratch disk is set to a hard drive that has more than 512MB of disk space available.

Solutions
A few solutions exist. Set the primary scratch disk to a hard drive of less than 512MB. The secondary scratch disk can be set to a drive that has more than 512MB available. You can also update to Photoshop version 3.04 or later, where the 512MB limitation has been removed. Run a disk utility (such as Norton Disk Doctor) to verify the integrity of the drive.

"Could not initialize Photoshop because not enough memory (RAM)"

Problem
We have never been told what causes this problem, but we have come across it from time to time and have had some success in correcting it.

Solutions

Adobe suggests a few things. First, try allocating more RAM to Photoshop. See the "Out of memory" error for a description of memory allocation. This procedure hasn't always worked for us, but it is simple and quick. So it's definitely worth a try before you go on.

You can also try deleting Photoshop's preferences file. To do so, follow these steps:

1. Open up your System folder.
2. Find the preferences folder and open it.
3. You should find a file called "Adobe Photoshop 4.0 Prefs." Drag this file to the trash and delete it.

Keep in mind that you will lose all of your custom settings. These include changes in the Preferences dialog box, any new commands or actions you've defined, and most anything you have changed from the default settings that were created when you installed Photoshop. Before you delete the preferences file, you may want to jot down these custom settings so that you can return Photoshop to its previous custom setup. Some items — such as brushes, actions, and color settings — can be saved out as separate files prior to deleting the preferences file. Then after Photoshop is up and running again, you can simply reload these files as needed. An example is the brushes floating palette:

1. Open the submenu at the top right of the brushes palette and select Save Brushes. Name the brushes whatever you like.
2. Then when Photoshop is fixed, go to the same submenu and select Load Brushes.
3. Find the file you have previously saved and open it. The default brushes will be replaced with your custom brush set.

If you have tried deleting the preferences file and are still experiencing problems, try using a disk utility program such as Norton Utilities or MacTools. These programs defragment your drive and can clean up any problems that may exist.

If the problem persists, delete Photoshop altogether and reload a fresh copy from your master disks or CD. And then as a final resort try reinstalling your system. After that, just punt and go home. It's probably two o'clock in the morning anyway, and your cat or dog is wondering where the heck is dinner.

This error can also appear with earlier Macintosh CPUs and system versions. Upgrade your Mac OS to at least 7.5.5 or later.

"There is not enough memory to open Photoshop"

Problem

This is a system error that occurs when you don't have enough available memory to open the program.

Solutions

Many possible solutions apply to this one. The easiest solution is quit all other programs before you open Photoshop. You may not have enough memory for the system, Photoshop, and the other programs to run at the same time. To see what programs are currently running, at the Finder, look for the little computer icon at the top right of your screen. Click and hold on the icon. At the bottom of the menu will be a list of all programs that are currently running. It should include the Finder and then other programs. Select and quit each one, and then try to open Photoshop.

If the problem persists, try allocating less memory to Photoshop. We know we've said in previous examples that a solution to memory problems is to allocate more memory, but in this case allocating less memory is the answer. At the Finder click Photoshop's icon once and select Get Info from the File menu. At the Preferred Size setting, type in a lower value than appears, but make sure the new value is equal to or greater than the Suggested Size. Then try opening Photoshop again.

If you still have no luck, go to the Control Panels and select Memory. Turn on Virtual Memory. When you select it, a third box should appear that allows you to set the amount of virtual memory. We recommend setting it at least 20MB larger than the available built-in memory. That's, of course, if you have 20MB of disk space available to accommodate virtual memory.

NOTE Normally, Adobe doesn't recommend using virtual memory with Photoshop. The reason is that Photoshop has its own virtual memory scheme known as Scratch Disk. But when your computer has little memory, using virtual memory may be your only option to get Photoshop up and running. If this option works for you, be prepared for your Mac to run more slowly than normal. Photoshop runs more efficiently without virtual memory turned on.

You can also try deleting Photoshop's preferences file, as we described earlier.

A RAM extension program such as RAM Doubler can take the place of your system's virtual memory. It handles the VM scheme a little better, but it is basically the same thing. You should see some improvement, but maybe not enough to warrant buying the program. Don't get us wrong. We like RAM Doubler and have used it in the past. With most programs it works fine. But for Photoshop, it may not be the answer.

Finally, try restarting your computer. This will free up any memory that has become fragmented. Just as hard disk memory becomes sluggish when it becomes fragmented, RAM memory becomes sluggish after continual use. Restarting your computer will defragment it.

"Could not open, could not save *filename* -36 or -39"

Problem
The file could not be opened, or saved, in Photoshop.

Solutions
A file may become irreparably damaged, and you may not have an opportunity to rescue the document. If the problem persists, you need to repair the hard drive, the system, or both. You should assume both the hard drive and system file to be suspect and make an effort to repair both hardware and software. First run a disk utility to test your drive. If the drive has many errors, you may need to reformat it. If problems persist, replace your hard drive. Constant writing problems on hard drives can be due to SCSI ID conflicts and improper termination, wrong jumper settings, and improper configurations. To resolve some of these problems, you may need to call upon an authorized Apple service technician.

After solving the hardware problem, install the most recent available system software on the repaired or new hard drive. Perform a fresh install of Adobe Photoshop. Try to create documents similar to those that originally had problems to ensure that your new configuration is working properly.

"Could not save as *filename* because the disk is full -34"

Problem
This problem occurs when you have run out of space on the disk drive on which you are saving the file.

Solutions
This can have a simple solution. If you have more than one drive, try saving the file onto the other drive. If you got this message while trying to save a file onto a floppy disk, the file is too big to fit on a single floppy. Save the file onto your hard drive first. Then you can use any of an assortment of compression utilities (including StuffIt, Compact Pro, or DiskDoubler) to shrink the file and/or segment the file across many disks. There are many such utilities to choose from, and if you do not have one of these in your software library, we strongly suggest going out and buying one as soon as you can.

Another solution is to use JPEG compression. Saving a file in the JPEG format can greatly reduce your file size. JPEG compression will routinely reduce your file size at a ratio ranging from 10:1 to 20:1. This means that a 10MB to 20MB file can easily be compressed to 1MB. Keep in mind that JPEG is a lossy compression scheme, which means that every time you save a file with JPEG compression, you lose a little of the original quality of the photograph. Repeated JPEG compression is not recommended, and you should always be concerned with data loss.

A better way to reduce file sizes is to choose the channels palette and select Split Channels from the flyaway menu. Then save one channel and copy it to a storage medium. Close the channel just saved and repeat the process for the remaining channels. Performing this action eliminates the need for JPEG compression.

Other Errors

Problems

Many other problems can occur when you use hardware or software insufficient for Photoshop requirements. Errors such as "Coprocessor not installed" or "Could not launch because . . ." can arise when you use older CPUs and system files.

Solutions

Photoshop is a high-performance application for professional use, and the newer versions require a complement of more recent hardware and software. If you encounter persistent problems, you may have to upgrade your hardware. When upgrading hardware, always try to use the most recent operating system available. Additionally, have authorized service personnel make all your hardware configurations. Be careful of mail-order bargains and hacker installations. Many problems will also occur with improper configurations.

CHAPTER TEN

WINDOWS SYSTEM
ERRORS

Many of the Macintosh system errors we discussed in the previous chapter may equally well appear on Windows machines. As a Windows user, however, you should also be aware of some peculiarities of this system. This chapter discusses workarounds for common Photoshop problems under Windows.

Error messages are not exclusive to the Mac user. System and program failures are equally possible on the Windows platform. Even if Windows has performed flawlessly running your office applications, you will find high-end graphics-intensive applications another matter, and you will encounter system errors as often as your Mac-user counterparts.

"Out of memory" or "Disk or scratch disk is full"

Problem
You have tried to open a Photoshop file that is too large for your current system configuration. You do not have enough RAM and/or hard disk space available on your computer to accommodate such a large file.

Solutions
We know that memory limitations are due to one of two factors: RAM or hard disk scratch space. If you have multiple applications open, try closing all programs and working only in Photoshop. If you have applications that load on startup, close all utilities and any startup applications to free as much RAM as possible. By default, Photoshop allocates 75 percent of available RAM to itself in Windows. If your problem persists, quit all applications, quit Photoshop, and then restart Photoshop with all programs closed.

As to scratch space solutions, many 486 and Pentium computers have enough bays to allow you to add internal hard drives to your computer. If you value your time, the cost of a second IDE or SCSI drive will be a small price to pay to realize increased performance from Photoshop. We urge you to consider purchasing a second drive and allocate your primary scratch space to the second drive. The Preferences for Plug-ins & Scratch Disk dialog box, shown in Figure 10-1, is where you make this allocation. Ted Padova, for instance, has allocated the primary scratch partition on the E drive of his Pentium and the secondary scratch space on the D drive.

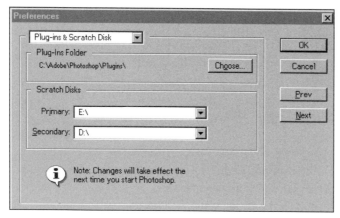

Figure 10-1
Ted's scratch disk space is allocated in this way on a
Pentium computer.

After reallocating scratch space, you will need to quit Photoshop and restart the program. Upon startup, Photoshop reassigns the scratch partitions. If you are using Windows for Workgroups 3.11, try turning off the 32-bit File Access option in the Virtual Memory dialog box.

"Could not complete your request because there is not enough memory (RAM)"

Problem
RAM limitations apply equally to Windows machines and Macintosh computers. If you start working with larger files and apply memory-intensive operations to those files, you may begin to experience this error message.

Solutions
As we described under "Out of memory," you can try to allocate more RAM to Photoshop. Photoshop running under Windows can adjust memory allocation in a different manner than it can on Mac machines. If you choose Preferences and select Memory

and Image Cache, you can control the physical memory allocated to Photoshop just as the Mac user identifies RAM requirements in the Get Info dialog box. When you choose Preferences ➪ Memory and Image Cache, a dialog box will appear as shown in Figure 10-2.

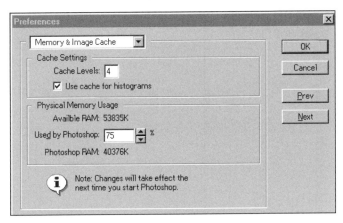

Figure 10-2
The Memory and Image Cache dialog box controls Photoshop memory use.

As we just stated, the default memory allocation is 75 percent of available memory. You can increase this amount, but be certain not to use 100 percent. Try to leave a small envelope of memory for system functions. You can also reduce the image caching to will free available RAM. The image cache will accept values between 1 and 8, with 1 allocating the least amount of memory for caching operations. You must restart Photoshop after making any changes to RAM allocation or the image cache.

"Could not initialize Photoshop because not enough memory (RAM)"

Problem
Upon launch, Photoshop will attempt to load in available RAM. If the RAM is not sufficient to load the program, you will be alerted to this fact. This error may or may not be related to the amount of memory you have available; it may be affected by the preferences or what the system reads at the time of launch.

Solutions
You can try deleting Photoshop's preferences file. To find it, look for the subfolder called Prefs in the Photoshop folder. Figure 10-3 shows the Photoshop directory hierarchy and the location of the Prefs folder.

Rename or delete this file

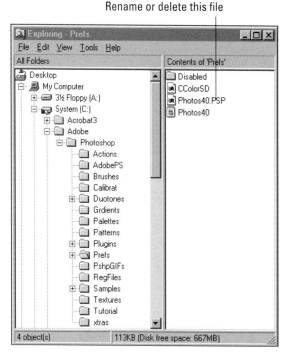

Figure 10-3
The Windows Photoshop Prefs folder is viewed in
Windows Explorer.

You can perform one of two actions with this Photos40.PSP file:

- Delete it. Then restart Photoshop; a new Photoshop preferences file will be created.

- Rename it. This will cause Photoshop to create a new preferences file without deleting the old one. If you wish to return to your original preferences, simply delete the current preference file and rename the old file back to Photos40.PSP, then restart Photoshop. You may wish to do this if you determine that the preferences file was not the problem after all.

If you have tried deleting the preferences file and are still experiencing problems, try using a disk utility program such as Norton Utilities to defragment and optimize your disk.

Another item to check is whether you have an auto compression utility installed on your computer. Many PC users have such a utility, but you would be best off eliminating it when working with Photoshop. Since Photoshop is constantly reading and writing to disk for the scratch space, using a compression utility will not only present problems but also slow your performance greatly.

"There is not enough memory to open Photoshop"

Problem

This is a system error that occurs when you don't have enough available memory to open the program.

Solutions

Many possible solutions exist for this one. The easiest solution is quit all other programs before you open Photoshop. You may not have enough memory for Windows, Photoshop, and the other programs to run at the same time. To see what programs are currently running, look at the status bar. Click any application names, quit the programs, and then try to relaunch Photoshop.

If the problem persists, try allocating less memory to Photoshop. We know that we have said previously that a solution to memory problems is to allocate more memory, but in this case allocating less memory is the answer. Choose Preferences ➪ Memory and Image Cache and set the percentage of memory allocated to Photoshop lower than the default 75 percent.

You can also try deleting Photoshop's preferences file as we described earlier.

Try restarting your computer. This frees up any memory that has become fragmented. Just as hard disk memory becomes sluggish when it becomes fragmented, RAM memory becomes sluggish after continual use. Restarting your computer will defragment it.

Another item to check is your extended memory. With just Windows running, go to DOS, type **MEM** at the C:\ prompt, and press Enter. You will see a readout of the memory allocation with extended memory listed, as shown in Figure 10-4. The total represents the amount of RAM you have installed. If the Free amount is very small and the Used amount is large, Windows is using up all your RAM. You will need to call Microsoft technical support to have them assist you in making proper changes.

"Could not save as *filename* because the disk is full -34"

Problem

This problem occurs when you have run out of space on the disk drive to which you are saving the file.

Solutions

This can have a simple solution. If you have more than one drive, try saving the file onto the other drive. If you got this message while trying to save a file onto a floppy disk, the file is too big to fit on a single floppy. Save the file onto your hard drive first. Then you can use an assortment of compression utilities to shrink the file and/or segment the file across many disks. You can use WinZip to compress some files with a lossless compression, but be aware that some formats may not offer much compression.

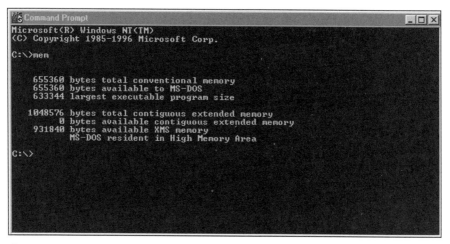

Figure 10-4
The MEM command in DOS shows you how memory is allocated by the operating system.

Another solution is to use JPEG compression. Saving a file in the JPEG format can greatly reduce your file size. JPEG compression will routinely reduce your file size at a ratio ranging from 10:1 to 20:1. This means that a 10MB to 20MB file could easily be compressed to 1MB. Keep in mind that JPEG compression is a lossy compression scheme, which means that every time you open and save a file with JPEG compression, you lose a little of the original quality of the photograph. Repeated JPEG compression is not recommended, and you should always be concerned with data loss.

A better solution to reduce file sizes is to choose the channels palette and select Split Channels from the flyaway menu. When you split the channels, you'll have a separate document for each channel, as shown in Figure 10-5.

Save one channel and copy it to a storage medium. Ideally, it would be a good idea to purchase a Zip drive if you have external storage no greater than a floppy. If you do purchase a Zip, the performance will be much faster with a SCSI device than with a parallel drive. If you split channels on a large file, you can copy each image to a separate Zip disk. If you are using the 100MB capacity cartridges, you can get approximately a 300MB file on three Zip cartridges using this method.

Solving Win32s Errors

Several errors can be identified as Win32s errors, including:

"At least one system component is out of date."
"Initialization of a dynamic link library failed."
"Invalid call to a dynamic link library."

Figure 10-5
An RGB image is shown with the three channels split.

Problem
Photoshop is finding duplicate versions of system-level files that are older than the ones it installs.

Solutions
The duplicate files need to be removed, leaving only the Photoshop files. To correct the problem, copy the installation files (contained in the Photoshop folder on the application CD-ROM) to a new folder on the hard drive. Then reboot Windows in minimized mode. In Windows 95, press the F5 key when you see "Starting Windows 95", and it will boot up in Safe Mode. (See your Windows documentation for how to accomplish this for the version of Windows you are running.) Once in minimized mode, run the installer from the hard drive by going to the Disk 1 folder and double-clicking the Setup icon (Setup.exe).

If you are running Photoshop for the first time under Windows 3.*x*, you may experience one of a variety of Win32s errors noted above. By removing these files and leaving only the Photoshop versions, you can allow Photoshop to launch without a hitch.

Other Win32s-related errors can happen under Windows 3.*x*. Since Photoshop is a 32-bit application, it must install Microsoft's Win32s files in order to run under a 16-bit operating system. Once this is done, various device drivers (such as video and scanner drivers) that were operating fine before Photoshop (or any 32-bit application) was installed may prove incompatible with Win32s.

Make it a point to contact the manufacturer of a given device for updated drivers when installing any major upgrades to software such as Photoshop. Since these drivers can change on an almost bimonthly basis, bookmark the companies' Web sites so that you can check them frequently.

APPENDIX A

ORGANIZING YOUR
FILES OUR WAY

By organizing your files in a consistent and efficient manner, you'll avoid serious problems with loss of time and save yourself some aggravating moments. This appendix offers some recommendations for creating an organizational scheme to keep track of your data.

Over the years in which we've produced virtually all of our graphic work on computers, three common file types have emerged: raster files (Photoshop), vector files (Illustrator or FreeHand), and page layout files (QuarkXPress or PageMaker). These three file types are essential for all graphic artists. But new file types will undoubtedly emerge as more and more programs become incorporated into the daily life of the production artist, such as LivePicture, Canvas, xRes, and 3-D programs of all types. The need to keep project files organized is paramount more than ever these days.

File organization is a very personal thing, like setting up the way your computer looks and feels. If you look at five different computers, you will probably see five different, sometimes polar opposite, ways in which files are organized. This is fine if only one person works with each set of files. But when you have a whole department of computer artists needing to access and work on common files, a file organization procedure is a must.

This appendix looks at the way we organize our files. You may, after reading this appendix, ask, "Why would anybody organize their files *that* way?!" Well, this is the way in which we do it, and since the author keyboard is under our fingers, you get to read our procedures. Even if you don't use our procedures, they may inspire you to set up your own. If you happen to like our concepts, use them. If not, start your own procedures.

NOTE The difference between the Macintosh OS and the Windows OS has decreased greatly over the years. Since 95 percent of the screen shots in this book are from the Macintosh, you may have suspected that we are Macintosh users. Even though this section shows examples of the Macintosh OS, the concepts can very easily be applied to Windows NT, Windows 95, and — to a lesser degree — Windows 3.*x.*

Using Filenames and Extensions Our Way

Giving a file an appropriate name is a very important part of file organization. Usually a name is used that best describes the content of the file. For example, a text file for a newsletter could be named "Newsltr.doc" or "Newsltr1-97.doc." The "1-97" in the second example shows the month and year the newsletter is produced.

When a number of similar files are produced, sequential numbers can afford an easy way to organize files. For example, throughout this book we've captured a number of screens to show examples of what we were writing about. The names of the files all started with "Fig" and then had two numbers split by a period to denote chapter number and figure number. For example "Fig 08.23" meant the twenty-third figure in Chapter 8. We also used a short description after the numbers to further describe the file, as shown in Figure A-1.

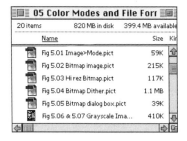

Figure A-1
These were the file-naming conventions used by the authors.

File extensions are also an important part of file-naming procedures. File extensions are the last part of the filename, usually three letters or numbers preceded by a period. In the example "Fig 08.23.TIF," the ".TIF" is considered the file extension.

Extensions allow you to tell the file type just by looking at the name, which often is all you have to go by. On the Macintosh, icons (in Icon view) or kind names (in List view) help you determine a file's type. Windows 95 now has similar Icon and List views; Windows 3.*x* did not. Under any viewing condition, however — be it Mac or Windows — you can always view the filename. And if your name has a known file extension, you can infer its type.

Sometimes extensions have two letters followed by a number, such as ".PS4." The letters usually denote the application used to create the file, and the number represents the version of the application. Thus ".PS4" stands for Photoshop 4.

Tables A-1 and A-2 list commonly used file extensions. File extensions can be virtually anything. Here are the ones that we have used or have come across on a regular basis. The idea is to use extensions that are familiar to everyone who potentially will work on the file.

TABLE A-1: APPLICATION FILES AND THEIR COMMON EXTENSIONS

APPLICATION	EXTENSION(S)
Photoshop	.PSD, .PSH, .PS3, .PS4
Illustrator	.Ill, .ART, .AI
PageMaker	.PM, .PM5, .PM6, .PM65
QuarkXPress	.XP, .QXP, .XPD
FreeHand	.FH, .FH5, .FH55, .FH7
Word	.MSW, .DOC, .WORD

TABLE A-2: STANDARD FILE FORMATS AND THEIR COMMON EXTENSIONS

FILE FORMAT	EXTENSION(S)
ASCII	.TXT
Encapsulated PostScript	.EPS
Tagged Image File Format	.TIF, .TIFF
PICT (Mac only)	.PCT, .PICT, .PICT2
PCX (Windows only)	.PCX
Windows Metafile	.WMF
Bitmap	.BMP
Scitex CT	.SCT
Adobe Acrobat	.PDF
Targa	.TGA
JPEG compressed	.JPG

Using Project Folders Our Way

Now that we have discussed how to name files that you create for any given project, where do you put them? Both the Mac and Windows can create folders, so we suggest creating project folders. This may seem a bit obvious, but let's take it all the way through the project and see what we end up with.

First we'll talk about what to name the project folder. In most cases this should be a no-brainer. Just give it the name of the project. If it's a newsletter for ABC Paint Products, then call it "ABC Paint Products Nwsltr." Taking this one step further, start a job numbering system. If you work on five jobs per year, job numbers may not be for you. If you work on 500 jobs per year, however, job numbers become essential. So include the job number in your naming scheme: "148 ABC Paint Nwsltr."

Now that you have a project folder defined, how should the files created for the project be organized inside the folder? One common mistake is to simply place all files relevant to the project in the project folder with no further organization. This is fine when a project only produces a small number of files — say, around 5–10 files. Beyond that number, however, it becomes harder and harder to distinguish what files are for what.

We recommend setting up a folder scheme for every job, so that anyone who opens the project folder can immediately recognize which file is ultimately used for what (see Figure A-2).

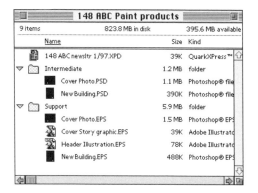

Figure A-2
Here is our project folder scheme.

The first-level job folder is reserved for all output files and for other organizational folders. Output files are the ones that are actually used for final output. Usually they are page layout documents from applications such as QuarkXPress and PageMaker, but they don't have to be. Any file that is used to create final art from an imagesetter, a film recorder, a mural printer, or a laser writer should be placed in that folder. More often than not, you'll have just one file, which makes things simple. But larger jobs could involve a number of final output files.

All the other items at this project level should be other organizational folders. We like to limit the number of these folders to two: Intermediate and Support.

Filling the "Intermediate" folder

The Intermediate folder is for all documents created that are not actually used for output. For example, text files that are placed into a page-layout program go here. Since text files are not linked but completely imported into page-layout documents, they are not needed when the page layout document is finally printed. Whenever we create a multilayered Photoshop file, we save it in two formats: first as a Photoshop file with all the layers intact, then as an EPS or TIFF file that we can place into the page-layout program and merge with the other elements of the project. The EPS or TIFF belongs in the Support folder (see the next section), but the Photoshop (layered) file belongs in the Intermediate folder, because it is not actually used for output. Any other file that is not a linked file for output should be placed in this folder, too. Inside this folder, you can create other folders to organize your files further — for instance, for fonts or client files.

Filling the "Support" folder

The Support folder is used for all files that are imported or placed into the output document and are required for output. These documents are considered to be linked documents. This means any files that are needed by the page-layout document for final output, such as graphic files imported from Photoshop or Illustrator.

For small jobs the Support folder should hold only documents. For larger jobs — catalogs, books, and projects with a large number of support files — more folders can be created inside the Support folder to organize the files even further. In a recent job, for instance, with 28 pages and multiple images per page, we created a folder inside the Support folder for each of the 14 page spreads. All support files associated with a spread were placed into their appropriate folder. This made it very easy to find any single file among the more than 100 files we ended up creating for the job. For a book with multiple chapters — such as *Photoshop Tech Support* — we created a folder for each chapter and its support documents, as shown in Figure A-3.

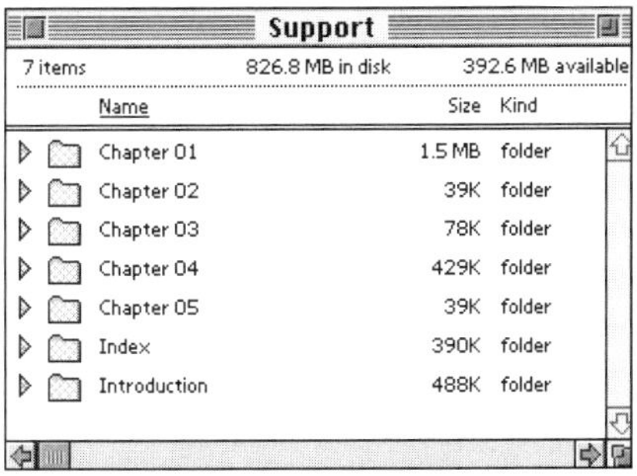

Figure A-3
These are the subfolders of the Support folder we created for this book project.

So that's it. This project folder scheme is just our way to manage what can often turn out to be a huge number of documents. The same concepts can be used to create many different folder schemes. One common element to all folder schemes is making sure everyone working with them *understands* and *follows* the basic structure. When you consider the ease in which files can be created and fill your hard disk's capacity, the need to set and follow project folder procedures becomes more obvious. With these procedures in place, you should be able to manage hundreds, if not thousands, of project files with ease.

Color Plate 1.

A *color cast* in a photo is a dominant color where there shouldn't be one, or an incorrect dominant color. Although color casts can appear anywhere, they usually appear in photos where no single color dominates, such as blue in a photo showing water or green in a photo showing grass.

The sample texture shown here could be considered a neutral color image. It really is a four-color image but looks close to a grayscale one. The first sample in the sequence shows what the image should look like. Because no single color dominates, the image contains almost equal amounts of cyan, magenta, and yellow. Black is used mostly for the shadows. Sometimes during the scanning process, one of the colors may become darker than the others, causing a color cast to appear. This is sometimes hard to detect but always easy to correct.

Create a Curves Adjustment layer in the Photoshop file. Determine which color needs to be manipulated and adjust the curves controls accordingly. If there is too much cyan in the image, start removing cyan until the image looks correct. You may need to make a few color proofs of the image to get the desired results. But after a while you should be able to come pretty close to what you want on your first or second try.

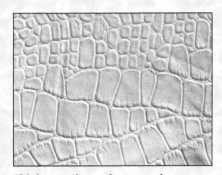

This image shows the true color.

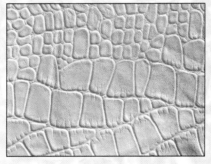

This image has a cyan cast.

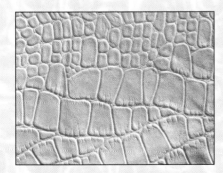

This image has a magenta cast.

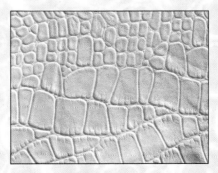

This image has a yellow cast.

Contrast is the difference between the lighter portions of an image (highlights) and its darker portions (shadows). If the image has the correct contrast, it will look rich and deep. If it doesn't, it will look dull and flat.

This problem is easy to detect and fix. To change the contrast of an image, add a Levels Adjustment layer to the Photoshop file. In the Levels dialog box there are five areas you can change. The three on the top slider bar are the ones you need to manipulate.

The black triangle on the left makes the shadow areas of the image darker as it is moved to the right or center of the bar. If the shadow portions of the image seem flat, then slide the black triangle to the right. The white triangle on the right makes the highlight areas of the image lighter as it is moved to the left or center of the bar. If the highlight portions of the image need to be brighter, then slide the white triangle to the left. The center gray triangle controls the midtones of the image. As you change the shadow and highlight triangles, you may then need to change the midtone triangle to make the image look correct.

The contrast is too high in this image.

The contrast is too low in this image.

Color Plate 3.

Sometimes colors appear dirty or muddy. This occurs when the four process colors are mixed together incorrectly. For example, a blue sky should mostly be cyan with a little magenta and black for toning. Grass is mainly green (made up of cyan and yellow) but when magenta is introduced, it becomes less defined, or muddy. As you correct more and more muddy colors, you'll understand when and where you can improve an image by adjusting the mix of the four process colors.

The tree and grass are pretty good but could use some improvement. With the Adjustment layer remove some magenta and add some cyan and yellow. This makes the grass greener overall.

The image of a tree in a grassy field and under a vivid sky is a great example of how muddy colors can change the overall look and perceived quality of an image. This is how the original image looks on the stock photo CD.

To start the modifying process, make a mask that separates the sky from the tree and grass. Create the mask using the Density Mask technique mentioned in this book.

Create two Adjustment layers. Set both Adjustment layers to Curves. The first Adjustment layer modifies the sky while the second layer modifies the tree and grass. Here the sky contains too much magenta, which makes it look more purple than blue. For the sky Adjustment layer, remove about half the magenta. Also remove traces of yellow in the sky.

Color Plate 4.

Memory colors are clearly recognizable to the average viewer. They are colors that people instinctively know how they should appear, without an original photograph for comparison. They include such colors as "sky blue" and "grassy green." It's crucial that these colors print correctly, or at least believably, for the viewer. If not, the photo will look fake.

The photos of this island scene show a memory color: the blue of the ocean. Here is the correct ocean blue.

By simply changing the ocean color, the image becomes unrealistic or even surreal.

Although this color is different than the correct image, the color is still a believable one for the ocean.

Color Plate 5.

Non-memory colors are not instinctively known, so they do not share the same problem as memory colors. For instance, this set of leaf photos represents non-memory colors. After the leaf was photographed, some artistic license was used to finalize the color and composition of the image. Which photo is the original one? Any of the three could be the original because there is really no color reference on which to base your decision.

This is the original image.

This ruby leaf is also quite attractive.

This image makes the leaf look like something from the Emerald City.

Color Plate 6.

Famed astro-photographer Tony Hallas desired a surrealistic effect for compositing two of his images: one of the Hale-Bopp comet and another of Mono Lake in California.

This is the original photograph of the spectacular Hale-Bopp comet.

This is the original photograph of Mono Lake.

Photography:

Tony Hallas

Digital imaging:

Michael Bacon

To create this composite image, digital imaging specialist Michael Bacon eliminated the sky out of Hallas's Mono Lake shot and brought the image of the Hale-Bopp comet in as a second layer. The original composite did not provide the effect desired, however, so Bacon took the original Mono Lake shot and split the channels, then merged the channels by swapping the red and blue, which provided a blue cast in the foreground area. The image was then composited and the comet's reflection in the lake was created from an inversed duplicate of the comet image. Many different effects and image moods can be created by splitting channels and reassembling them in different orders.

Color Plate 7.

Compositing images in Adobe Photoshop always presents a challenge. To create a sense of smooth blending between images without an artificial look requires both artistic skill and an advanced knowledge of using many Photoshop features. To create the composite image you see here, photographer Christopher Zsarnay of Z-Studios corroborated with designer Ray Hennessy of Applied Concepts to create Zsarnay's self-promotion image.

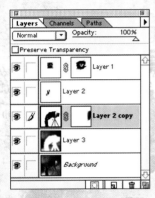

Hennessy made use of layers and channels to create the composite image. He first duplicated the background and blurred the original background. Then he eliminated the central figure with a feathered edge. The third layer included a sharp detail of the central figure with a Layer Mask, which ghosted out the end of the computer monitor. The fourth layer showed the keyboard image as you see it along Zsarany's sleeve. Another layer was created to bring the detail of the face appearing over the camera hood.

The composite image was then flattened and saved as a new document in preparation for the type. The embossing of the type and the logo was created by applying the Emboss filter in alpha channels. The channel data was loaded as a selection where the Levels adjustment was used to create highlight and shadow effects.

Photography:

Christopher Zsarnay

Digital Imaging:

Ray Hennessy

Color Plate 8.

Vector illustrations created in programs like Adobe Illustrator and Macromedia FreeHand can present printing problems when files get complex and the number of anchor points is extraordinary. An example of this is an illustration created by graphic designer Sandy Fox in Macromedia FreeHand.

Here you can see the complexity of the illustrated artwork and the massive amount of points involved. The original series of images were duplicated and reduced to 25 percent, then placed aside the original on a tabloid page. This file, when output to a high-end imagesetter, RIPed over eight hours without printing the first plate.

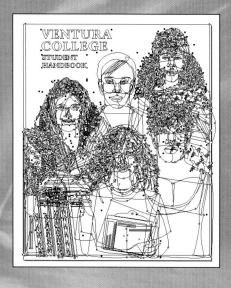

The file was eventually opened in Photoshop and rasterized with Photoshop's rasterizer at 300 dpi. The file was then saved as an EPS. It printed four separations in less than 30 minutes, with no image degradation compared to the original vector file.

Concept and design:

Sandy Fox

APPENDIX B

PHOTOSHOP'S
INSTALLATION FOLDERS
AND FILES

When you install Photoshop, as we covered in Chapter 1, the default installation of the files are located in separate folders. The hierarchy of those folders resulting from the installation is listed in here for your reference.

Macintosh Installation Files

Adobe Photoshop 4.0 *f*
Adobe Photoshop® 4.0
Help for Adobe Photoshop®
Help With QuickHelp™
QuickHelp™ 4.1.0
PshpLink.htm
PshpGIFs folder
    1topbar.gif
    2homebar.gif
    3rd.gif
    4prodbar.gif
    adobe.gif
    photoshp.gif
    ps.gif
    search.gif
    sm3rd.gif
    smadobe.gif
    smdisk.gif

smpage.gif
smplugin.gif
smsearch.gif
smsupprt.gif
smtips.gif
smwhdisk.gif
support.gif
tips.gif
walkinmn.gif
Goodies
Brushes & Patterns
Assorted Brushes
Drop Shadow Brushes
PostScript Patterns
Arrowheads
Deco
Diamonds/cubes
Drunkard's path
Herringbone 1
Herringbone 2
India
Intricate surface
Laguna
Mali primitive
Mayan bricks
Mezzotint-shape
Optical checkerboard
Pinwheel
Random V's
Scallops
Spiked
Undulating dot gradation
Waves
Weave-Y
Wrinkle
Square Brushes
Calibration
Gamma
Separation Sources
CMYK Colors
Lab Colors
Olé No Moiré
Color Palettes

ANPA Colors
FOCOLTONE Colors
PANTONE Colors (Coated)
PANTONE Colors (Process)
PANTONE Colors (ProSim)
PANTONE Colors (Uncoated)
System Palette
TOYO Colors
TRUMATCH Colors
Duotone Presets
Duotones
Gray/Black Duotones
424 bl 1
424 bl 2
424 bl 3
424 bl 4
Cool Gray 7 bl 1
Cool Gray 7 bl 2
Cool Gray 7 bl 3
Cool Gray 7 bl 4
Cool Gray 9 bl 1
Cool Gray 9 bl 2
Cool Gray 9 bl 3
Cool Gray 9 bl 4
gray 423 bl
gray 423 bl soft
gray 423 bl very soft
Warm Gray 11 bl 1
Warm Gray 11 bl 2
Warm Gray 11 bl 3
Warm Gray 11 bl 4
Warm Gray 8 bl 1
Warm Gray 8 bl 2
Warm Gray 8 bl 3
Warm Gray 8 bl 4
PANTONE® Duotones
144 orange (25%) bl 1
144 orange (25%) bl 2
144 orange (25%) bl 3
144 orange (25%) bl 4
144 orange bl 80% shad
159 dk orange bl 1
159 dk orange bl 2

159 dk orange bl 3
159 dk orange bl 4
327 aqua (50%) bl 1
327 aqua (50%) bl 2
327 aqua (50%) bl 3
327 aqua (50%) bl 4
478 brown (100%) bl 1
478 brown (100%) bl 2
478 brown (100%) bl 3
478 brown (100%) bl 4
506 burgundy (75%) bl 1
506 burgundy (75%) bl 2
506 burgundy (75%) bl 3
506 burgundy (75%) bl 4
527 purple (100%) bl 1
527 purple (100%) bl 2
527 purple (100%) bl 3
527 purple (100%) bl 4
blue 072 bl 1
blue 072 bl 2
blue 072 bl 3
blue 072 bl 4
blue 286 bl 1
blue 286 bl 2
blue 286 bl 3
blue 286 bl 4
brown 464 bl 1
brown 464 bl 2
brown 464 bl 3
brown 464 bl 4
green 3405 bl 1
green 3405 bl 2
green 3405 bl 3
green 3405 bl 4
green 349 bl 1
green 349 bl 2
green 349 bl 3
green 349 bl 4
mauve 4655 bl 1
mauve 4655 bl 2
mauve 4655 bl 3
mauve 4655 bl 4
red 485 bl 1

red 485 bl 2
red 485 bl 3
red 485 bl 4
Process Duotones
cyan bl 1
cyan bl 2
cyan bl 3
cyan bl 4
magenta bl 1
magenta bl 2
magenta bl 3
magenta bl 4
yellow bl 1
yellow bl 2
yellow bl 3
yellow bl 4
Quadtones
Gray Quadtones
Bl CG10 CG4 WmG3
Bl CG10 WmG3 CG1
Bl CG10 WmG4 CG3
Bl WmG9 CG6 CG3
PANTONE® Quadtones
Bl 430 493 557
Bl 431 492 556
Bl 541 513 5773
Bl 75% 50% 25%
Process Quadtones
CMYK cool
CMYK ext wm
CMYK neutral
CMYK very cool
CMYK very wm
CMYK wm
Tritones
Gray Tritones
Bl 404 WmGray 401 WmGray
Bl 409 WmGray 407 WmGray
Bl Cool Gray 10 WmGray 1
Bl for dark CG9 CG2
Bl for low con CG9 CG2
Bl normal CG9 CG2
Bl soft CG9 CG2

Bl WmGray 7 WmGray 2

PANTONE® Tritones

Bl 165 red orange 457 brown

Bl 172 orange 423 gray

Bl 313 aqua 127 gold

Bl 334 green 437 mauve

Bl 340 green 423 gray

Bl 437 burgundy 127 gold

Bl 50% 25%

Process Tritones

BCY green 1

BCY green 2

BCY green 3

BCY green 4

BMC blue 1

BMC blue 2

BMC blue 3

BMC blue 4

BMY brown 1

BMY brown 2

BMY brown 3

BMY brown 4

BMY red 1

BMY red 2

BMY red 3

BMY red 4

BMY sepia 1

BMY sepia 2

BMY sepia 3

BMY sepia 4

Plug-ins

ColorSync

ColorSync Support

csynres.rsl

Embed Watermark

Read Watermark

Displacement maps

12 sided (25%)

Cees (10%)

Crumbles

Fragment layers

Honeycomb (10%)

Mezzo effect

Pentagons (10%)
Random strokes(25%)
Rectangular tiles (10%)
Schnable Effect
Streaks pattern
Twirl pattern

Effects

Accented Edges
Angled Strokes
Bas Relief
Chalk & Charcoal
Charcoal
Chrome
Colored Pencil
Conté Crayon
Craquelure
Crosshatch
Cutout
Dark Strokes
Diffuse Glow
Dry Brush
Film Grain
Fresco
Glass
Glowing Edges
Grain
Graphic Pen
Halftone Pattern
Ink Outlines
Mosaic Tiles
Neon Glow
Note Paper
Ocean Ripple
Paint Daubs
Palette Knife
Patchwork
Photocopy
Plaster
Plastic Wrap
Poster Edges
Reticulation
Rough Pastels
Smudge Stick

Displace
Pinch
Polar
Ripple
Shear
Spherize
Twirl
Wave
ZigZag
Extrude
Lens Flare
Lighting FX
Lighting Effects
Texture Fill
Lighting Styles
2 o'clock Spotlight
Blue Omni
Circle of Light
Crossing
Crossing Down
Default
Five Lights Down
Five Lights Up
Flashlight
Flood Light
Parallel Directional
RGB Lights
Soft Direct Lights
Soft Omni
Soft Spotlight
Three Down
Triple Spotlight
Mezzotint
NTSC Colors
Pointillize
Radial Blur
Smart Blur
Solarize
Tiles
Variations
Wind
Import/Export
Anti-Aliased PICT

GIF89a
    About GIF89a Export
    GIF89a Export
Paths to Illustrator
PICT Resource
Quick Edit
TWAIN
Parser
    Adobe Illustrator® Paths Parser
    EPS Parser
Read Me
Samples folder
    About Samples
    Ball
    Brooch
    Fruit
    Hands
    Leaf
    Mallorca
    Shoes
    Tools
Tutorial folder
    Fish
    Frame
    Tour1.psd

Windows Installation Files

Adobe Photoshop 4.0 *f*
Adobe Photoshop® 4.0
Actions
Brushes
    Assorted.abr
    Shadows.abr
    Square.abr
Calibrat
    Cmyk.tif
    Lab.tif
    Testpict.jpg
Duotones
    Duotone
        Gray
            423-1.ado

423-2.ado
423-3.ado
424-1.ado
424-2.ado
424-3.ado
424-4.ado
Cg7-1.ado
Cg7-2.ado
Cg7-3.ado
Cg7-4.ado
Cg9-1.ado
Cg9-2.ado
Cg9-3.ado
Cg9-4.ado
Wg11-1.ado
Wg11-2.ado
Wg11-3.ado
Wg11-4.ado
Wg8-1.ado
Wg8-2.ado
Wg8-3.ado
Wg8-4.ado

PMS

072-1.ado
072-2.ado
072-3.ado
072-4.ado
144-1.ado
144-2.ado
144-3.ado
144-4.ado
144-5.ado
159-1.ado
159-2.ado
159-3.ado
159-4.ado
286-1.ado
286-2.ado
286-3.ado
286-4.ado
327-1.ado
327-2.ado
327-3.ado

327-4.ado
3405-1.ado
3405-2.ado
3405-3.ado
3405-4.ado
349-1.ado
349-2.ado
349-3.ado
349-4.ado
464-1.ado
464-2.ado
464-3.ado
464-4.ado
4655-1.ado
4655-2.ado
4655-3.ado
4655-4.ado
478-1.ado
478-2.ado
478-3.ado
478-4.ado
485-1.ado
485-2.ado
485-3.ado
485-4.ado
506-1.ado
506-2.ado
506-3.ado
506-4.ado
527-1.ado
527-2.ado
527-3.ado
527-4.ado

Process

Ck-1.ado
Ck-2.ado
Ck-3.ado
Ck-4.ado
Mk-1.ado
Mk-2.ado
Mk-3.ado
Mk-4.ado
Yk-1.ado

                Yk-2.ado
                Yk-3.ado
                Yk-4.ado

Quadtone
    Gray
            Cg10-1w3.ado
            Cg10-3w4.ado
            Cg10-4w3.ado
            Wg9cg6-3.ado
    Pms
            430-493.ado
            431-492.ado
            541-513.ado
            75%50%25.ado
    Process
            Cmykblue.ado
            Cmykbrwn.ado
            Cmykcool.ado
            Cmykexwm.ado
            Cmykneut.ado
            Cmykwarm.ado

Tritone
    Gray
            404-401.ado
            409-407.ado
            Cg10-wg1.ado
            Cg9cg2-1.ado
            Cg9cg2-2.ado
            Cg9cg2-3.ado
            Cg9cg2-4.ado
            Wg7-wg2.ado
    Pms
            165-457.ado
            172-423.ado
            313-127.ado
            334-437.ado
            340-423.ado
            437-127.ado
            Bl50%25%.ado
    Process
            Cygreen1.ado
            Cygreen2.ado
            Cygreen3.ado

Cygreen4.ado
Mc-blue1.ado
Mc-blue2.ado
Mc-blue3.ado
Mc-blue4.ado
My-brwn1.ado
My-brwn2.ado
My-brwn3.ado
My-brwn4.ado
My-red-1.ado
My-red-2.ado
My-red-3.ado
My-red-4.ado
Mysepia1.ado
Mysepia2.ado
Mysepia3.ado
Mysepia4.ado

Grdients
    Colrharm.grd
    Metals.grd
    Spec_efx.grd
Palettes
    Anpa.aco
    Default.aco
    Focolton.aco
    Ptcoated.aco
    Ptproces.aco
    Ptprosim.aco
    Ptuncoat.aco
    Toyo.aco
    Trumatch.aco
Patterns
    Arrows.ai
    Checker.ai
    Deco.ai
    Diamonds.ai
    Drunkard.ai
    Herring1.ai
    Herring2.ai
    India.ai
    Intricat.ai
    Laguna.ai
    Mali.ai

Mayan.ai
Pinwheel.ai
Randomv.ai
Shells.ai
Spiked.ai
Undulate.ai
Waves.ai
Weave-y.ai
Wrinkle.ai
Plugins
  Digimarc
    Digimarc.ini
    Digiread.8bf
    Digisign.8bf
  Effects
    accented.8bf
    angledst.8bf
    basrelie.8bf
    chalkcha.8bf
    charcoal.8bf
    chrome.8bf
    coloredp.8bf
    contecra.8bf
    craquelu.8bf
    crosshat.8bf
    cutout.8bf
    darkstro.8bf
    diffuseg.8bf
    drybrush.8bf
    filmgrai.8bf
    fresco.8bf
    glass.8bf
    glowinge.8bf
    grain.8bf
    graphicp.8bf
    halftone.8bf
    inkoutli.8bf
    mosaic.8bf
    neonglow.8bf
    notepape.8bf
    paintdau.8bf
    palettek.8bf
    patchwor.8bf

photocop.8bf
plaster.8bf
plasticw.8bf
postered.8bf
reticula.8bf
ripple.8bf
roughpas.8bf
smudgest.8bf
spatter.8bf
sponge.8bf
sprayeds.8bf
stainedg.8bf
stamp.8bf
sumi-e.8bf
texturiz.8bf
tornedge.8bf
underpai.8bf
watercol.8bf
waterpap.8bf

Export
GIF89Exp.8be
Paths8b.8be
Extensns
Ccms.8bx
FastCore.8bx
MThread.8bx
Filters
Dispmaps
12sided.psd
Cees.psd
Crumbles.psd
Fragment.psd
Honeycmb.psd
Mezzo.psd
Pentagon.psd
Random.psd
Schnable.psd
Streaks.psd
Tiles.psd
Twirl.psd
LtStyles
2amspot
3down

        3spots
        5down
        5up
        Blueomni
        Circle
        Crossing
        Default
        Flash
        Flood
        Parallel
        Rgblight
        Softlite
        Softomni
        Softspot
        Xdown
    Clouds8b.8bf
    Colort8b.8bf
    Crysta8b.8bf
    DeInte8b.8bf
    Displa8b.8bf
    Extrud8b.8bf
    Flare8b.8bf
    Lighting.8bf
    Mezzo8b.8bf
    Ntsc8b.8bf
    Pinch8b.8bf
    Pointi8b.8bf
    Polar8b.8bf
    Radial8b.8bf
    Ripple8b.8bf
    Shear8b.8bf
    Solar8b.8bf
    Spheri8b.8bf
    Smooth.8bf
    Texture.8bf
    Tiles8b.8bf
    Twirl8b.8bf
    Vary8b.8bf
    Wave8b.8bf
    Wind8b.8bf
    ZigZag8b.8bf
Formats
    aipaths.8by

                    Bmp8b.8bi
                    EPSParsr.8by
                    Filmst8b.8bi
                    Gif8b.8bi
                    Pcdform.8bi
                    Pcx8b.8bi
                    Pixar8b.8bi
                    png8b.8bi
                    Targa8b.8bi
            Import
                    QuickEd.8bp
                    Twain_32.8ba
                    Twain8b.8ba
    Prefs
        CColorSD
        Photos40.ini
        Photos40.psp
    Pshpgifs
        1topbar.gif
        2homebar.gif
        3rd.gif
        4prodbar.gif
        Adobe.gif
        Photoshp.gif
        Ps.gif
        Search.gif
        Sm3rd.gif
        Smadobe.gif
        Smdisk.gif
        Smpage.gif
        Smplugin.gif
        Smsearch.gif
        Smsupprt.gif
        Smtips.gif
        Smwhdisk.gif
        Support.gif
        Tips.gif
        Walkinmn.gif
    RegFiles
        Connect.gif
        Cramapi.dll
        Dial.gif
        Eur.ctl

        Eur.wmf
        Faxus.wmf
        Intro.gif
        Magaz1.gif
        Magaz2.gif
        Mailform.ctl
        Mailus.wmf
        Pipedlg.dat
        Pipeline.dll
        Pipeline.ini
        Pipermd.dll
        Register.exe
        Regprint.ctl
        Row.ctl
        Row.wmf
        Scrn1pc.gif
        Scrn2pc.gif
        Scrn3pc.gif
        Scrn4pc.gif
        Scrn5oth.gif
        Scrn5usa.gif
        Sslib.dll
        Thanks.gif
        Uschtfax.gif
        Wallppr.bmp
        Warning.gif
    Samples
        Tutorial
            Fish.jpg
            Frame.jpg
            Tour1.psd
        Ball.psd
        Brooch.psd
        Fruit.jpg
        Hands.jpg
        Leaf.psd
        Mallorca.jpg
        Samples.wri
        Shoes.jpg
        Tools.jpg
    Xtras
        Twain32.dll
    Textures

Aomeba.psd
Bark.psd
Blistpnt.psd
Bricks.psd
Burlap.psd
Canvas.psd
Carpet.psd
Cavier.psd
Clouds.psd
Cndrblks.psd
Concrete.psd
Confetti.psd
Denim1.psd
Denim2.psd
Dgnscls1.psd
Dgnscls2.psd
Drvnsnow.psd
Feathers.psd
Filssmth.psd
Footprts.psd
Frstdgls.psd
Frznrain.psd
Gauze.psd
Glassblk.psd
Irshsthr.psd
Knurl.psd
Leathr1.psd
Leathr2.psd
Lichen.psd
Lines.psd
Loosthds.psd
Mtns1.psd
Mtns2.psd
Noise.psd
Paper.psd
Papr_reg.psd
Papr_rgh.psd
Paprcnvs.psd
Paprfibr.psd
Paprfine.psd
Paprrghr.psd
Paprwtcl.psd
Paprxrgh.psd

Pinebark.psd
Puzzle.psd
Readme.wri
Rosette.psd
Rustflks.psd
Scrndoor.psd
Shagrug.psd
Shdplst1.psd
Shdplst2.psd
Shngls1.psd
Shngls2.psd
Snakskin.psd
Sphrgrid.psd
Sprsnois.psd
Strands1.psd
Strands2.psd
Stucco1.psd
Stucco2.psd
Stucco3.psd
Styrbals.psd
Textures.wri
Thckhair.psd
Tilsbmpy.psd
Towel.psd
Tread.psd
Weave1.psd
Weave2.psd
Weave3.psd
Weave4.psd
Weave5.psd
Weave6.psd
Weave7.psd
Weave8.psd
Web.psd

Photoshop
Adobeui.fon
Agm.dll
Csdtrn32.dll
Deisl1.isu
Kicccmsg.swb
Kiccres.rsl
Photos01.dll
Photos02.dll

Photoshp.exe
Photoshp.hlp
Photoshp.reg
Plugin.dll
Pshplink.htm
Psicon.dll
Psreadme.wri
Psut16.dll
Psut32.dll
Psut9516.dll
Psut9532.dll
Typelibrary.tlb

APPENDIX C

DESIGNER'S GUIDE TO
DIGITAL PREPRESS

In Chapter 4 we discussed proper formats for digital imaging and the color modes associated with those formats. In Chapter 8 we talked about avoiding printing problems and recommended workarounds to solve many imaging errors. All of the steps mentioned in this book won't mean a hill of beans if you follow our recommendations and still get stuck with some serious color problems, separation problems, or any of the many things that can go wrong at the print shop. This appendix is offered as a road map to guide you through high-end digital prepress. If you follow the rules here, you may wind up saving time, money, and much frustration.

Several steps must be taken in sequence if you hope to gain control over your jobs and achieve predictable results when working with Photoshop or any other program. Look at these steps in sequential order and perform them religiously for each job intended for press. For our example, we'll assume you wish to obtain color separations and have them printed at your local commercial printer.

Step 1. Talk to the Printer

The first step in your journey to successful imaging is to talk to your printer to determine what it will need as composed film. The printer will discuss with you the requirements for the halftone frequency of your files, the paper stocks, any expected dot gain, and other special considerations to produce the film for the job.

Step 2. Talk to the Service Bureau

Assuming your job will be output to an imagesetter at a local service bureau, you should take the information provided by the printer to the service bureau and discuss the requirements for generating composed film. (If your printer is producing the digital separations, it will be able to discuss both the imaging and printing needs with you.) The service bureau personnel will talk to you about the resolution you need in your Photoshop images, the preferred programs to use, and the file formats recommended for your images. This latter point is most important — listen to the technicians and try to meet their recommendations. If you don't have a $100,000 imagesetter in your backyard, listen to the people who run them daily. They know what they are talking about.

Step 3. Obtain Your Scanned Images

If you intend to produce a high-quality job, you will be best served by acquiring high-end drum scans. If you try to squeak by with flatbed scans for a high-quality job, your customer may be dissatisfied with the results, and you can wind up eating the whole job. Keep in mind that you get what you pay for — if your customer demands high-end, you can't cut corners on your Photoshop images.

Step 4. Obtain a Prepress Proof

Assemble your design as prescribed by your printer and service center and purchase a color prepress proof. There are many different color composite printers out there, but only a handful show you what your printed piece will look like off the press. Instruments such as an IRIS printer or a 3M dye-sub proofer are your best bet. If in doubt, ask the service center to show you samples of prepress proofs and color separations to see how they match. Some proofing systems display a color shift for which you should be prepared to compensate.

Step 5. Print Laser Separations

Assuming your color from the proofing system appears as you wish, your next step is to print separations yourself off your laser printer. So far, all you know about your job is that it prints fine on a color printer. You really don't know if a color was spec'd as a spot color or whether your Photoshop file will separate properly. If you run separations at the service center and something goes awry, you may be in for some extra costs before the final separations are printed properly.

Step 6. Export Your Job to a Storage Cartridge

One of the most common problems experienced at imaging centers is missing links or fonts. You should use features such as Collect for Output in QuarkXPress or Save for Service Provider in Adobe PageMaker 6.5, and then double-check your job to assure that all associated files are brought to the imaging center. A missing link can cause you to eat the first round of film once again and have to print your separations a second time.

Step 7. Order Your Film Separations

When you take your job to the service center, they will have an order form for you to complete thoroughly. If you neglect to fill out the form properly, including such items as halftone frequency, number of colors, fonts included, special imaging issues, and the like, you could wind up with useless film once again.

Step 8. Order a Color Proof from the Film

After your film has been separated, you should always order a Matchprint, Cromalin, or similar type of proof. Imagesetters may print separated files differently than the laser proofs. If you submit your laser separations along with your prepress proof to the imaging center and follow their directions precisely, they will most often reprint your job at no cost if the imaging equipment failed to produce the proper separations. Your visible evidence of the file separating properly will be your proof made directly from the separated film.

Step 9. Have Your Customer Sign Off on the Proof

Before you begin to incur expensive printing costs, always have your customer agree to the color proof generated from the separated film and sign off on it. Give a copy of your approval form to the customer and keep a copy for your records. If the customer doesn't like the print job, this form will be your recourse to collect payment.

Step 10. Perform a Press Check

Up to this point everything has moved along well, but your job has not yet been printed at the print shop. When the printer is ready to put the job on press, you need to be in attendance to see the first run. If colors need to be adjusted, this is the time to have the press operator make those adjustments. Since your client signed off on the proof, you had better make certain the printed piece looks like the proof!

If you follow these ten rules and do not eliminate a single step, you will rarely experience a problem, and you will complete many successful imaging jobs. We care about you and want to see you succeed. With Photoshop as your tool and *Photoshop Tech Support* as your guide, you cannot fail!

APPENDIX D

ABOUT THE CD-ROM

The Photoshop Tech Support companion CD-ROM includes many nifty items you can use in your everyday work. For starters, there's a fully searchable, on-screen version of the book in Adobe Acrobat (PDF) format. The CD-ROM also includes numerous exclusive software tools, such as actions; demos from Adobe Systems, Andromeda, Chroma Graphics, Equilibrium, Extensis, MetaTools, Vivid Details, and others; Photoshop plug-ins and utilities; Web links (pointers to a number of Photoshop-related sites on the World Wide Web); royalty-free images; and more.

This CD-ROM can be used in both Macintosh and Windows environments. Macintosh users can access files using the Finder. With Windows 95 or NT 4.0, access the software with My Computer or Windows Explorer.

To take advantage of all the resources on the CD-ROM, Macintosh users should be running System 7.0 or later and should have at least 8MB of RAM, a 68040 or PowerPC processor, and at least a 640×480 256-color display. Windows 95 or NT 4.0 users should be running a 80486 or Pentium computer with 16MB of RAM, 20MB of hard disk space, and at least a 640×480 256-color display.

Of course, you'll need a CD-ROM drive and plenty of hard disk space for either platform. Most of the CD-ROM's content is self-explanatory.

Following is a description of products you'll find on the companion CD-ROM. We'll explain how to use or install them and provide additional contact information for the company or individual responsible for creating these products.

TIP Be sure to read the main Read Me file on the CD-ROM for updated information about the contents. In fact, whenever you see a file called "Read Me" in a folder, be sure to read it. It's a message from the creator of the product that usually contains important information about installing the software and often lists new features and enhancements made since the last version came out — as well as known bugs that either exist or have been fixed from earlier editions. It's worth checking out before you boldly forge ahead!

Photoshop Tech Support, On-Screen Edition

This is a fully searchable, electronic version of the book you now hold in your hands, complete with all the artwork, in Adobe Acrobat (PDF) format. Using these files you can have the book on-screen in one window while you work with Photoshop in another. If you have Photoshop questions or run into problems while you're working, you can easily search for guidance or related techniques without having to flip through the pages of the printed book. (For both Macintosh and Windows.)

Usage: Double-click the Photoshop Tech Support chapter icon in the Photoshop Tech Support folder.

 NOTE You must first install the Acrobat Reader, which you can find on the CD-ROM.

Acrobat Reader

This is the Acrobat Reader 3.0 software required to view the on-screen edition of the book. Adobe Acrobat software lets you access documents in their original form, independent of computer platform. With the Acrobat Reader on the CD-ROM, you can view, navigate, print, and present any Portable Document Format (PDF) file. (For both Macintosh and Windows.)

Macintosh installation: Double-click the Reader 3.0 Installer icon in the Adobe Acrobat Reader folder.

Windows Installation: Run Install Acrobat Reader 3.exe from the Adobe Acrobat Reader folder.

Contact: Adobe Systems Incorporated, 345 Park Avenue, San Jose, California 95110-2704, (408) 536-6000, http://www.adobe.com

Web Links

On the CD-ROM is an HTML file containing several links to Photoshop-related Web sites. Some are corporate (Adobe Systems), while others are maintained by support groups or Photoshop professionals. (For both Macintosh and Windows.)

Usage: Load your favorite Web browser and choose File ⇨ Open to open PSTS-links.html. Click on any link indicated, and your browser will send you to that Web site automatically.

Images

The CD-ROM contains many great background images and TIFFs you can use either in your work or personal artistic efforts. There is also a gallery of Photoshop images you can use for inspiration. The following products can be found in the Images folder.

Texture Farm

These superb photographic-quality background images in Kodak Photo CD format are samples from the Texture Farm Terra Incognita and Terra Firma Collections, created by photographer David Wasserman and digital artist Fred Smith. These original images are digitally altered images of fauna, flora, and natural phenomena. (For both Macintosh and Windows.)

Usage: Load these files from the Texture Farm folder and adjust the resolution.
Contact: Texture Farm, PO Box 460417, San Francisco, California 94146-0417, (415) 284-6180

VCA Images

The Awards.pdf file is a visual tour of professional artwork by advertising professionals from Ventura County, California, who were all winners of the 1996 Ventura County Advertising Awards. Most of the work contained on the CD-ROM, as well as the graphics to create the presentation, were digitally manipulated with Adobe Photoshop. All the screens in this file were Photoshop images placed in Adobe PageMaker and converted to PDFs, then assembled in Adobe Acrobat Exchange. (For both Macintosh and Windows.)

Usage: Awards.pdf is in the VCA Images folder. It's an Adobe Acrobat file that can be viewed with the Acrobat Reader 3.0 software on the CD-ROM.
Contact: Z Studios, 2085 Sperry Drive, Suite A, Ventura, California 93003, ZStudios@west.net

WARNING Unlike the royalty-free images from Vivid Details, the material contained in Awards.pdf is the property of the respective contributors. No material may be reproduced in any form without the permission of the artist who owns the copyright.

Vivid Details

This collection of royalty-free photos (TIFFs) is provided by Vivid Details, creators of Test Strip, a Photoshop plug-in exclusively designed for color correction. These images are suitable for use online or in print. (For both Macintosh and Windows.)

Usage: Open the TIFF files in the Vivid Details folder.

Contact: Vivid Details, 8228 Sulphur Mountain Road, Ojai, California 93023, (805) 646-0217, http://www.vividdetails.com

Utilities

The CD-ROM also contains several useful utilities. They can be found in the Utilities folder.

Conflict Catcher

Conflict Catcher 4 from Casady & Greene won a perfect five-star rating from *Macworld* magazine (July, 1997). Conflict Catcher is a utility for startup file management and conflict identification. (For the Macintosh only.)

Installation: Double-click the CC Installer icon in the Conflict Catcher 4.0 Demo folder.

Contact: Casady & Greene, Inc., 22734 Portola Drive, Salinas, California 93908-1119, (800) 359-4920, http://www.casadyg.com

DeBabelizer

We've enclosed a full demo of the premiere graphics translator for Macintosh on the CD-ROM. It reads and writes 64 graphics formats. (For the Macintosh only.)

Installation: Double-click the DeBabelizer Demo 1.6.5 icon in the DeBabelizer 1.6.5 Demo folder.

Contact: Equilibrium, 3 Harbor Drive, Suite 111, Sausalito, California 94965, (415) 332-4343, http://www.equilibrium.com

DEBABELIZER LITE LE

This "lite" version of the award-winning Macintosh graphics translator reads and writes BMP, GIF, PICT, and TIFF (Macintosh and PC) files. (For the Macintosh only.)

Installation: Double-click the DeBabelizer Lite LE icon in the DeBabelizer Lite LE folder.

DEBABELIZER PRO

Equilibrium's DeBabelizer Pro for Windows 95 and NT 4.0 is *the* comprehensive, automated 32-bit application for anyone working with graphics, animations, and digital video in multimedia, Web, and desktop productions. It reads and writes a very large number of graphics formats. (For Windows 95 and NT 4.0 only.)

Installation: Run Setup.exe in the DeBabelizer Pro for Windows folder.

Graphic Converter

This utility, as the name suggests, converts graphics from one format to another. The list of supported formats is impressive and can convert entire folders at once. (For the Macintosh only.)

Installation: Double-click the GraphicConverter 2.5.1 icon in the Graphic Converter folder.

Contact: Lemke Software, Erich-Heckel-Ring 8a, 31228 Peine, Germany, `http://www.goldinc.com/Lemke/`

JPEGView

Aaron Giles created this simple but versatile utility to view JPEG files. It's great for looking at graphics without having to open Photoshop. (For the Macintosh only.)

Installation: Double-click the JPEGView icon of your choice in the JPEGView folder.

Contact: Aaron Giles, `AGiles@aol.com`

SoftwareFPU

SoftwareFPU enables applications requiring a Floating Point Unit (FPU) chip to work on computers that don't have the chip physically installed, such as the IIsi, IIvi, LC series, Classic II & Color Classic series, Performa series, Power Macintosh, and some models of PowerBook, PowerBook Duo, and Quadra series. (For the Macintosh only.)

Installation: Double-click the appropriate SoftwareFPU icon for your hardware in the SoftwareFPU folder.

Contact: John Neil & Associates, PO Box 2156, Cupertino, California 95015, (415) 905-3000, `http://www.jna.com`

TechTool

TechTool is the utility of choice for certain housekeeping duties such as deleting the Macintosh desktop file (a better alternative to rebuilding it), zapping parameter RAM, testing for damaged system files, and displaying system information about your Macintosh. It is distributed as freeware.

Installation: Double-click the TechTool 1.1.3 icon in the TechTool folder.

Contact: MicroMat Computer Systems, 8934 Lakewood Drive #273, Windsor, California 95492

Transparency

Aaron Giles created this "quick and dirty utility" for creating transparent GIF images. It sets the transparency index in GIF images. Transparent GIF images are most commonly used as inline images on Web pages. (For the Macintosh only.)

Installation: Double-click the Transparency icon in the Transparency folder.

Contact: Aaron Giles, `AGiles@aol.com`

Plug-ins

We did some major trolling on the Internet and World Wide Web to come up with the numerous Photoshop plug-ins you see here. Most are full-functioning, some are demos, but all deserve a look to see if they can fit into your daily work. The following plug-ins can be found in the Plug-ins folder.

To install a plug-in simply drag it from the folder on the CD-ROM to the Photoshop Plug-ins folder and restart Photoshop. Some of these may only work with the Macintosh version of Photoshop.

Chris's Filters

Chris Cox has created some interesting filters that he's put in this collection. For instance, Average makes it easy for photographs to look like stained glass. They're meant for fairly specific uses, but you should find them helpful. (For the Macintosh only.)

Installation: Drag the plug-ins from the Chris's Filters 3.0 folder to the Photoshop Plug-ins folder.
Contact: Chris Cox, `http://www.teleport.com/~ccox/`

Colleen's Photoshop Fun Pack

Hugh Kawahara is a busy fellow. His pack of filter plug-ins includes Adjust Saturation, Create B/W, Kwick Mask, Rotate Color, and Modulate Color. He distributes his software as "charity-ware." If you appreciate it, please make a donation of whatever you think the filters are worth to any charitable organization in any part of the world. (For the Macintosh only.)

Installation: Drag the plug-in you want to use from the Colleen's Photoshop Fun Pack folder to the Photoshop Plug-ins folder.
Contact: Hugh Kawahara, `http://pw1.netcom.com/~kawahara/`

Dither Filter Package

This package contains VGDither and PNDither, two plug-ins that dither grayscale images to black and white in order to compensate for the dot gain produced by "bilevel devices," such as laser printers. (For the Macintosh only.)

Installation: Drag the plug-ins from the DitherFilters-1.8 folder to the Photoshop Plug-ins folder.
Contact: David Hull, `hull@cs.uiuc.edu`

Expression

This plug-in creates "groovy abstract art" in Photoshop and "psychedelic movies" in Adobe Premiere. The author also says it's a fun way to explore arithmetic. (For the Macintosh only.)

Installation: Drag the plug-in from the Expression folder to the Photoshop Plug-ins folder.
Contact: Jim Bumgardner, `http://www.thepalace.com/jbum/`

Frame

Frame is a plug-in that creates borders around pictures or selection areas. You can define the thickness and washout values of your borders. (For the Macintosh only.)

Installation: Drag the plug-in from the Frame folder to the Photoshop Plug-ins folder.

Contact: Kas Thomas, ECurrent@aol.com

Frosty

Frosty puts a variable frost look on any selected area of an image. This plug-in is distributed as "jobware," showcasing the author's programming experience. (For the Macintosh only.)

Installation: Drag the plug-in from the Frosty folder to the Photoshop Plug-ins folder.

Contact: Neil Schulman, nwcs@delphi.com

Garden Tools

This suite contains three filters — VectorGraph, Radar, and Lumpy Noise. Vector-Graph maps the direction of shading and tends to yield a metallic-looking, embossed image. Radar creates the effect of a radial sweep radar image. Lumpy Noise adds noise with a desired grain size. (For the Macintosh only.)

Installation: Drag the plug-in you want to use from the Garden Tools folder to the Photoshop Plug-ins folder.

Contact: Paul Badger, Paul_Badger@kagi.com

PhotoNavigator

PhotoNavigator creates a small, resizable floating palette within Photoshop that contains a thumbnail representation of an entire image. With this palette you can point, click, and drag around the image without having to wait for the screen to continually redraw. This product is freeware. (For the Macintosh only.)

Installation: Drag the plug-ins in the PhotoNavigator folder to the Photoshop Plug-ins folder.

Contact: Extensis Corporation, (800) 796-9798, http://www.extensis.com

PhotoTools

PhotoTools from Extensis consists of eight productivity and "everyday effects" plug-in tools that address many of the most requested features from a variety of Photoshop users. (For both Macintosh and Windows.)

Macintosh installation: Double-click the PhotoTools 1.1 Installer icon in the PhotoTools folder.

Windows installation: Run Setup.exe in the Disk 1 subfolder, found in the US-setup folder in the PhotoTools folder.

Contact: Extensis Corporation, (800) 796-9798, http://www.extensis.com

RetroScan

This plug-in simulates the effect of rescanning a noisy TV signal. As the author of this plug-in puts it, "It provides an easy way to achieve the fashionable 'cyber punk' effect for print, multimedia, and video." (For the Macintosh only.)

Installation: Drag the plug-in from the RetroScan folder to the Photoshop Plug-ins folder.

Contact: Rob Gonsalves, Deep Devices, PO Box 620038, Newton Lower Falls, Massachusetts 02162, `http://members.aol.com/deepdevice/index.html`

SISNIKK Pro

SISNIKK Pro is a Photoshop plug-in pack for professional high-quality single-image stereogram development. Single-image stereograms are pictures containing hidden 3-D information. When you focus your eyes beyond the page, elements begin to float all over the image and objects pop out of the surface. (For the Macintosh only. The Windows version was not available at press time.)

Installation: Drag the SISNIKK demo icons from the SISNIKK Pro Demo folder to the Photoshop Plug-ins folder.

Contact: M.M.M. Software, `http://www.mmmsoft.com`

Actions

The Actions folder contains many really cool Photoshop actions. Not only will they save you a lot of time, but they'll add luster to your creations. Action files work for both Macintosh and Windows.

Nick Ustinov has a Web page devoted to many cool Photoshop tricks, which you can find at `http://www.cooltype.com`. From him we've compiled the following actions: Chalk, Fire, Oil, and Pencil.

Tile Maker action comes from Robbyn Kenyon.

Carvium, Chromium, Glassium, and Woodenizer (for Windows only) come from the creative hands of Steven Alexander.

Usage: Activate the Action palette. Under the Action submenu select Load Actions and open the desired action files from the appropriate folder. The new action will appear at the bottom of the Action list. If you select Replace Actions, all your current actions will be replaced with the new ones.

Contacts: Nick Ustinov (who hails from Latvia!) can be reached at `nick@bit.lv`. Robbyn Kenyon can be reached at `moonwolf@tiac.net`. Steven Alexander has a Web page at `http://www.intertech.net/alex/`.

TIP If you really want to see what's hip in the world of Photoshop 4.0 actions, go on the Web and link to the Action XChange at `http://jmc.mit.edu /photoshp`.

Demos

Several software demos are included in the Demos folder on the CD-ROM. Installation procedures are included in their respective folders.

Adobe Dimensions 3.0

A trial (save-disabled) version of Adobe Dimensions 3.0. (For both Macintosh and Windows.)

Macintosh installation: Double-click the Adobe Dimensions 3.0 Installer icon in the Disk 1 subfolder in the Adobe Dimensions 3.0 Tryout folder.

Windows installation: Run Setup.exe from the Adobe Dimensions 3.0 Tryout folder.

Contact: Adobe Systems Incorporated, 345 Park Avenue, San Jose, California 95110-2704, (408) 536-6000, `http://www.adobe.com`

Adobe Illustrator 7.0

A trial (save-disabled) version of what we think is the best vector drawing program available, namely Illustrator 7.0. Not only is it the program of choice, it works best in conjunction with Photoshop. (For both Macintosh and Windows.)

Macintosh installation: Double-click the Install Adobe Illustrator 7.0 icon in the Install-Disk 1 subfolder in the Adobe Illustrator 7.0 Tryout folder.

Windows installation: Run Setup.exe from the Adobe Illustrator 7.0 Tryout folder.

Contact: Adobe Systems Incorporated, 345 Park Avenue, San Jose, California 95110-2704, (408) 536-6000, `http://www.adobe.com`

Adobe Photoshop 4.0

A trial (save-disabled) version of Photoshop 4.0, just in case you haven't yet upgraded from your current (older) version. (For both Macintosh and Windows.)

Macintosh installation: Double-click the Install Adobe Photoshop Tryout icon in the Install-Disk 1 subfolder in the Adobe Photoshop 4.0.1 Tryout folder.

Windows installation: Run Setup.exe from the Disk1 subfolder in the Adobe Photoshop 4.0 Tryout folder.

Contact: Adobe Systems Incorporated, 345 Park Avenue, San Jose, California 95110-2704, (408) 536-6000, `http://www.adobe.com`

Andromeda Series Filters

Andromeda Software has created a series of filters, each for a specific use. Series 1 consists of photography filters, Series 2 contains 3-D filters, and Series 3 contains screens filters (for mezzotinting and digital engraving). There's a lot to explore in each of them. (For both Macintosh and Windows.)

Installation: Read the Readme file in the appropriate Series subfolder in the Andromeda Software Inc. folder for more information.

Contact: Andromeda Software, 699 Hampshire Road, Suite 109, Thousand Oaks, California 91361, (800) 547-0055, `http://www.andromeda.com`

Chromatica

Chromatica is a plug-in for Photoshop that makes selecting objects, recoloring, and edge blending effortless. It consists of four tools. ChromaMask lets you select objects without having to use the magic wand and lasso tools. ChromaColor enables you to change colors without having to "dump" color with a bucket or guess with color sliders. EdgeWizard addresses the problem of unnatural edges or remnant pixels that remain after an object has been recolored, allowing you to blend edges in one step. ChromaPalette lets you create an unlimited number of dazzling color effects by using the colors from one image to recolor another image. (For both Macintosh and Windows.)

Macintosh installation: Double-click the Chromatica Installer icon in the Chromatica folder.

Windows installation: Run Setup.exe from the Disk1 subfolder in the Chromatica folder.

Contact: Chroma Graphics, Inc., 577 Airport Boulevard, Suite 730, Burlingame, California 94010-2020, (888) 824-7662, `http://www.chromagraphics.com`

Convolver

An award-winning special effects and texture generator for Photoshop, Convolver lets you explore and design custom image effects such as blurring, sharpening, embossing, tinting, color contrasting, Gaussian blurring, and unsharp masking — all in real time. Convolver's interface also allows you to define complex filters and preview their effects quickly and easily. (For both Macintosh and Windows.)

Macintosh installation: Double-click the KTP Convolver Demo icon in the Convolver folder.

Windows installation: Run Setup.exe in the Convolver folder.

Contact: MetaTools, 6303 Carpinteria Avenue, Carpinteria, California 93013, (805) 566-6200, `http://www.metatools.com`

Eye Candy

Eye Candy 3.0 makes your special effects more spectacular and easier to create than ever before. This new version doubles the number of filters and adds the most advanced previews of any filter set. (For both Macintosh and Windows.)

Macintosh Installation: Double-click the Install Eye Candy 3.0.1 Demo icon in the Eye Candy folder.

Windows Installation: Run ECPatch.exe in the Eye Candy folder.

Contact: Alien Skin Software, 322 Chapanoke Road, Suite 101, Raleigh, North Carolina 27603-3400, (919) 662-4934, `http://www.alienskin.com`

HoloDozo

HoloDozo is a set of 28 plug-ins for Photoshop, Premiere, Director 5.0, and other Photoshop-compatible applications that "frees you from the time-consuming drudgery of 3-D work." (For the Macintosh only.)

Installation: Double-click the HoloDozoDemo icon in the M.M.M. Software folder.

Contact: M.M.M. Software, `http://www.mmmsoft.com`

TIP Since HoloDozo requires QuickDraw 3D from Apple Computer (any version from 1.0.4 to 1.5.1 will do), you can download the QuickDraw 3D extensions for free from the M.M.M. Software Web site mentioned above, or directly from Apple Computer by clicking the Download link at `http://quickdraw3d.apple.com`.

Intellihance

Intellihance is a powerful image-enhancement filter that makes improvements based on individual image needs, eliminating up to 12 steps in Photoshop that are required to enhance images. (For both Macintosh and Windows.)

Macintosh installation: Double-click the Intellihance 3.0 Installer icon in the Intellihance folder.

Windows installation: Run Setup.exe from the Intellihance folder.

Contact: Extensis Corporation, (800) 796-9798, `http://www.extensis.com`

Kai's Power Tools

Kai's Power Tools is a set of award-winning plug-ins for Photoshop that allows you to create stunning digital special effects. (For both Macintosh and Windows.)

Macintosh installation: Double-click the KPT3 Demo Install icon in the Kai's Power Tools folder and follow the instructions.

Windows installation: Run Setup.exe in the Kai's Power Tools folder.

Contact: MetaTools, 6303 Carpinteria Avenue, Carpinteria, California 93013, (805) 566-6200, `http://www.metatools.com`

Mask Pro

Mask Pro is a powerful Photoshop plug-in that takes the pain out of creating image masks. Its color-matching technology and vector-based clipping paths reduce the time it takes to create professional-quality masks. (For the Macintosh only as of press time.)

Installation: Double-click the Mask Pro 1.0 Demo Installer icon in the Mask Pro folder.

Contact: Extensis Corporation, (800) 796-9798, http://www.extensis.com

Author Contributions

When Ken Oyer and Ted Padova aren't writing or teaching others about Photoshop, they're actively making their Photoshop lives easier. That's right, these guys are *creative*! Their contributions to this book can be found in the Author Contributions folder.

Ken's Brushes

From Ken Oyer we have a set of custom brush files that you can load into Photoshop. (For the Macintosh only.)

Usage: Activate the Brushes palette in Photoshop. Select Load Brushes and open the Ken's Brushes file. The new brushes will appear under your current brushes. If you select Replace Brushes, the new set of brushes will replace your old set of brushes.

Contact: Ken Oyer, KAOyer@cts.com

Ted's Dots

From Ted Padova we get a collection of custom PostScript dot patterns. These are described in Chapter 8. (For both Macintosh and Windows.)

Usage: While in Photoshop, access the Page Setup menu and click the Screen Button. Load the dot pattern by clicking the Load button and navigating to the Ted's Dots folder to load the respective pattern.

Contact: Ted Padova, The Image Source, 4532 Telephone Road, Ventura, California 93003, (805) 676-1000, ted@imgsrc.com

Illustrator Colors

In Chapter 7 is a discussion of creating a custom color palette for use with Adobe Illustrator.

Usage: Read the directions in Chapter 7 under "Avoiding color problems." The file is in the Author Contributions folder. On the Macintosh it's called Illustrator Colors; in Windows it's called Illcolor.api.

GLOSSARY

ACTION A form of a macro application tool to automate Photoshop tasks.

ADJUSTMENT LAYER A layer used to affect the brightness values of all layers below the adjustment layer without affecting the image data.

ALPHA CHANNEL A grayscale division of a color mode to represent a single color, or a holding place for saved selections, masks, or specific areas to be isolated in an image.

ANTIALIASING Varying levels of gray at the edge pixels in an image, type, or a selection to provide a visual perception of smoothing.

BACKGROUND Analogous to a painter's canvas, the background contains pixels regardless of any applied image data. The background of a newly created document will accept the current background color by default.

BANDING The result of printing gradients with too little resolution, which results in bands of gray values as opposed to a smooth transition of tones.

BÉZIER CURVE A curved path created with two anchor points from which extend two directional lines that ultimately describe a curve.

BITMAP A single channel image with two gray levels (black and white).

BLEED The image area that extends beyond the cut marks in a printed document.

BRIGHTNESS Usually expressed in Photoshop terms as a single value, one of three used to describe an image. The other two are *hue* and *saturation*. Brightness applies to light intensities (ranging from light to dark) without affecting color.

BURN To focus concentrated light in an image area, resulting in a darker exposure.

CALIBRATION The process of bringing one's monitor into correspondence with printing devices. Tools used for calibrating color in Photoshop are the Gamma Control Panel (Macintosh), the Calibrate button available via File ⇨ Color Settings (Windows), Monitor Setup, Printing Inks Setup, and Separation Setup.

CCD A charge-coupled device, composed of light-sensitive diodes and used in low-end scanners. A CCD yields scans that are less sharp and have a poorer dynamic range than do PMT systems.

CHANNEL Similar to an *alpha channel*, one of the grayscale images used to define the color in an image. In terms of CMYK separations, a channel corresponds to the plates separated for process-color offset printing.

CHROMALIN A trademarked color-proofing system developed by DuPont that provides a composite proof from separated film.

CMYK Cyan, magenta, yellow, and black process colors, typically used as a mode for composite color printing devices and film separations.

COLOR SEPARATION The process of separating the individual colors in an image in preparation for offset printing. In terms of process color separations, color images are divided into four separate printed documents, one for each of the CMYK values.

CONTINUOUS-TONE Of a file that contains graduated values from black to white. In color images these black-and-white values are represented in individual channels.

CONTRAST Distinctions between brightness values in highlights, midtones, and shadows.

CROP To isolate a portion of an image and cut out the area existing beyond that portion.

CROP MARKS Small lines existing outside the image area, defining the final trim size of the printed document.

CUSTOM COLOR Of spot color values selected from individual color libraries such as Pantone coated, APNA, TOYO, TRUMATCH, and so on.

DCS Desktop Color Separation, a format used for process color separation that breaks a CMYK image into five separate files, one file for each of the CMYK plates and a fifth preview file for placement in a layout or illustration program.

DITHERING A method of creating an illusion of a continuous tone with fewer than the necessary shades to truly represent a continuous tone.

DODGE To hold back brightness in an image, resulting in a lighter exposure.

DOT GAIN The process of dots swelling and expanding to yield an overall darker image. On printing presses the dot gain is due to paper absorption of inks, which results in a larger dot as the ink is absorbed.

DOUBLE BUMP To run paper through an ink color twice on a printing press to add more saturation to a given color.

DPI Dots per inch.

DRUM SCANNER A high-end scanning device usually found at service centers, service bureaus, and commercial print shops. Drum scanners provide greater detail in shadows and more authentic digital representations of photographs, transparencies, and negatives than desktop scanners.

DUOTONE Of a grayscale image with two spot color values.

EMULSION The light-sensitive portion of film or paper that accepts exposure.

EPS Encapsulated PostScript, a file format for transporting images to and from PostScript applications in preparation for printing on PostScript devices.

FILTER In Photoshop, filters rearrange or change pixels to affect the brightness, hue, and saturation values.

FREQUENCY The lines per inch of the printed document, commonly referred to as halftone frequency.

FUZZINESS A control for adjusting antialiasing edge pixels in terms of the brightness values.

GAMMA A mathematically defined function that controls the midtone ranges based on a curve (as opposed to a linear control) for brightness values.

GAMUT Gamut expresses the available colors in a given color mode. The RGB color gamut contains over 16.7 million individual colors.

GIF Originally developed for CompuServe to exchange image files between computer systems, the format is widely used on the World Wide Web.

GIF89A An upgraded GIF format that enables transparency and interlacing.

GRADIENT A representation of a transition of tones from one color or brightness value to another.

GRAYSCALE Of an image that is stripped of all color and varies between black, white, and intermediate grays.

HALFTONE The process of taking a continuous tone image and redefining it with a screen that produces dots. Halftones are prepared for offset printing and measured in lines per inch.

HEXACHROME A six-color separation with the four process colors of CMYK and separate plates for green and yellow.

HIGHLIGHT The brightest portion of an image. Highlights can be created with photo flash, sunlight, or direct light in a photograph.

HISTOGRAM A graphic chart displaying frequencies of the distinct 256 gray levels along an axis.

HSB Hue, saturation, and brightness. A three-channel image is displayed in these values as opposed to red, green, and blue.

HUE Hue defines the color in an image.

IMAGESETTER A high-resolution printing device capable of printing on resin-coated paper, film, and/or printing plates.

INDEXED COLOR A color mode applied to an image represented in one channel that uses a lookup table to draw color for 256 values.

JPEG A lossy compression scheme developed by the Joint Photographic Expert Group.

LAYER A feature of a Photoshop image that is analogous to a piece of clear acetate. A layer is transparent by default.

LAB A color mode that mathematically defines all perceptible color within our visual universe.

LPI Lines per inch, typically used with halftones to describe the size of the dots in the final printed document.

INTERPOLATION A method of mathematically creating or eliminating pixels to add to or take away from the existing image.

LINE ART Images, usually illustrations, that are represented in two-color values (black and white).

LOSSLESS Said of a class of compression scheme, lossless signifies that compression will not affect image quality.

LOSSY Said of a class of compression scheme, lossy signifies that compression will eliminate pixels during the compression process.

LZW A lossless compression scheme.

MATCHPRINT A trademarked color proofing system developed by 3M Company that provides a composite proof from separated film.

MIDTONE A tone falling between the highlight and the shadow in an image.

MONOTONE Of a single-color image.

MOIRÉ PATTERN A pattern resulting from printing colors at too similar angles. Such a pattern is usually undesirable in the printed document.

MULTICHANNEL Of a Photoshop file containing more than one channel.

OBJECT-ORIENTED Of an element or an image that is defined in terms of its file structure as an object. Such objects are device dependent and carry no inherent resolution.

OPTICAL RESOLUTION In scanning terms, the true resolution of the scanning device, as opposed to the interpolated resolution.

PCX An indexed color format originally created by Zsoft Corporation that now has five standards resulting from independent refinement of the format.

PICT A file format originally developed by Apple Computer for graphic representation. PICT files are used for screen graphics and QuickDraw printing devices.

PICT RESOURCE A file for Macintosh computers usually used for startup screens.

PIXEL A dot as it is displayed on a computer screen.

PMS Pantone Matching System, the most common spot color system used by commercial printers. It is used for mixing colors to create pigments that remain consistent throughout the industry.

PMT Photo multiplier tubes are light-sensitive tubes that detect very low levels of light. Typically found in drum scanners, PMTs offer an impressive dynamic range that provides great detail in shadows.

PNG Portable Network Graphics is a new format designed for use on the World Wide Web.

POSTSCRIPT A trademarked page description language developed by Adobe Systems, Inc. that is used to translate the computer screen image to a form useful on PostScript printing devices.

PPI Pixels per inch.

PREPRESS PROOF A composite proof usually generated from a high-quality printing instrument such as a dye sublimation printer or an IRIS inkjet printer. Prepress proofs are printed prior to final film separations.

PROGRESSIVE JPEG A JPEG format that enables an interlacing effect similar to that for GIF89a files when viewed on the World Wide Web.

PROCESS COLOR The use of CMYK inks to print a complete complement of color in offset printing.

QUADTONE A grayscale image created with four spot colors.

RAM Random access memory, a hardware component in a computer that stores data. RAM is volatile, in that data are maintained in RAM only while the computer is on. Upon shutdown or in a computer crash, all data in RAM are lost.

RASTERIZATION The process of converting object-oriented art to a raster image, which is displayed in pixels as opposed to objects. In printing processes, rasterization converts the computer screen data to dots for printing.

REGISTRATION MARKS Small lines and circles placed beyond an image area in a separation used to align the composite printed document.

RESAMPLE To change the resolution in an image. The new resolution is calculated through various interpolation methods.

RGB Red, green, and blue, a three-channel color mode most commonly used for scanned images and screen views.

RIP Raster image processor, an interpreter that rasterizes images in preparation for PostScript printing devices.

ROSETTE A collection of dots from separated images that yields desirable results because all colors print at proper angles. A rosette pattern is desirable, whereas a moiré pattern is not.

SATURATION A measure of the amount of gray in an image. As saturation is decreased, the amount of gray is increased, whereas an increase in saturation decreases the amount of gray.

SCANNING The process of converting analog images to digital form.

SCREEN ANGLE The angle at which each color in a separation is printed. Typically to prevent a moiré in an image, colors must be printed with 30-degree spreads between angles.

SHADOW The darkest portion of an image.

SPI Samples per inch.

SPOT COLOR A color value assigned individually. Whereas red as a process color may involve a mixture of magenta and yellow, red as a single color would be a spot color.

TIFF Tagged Image File Format, a format first developed by Aldus Corporation, was created to exchange image files between computer platforms.

TRAP The process of overprinting the edge color of one value on top of another to ensure that ink is applied over any gaps despite any paper movement in the printing process.

TRITONE Of a grayscale image created with three spot colors.

VIRTUAL MEMORY A means of using hard disk space as an extension of RAM.

INDEX

DUMMIES PRESS™

BOOK SERIES FROM IDG

IDG BOOKS WORLDWIDE

10/31/95

The Fun & Easy Way™ to learn about computers and more!

Windows® 3.11 For Dummies,® 3rd Edition
by Andy Rathbone

ISBN: 1-56884-370-4
$16.95 USA/
$22.95 Canada

SUPER STAR

Mutual Funds For Dummies™
by Eric Tyson

ISBN: 1-56884-226-0
$16.99 USA/
$22.99 Canada

SUPER STAR

DOS For Dummies,® 2nd Edition
by Dan Gookin

ISBN: 1-878058-75-4
$16.95 USA/
$22.95 Canada

SUPER STAR

The Internet For Dummies,® 2nd Edition
by John Levine & Carol Baroudi

ISBN: 1-56884-222-8
$19.99 USA/
$26.99 Canada

Personal Finance For Dummies™
by Eric Tyson

ISBN: 1-56884-150-7
$16.95 USA/
$22.95 Canada

SUPER STAR

PCs For Dummies,® 3rd Edition
by Dan Gookin & Andy Rathbone

ISBN: 1-56884-904-4
$16.99 USA/
$22.99 Canada

Macs® For Dummies,® 3rd Edition
by David Pogue

ISBN: 1-56884-239-2
$19.99 USA/
$26.99 Canada

SUPER STAR

The SAT® I For Dummies™
by Suzee Vlk

ISBN: 1-56884-213-9
$14.99 USA/
$20.99 Canada

SUPER STAR

Here's a complete listing of IDG Books' ...For Dummies® titles

Title	Author	ISBN	Price
DATABASE			
Access 2 For Dummies®	by Scott Palmer	ISBN: 1-56884-090-X	$19.95 USA/$26.95 Canada
Access Programming For Dummies®	by Rob Krumm	ISBN: 1-56884-091-8	$19.95 USA/$26.95 Canada
Approach 3 For Windows® For Dummies®	by Doug Lowe	ISBN: 1-56884-233-3	$19.99 USA/$26.99 Canada
dBASE For DOS For Dummies®	by Scott Palmer & Michael Stabler	ISBN: 1-56884-188-4	$19.95 USA/$26.95 Canada
dBASE For Windows® For Dummies®	by Scott Palmer	ISBN: 1-56884-179-5	$19.95 USA/$26.95 Canada
dBASE 5 For Windows® Programming For Dummies®	by Ted Coombs & Jason Coombs	ISBN: 1-56884-215-5	$19.99 USA/$26.99 Canada
FoxPro 2.6 For Windows® For Dummies®	by John Kaufeld	ISBN: 1-56884-187-6	$19.95 USA/$26.95 Canada
Paradox 5 For Windows® For Dummies®	by John Kaufeld	ISBN: 1-56884-185-X	$19.95 USA/$26.95 Canada
DESKTOP PUBLISHING/ILLUSTRATION/GRAPHICS			
CorelDRAW! 5 For Dummies®	by Deke McClelland	ISBN: 1-56884-157-4	$19.95 USA/$26.95 Canada
CorelDRAW! For Dummies®	by Deke McClelland	ISBN: 1-56884-042-X	$19.95 USA/$26.95 Canada
Desktop Publishing & Design For Dummies®	by Roger C. Parker	ISBN: 1-56884-234-1	$19.99 USA/$26.99 Canada
Harvard Graphics 2 For Windows® For Dummies®	by Roger C. Parker	ISBN: 1-56884-092-6	$19.95 USA/$26.95 Canada
PageMaker 5 For Macs® For Dummies®	by Galen Gruman & Deke McClelland	ISBN: 1-56884-178-7	$19.95 USA/$26.95 Canada
PageMaker 5 For Windows® For Dummies®	by Deke McClelland & Galen Gruman	ISBN: 1-56884-160-4	$19.95 USA/$26.95 Canada
Photoshop 3 For Macs® For Dummies®	by Deke McClelland	ISBN: 1-56884-208-2	$19.99 USA/$26.99 Canada
QuarkXPress 3.3 For Dummies®	by Galen Gruman & Barbara Assadi	ISBN: 1-56884-217-1	$19.99 USA/$26.99 Canada
FINANCE/PERSONAL FINANCE/TEST TAKING REFERENCE			
Everyday Math For Dummies™	by Charles Seiter	ISBN: 1-56884-248-1	$14.99 USA/$22.99 Canada
Personal Finance For Dummies™ For Canadians	by Eric Tyson & Tony Martin	ISBN: 1-56884-378-X	$18.99 USA/$24.99 Canada
QuickBooks 3 For Dummies®	by Stephen L. Nelson	ISBN: 1-56884-227-9	$19.99 USA/$26.99 Canada
Quicken 8 For DOS For Dummies,® 2nd Edition	by Stephen L. Nelson	ISBN: 1-56884-210-4	$19.95 USA/$26.95 Canada
Quicken 5 For Macs® For Dummies®	by Stephen L. Nelson	ISBN: 1-56884-211-2	$19.95 USA/$26.95 Canada
Quicken 4 For Windows® For Dummies,® 2nd Edition	by Stephen L. Nelson	ISBN: 1-56884-209-0	$19.95 USA/$26.95 Canada
Taxes For Dummies,™ 1995 Edition	by Eric Tyson & David J. Silverman	ISBN: 1-56884-220-1	$14.99 USA/$20.99 Canada
The GMAT® For Dummies™	by Suzee Vlk, Series Editor	ISBN: 1-56884-376-3	$14.99 USA/$20.99 Canada
The GRE® For Dummies™	by Suzee Vlk, Series Editor	ISBN: 1-56884-375-5	$14.99 USA/$20.99 Canada
Time Management For Dummies™	by Jeffrey J. Mayer	ISBN: 1-56884-360-7	$16.99 USA/$22.99 Canada
TurboTax For Windows® For Dummies®	by Gail A. Helsel, CPA	ISBN: 1-56884-228-7	$19.99 USA/$26.99 Canada
GROUPWARE/INTEGRATED			
ClarisWorks For Macs® For Dummies®	by Frank Higgins	ISBN: 1-56884-363-1	$19.99 USA/$26.99 Canada
Lotus Notes For Dummies®	by Pat Freeland & Stephen Londergan	ISBN: 1-56884-212-0	$19.95 USA/$26.95 Canada
Microsoft® Office 4 For Windows® For Dummies®	by Roger C. Parker	ISBN: 1-56884-183-3	$19.95 USA/$26.95 Canada
Microsoft® Works 3 For Windows® For Dummies®	by David C. Kay	ISBN: 1-56884-214-7	$19.99 USA/$26.99 Canada
SmartSuite 3 For Dummies®	by Jan Weingarten & John Weingarten	ISBN: 1-56884-367-4	$19.99 USA/$26.99 Canada
INTERNET/COMMUNICATIONS/NETWORKING			
America Online® For Dummies,® 2nd Edition	by John Kaufeld	ISBN: 1-56884-933-8	$19.99 USA/$26.99 Canada
CompuServe For Dummies,® 2nd Edition	by Wallace Wang	ISBN: 1-56884-937-0	$19.99 USA/$26.99 Canada
Modems For Dummies,® 2nd Edition	by Tina Rathbone	ISBN: 1-56884-223-6	$19.99 USA/$26.99 Canada
MORE Internet For Dummies®	by John R. Levine & Margaret Levine Young	ISBN: 1-56884-164-7	$19.95 USA/$26.95 Canada
MORE Modems & On-line Services For Dummies®	by Tina Rathbone	ISBN: 1-56884-365-8	$19.99 USA/$26.99 Canada
Mosaic For Dummies,® Windows Edition	by David Angell & Brent Heslop	ISBN: 1-56884-242-2	$19.99 USA/$26.99 Canada
NetWare For Dummies,® 2nd Edition	by Ed Tittel, Deni Connor & Earl Follis	ISBN: 1-56884-369-0	$19.99 USA/$26.99 Canada
Networking For Dummies®	by Doug Lowe	ISBN: 1-56884-079-9	$19.95 USA/$26.95 Canada
PROCOMM PLUS 2 For Windows® For Dummies®	by Wallace Wang	ISBN: 1-56884-219-8	$19.99 USA/$26.99 Canada
TCP/IP For Dummies®	by Marshall Wilensky & Candace Leiden	ISBN: 1-56884-241-4	$19.99 USA/$26.99 Canada

Microsoft and Windows are registered trademarks of Microsoft Corporation. Mac is a registered trademark of Apple Computer. SAT is a registered trademark of the College Entrance Examination Board. GMAT is a registered trademark of the Graduate Management Admission Council. GRE is a registered trademark of the Educational Testing Service. America Online is a registered trademark of America Online, Inc. The "...For Dummies Book Series" logo, the IDG Books Worldwide logos, Dummies Press, and The Fun & Easy Way are trademarks, and ---- For Dummies and ... For Dummies are registered trademarks under exclusive license to IDG Books Worldwide, Inc., from International Data Group, Inc.

For scholastic requests & educational orders please call Educational Sales at 1. 800. 434. 2086

FOR MORE INFO OR TO ORDER, PLEASE CALL ▶ 800. 762. 2974

For volume discounts & special orders please call Tony Real, Special Sales, at 415. 655. 3048

The Internet For Macs® For Dummies, 2nd Edition	by Charles Seiter	ISBN: 1-56884-371-2	$19.99 USA/$26.99 Canada
The Internet For Macs® For Dummies® Starter Kit	by Charles Seiter	ISBN: 1-56884-244-9	$29.99 USA/$39.99 Canada
The Internet For Macs® For Dummies® Starter Kit Bestseller Edition	by Charles Seiter	ISBN: 1-56884-245-7	$39.99 USA/$54.99 Canada
The Internet For Windows® For Dummies® Starter Kit	by John R. Levine & Margaret Levine Young	ISBN: 1-56884-237-6	$34.99 USA/$44.99 Canada
The Internet For Windows® For Dummies® Starter Kit, Bestseller Edition	by John R. Levine & Margaret Levine Young	ISBN: 1-56884-246-5	$39.99 USA/$54.99 Canada

MACINTOSH

Mac® Programming For Dummies®	by Dan Parks Sydow	ISBN: 1-56884-173-6	$19.95 USA/$26.95 Canada
Macintosh® System 7.5 For Dummies®	by Bob LeVitus	ISBN: 1-56884-197-3	$19.95 USA/$26.95 Canada
MORE Macs® For Dummies®	by David Pogue	ISBN: 1-56884-087-X	$19.95 USA/$26.95 Canada
PageMaker 5 For Macs® For Dummies®	by Galen Gruman & Deke McClelland	ISBN: 1-56884-178-7	$19.95 USA/$26.95 Canada
QuarkXPress 3.3 For Dummies®	by Galen Gruman & Barbara Assadi	ISBN: 1-56884-217-1	$19.95 USA/$26.99 Canada
Upgrading and Fixing Macs® For Dummies®	by Kearney Rietmann & Frank Higgins	ISBN: 1-56884-189-2	$19.95 USA/$26.95 Canada

MULTIMEDIA

Multimedia & CD-ROMs For Dummies, 2nd Edition	by Andy Rathbone	ISBN: 1-56884-907-9	$19.99 USA/$26.99 Canada
Multimedia & CD-ROMs For Dummies, Interactive Multimedia Value Pack, 2nd Edition	by Andy Rathbone	ISBN: 1-56884-909-5	$29.99 USA/$39.99 Canada

OPERATING SYSTEMS:

DOS

MORE DOS For Dummies®	by Dan Gookin	ISBN: 1-56884-046-2	$19.95 USA/$26.95 Canada
OS/2® Warp For Dummies, 2nd Edition	by Andy Rathbone	ISBN: 1-56884-205-8	$19.99 USA/$26.99 Canada

UNIX

MORE UNIX® For Dummies®	by John R. Levine & Margaret Levine Young	ISBN: 1-56884-361-5	$19.99 USA/$26.99 Canada
UNIX® For Dummies®	by John R. Levine & Margaret Levine Young	ISBN: 1-878058-58-4	$19.95 USA/$26.95 Canada

WINDOWS

MORE Windows® For Dummies, 2nd Edition	by Andy Rathbone	ISBN: 1-56884-048-9	$19.95 USA/$26.95 Canada
Windows® 95 For Dummies®	by Andy Rathbone	ISBN: 1-56884-240-6	$19.99 USA/$26.99 Canada

PCS/HARDWARE

Illustrated Computer Dictionary For Dummies, 2nd Edition	by Dan Gookin & Wallace Wang	ISBN: 1-56884-218-X	$12.95 USA/$16.95 Canada
Upgrading and Fixing PCs For Dummies, 2nd Edition	by Andy Rathbone	ISBN: 1-56884-903-6	$19.99 USA/$26.99 Canada

PRESENTATION/AUTOCAD

AutoCAD For Dummies®	by Bud Smith	ISBN: 1-56884-191-4	$19.95 USA/$26.95 Canada
PowerPoint 4 For Windows® For Dummies®	by Doug Lowe	ISBN: 1-56884-161-2	$16.99 USA/$22.99 Canada

PROGRAMMING

Borland C++ For Dummies®	by Michael Hyman	ISBN: 1-56884-162-0	$19.95 USA/$26.95 Canada
C For Dummies, Volume 1	by Dan Gookin	ISBN: 1-878058-78-9	$19.95 USA/$26.95 Canada
C++ For Dummies®	by Stephen R. Davis	ISBN: 1-56884-163-9	$19.95 USA/$26.95 Canada
Delphi Programming For Dummies®	by Neil Rubenking	ISBN: 1-56884-200-7	$19.99 USA/$26.99 Canada
Mac® Programming For Dummies®	by Dan Parks Sydow	ISBN: 1-56884-173-6	$19.95 USA/$26.95 Canada
PowerBuilder 4 Programming For Dummies®	by Ted Coombs & Jason Coombs	ISBN: 1-56884-325-9	$19.99 USA/$26.99 Canada
QBasic Programming For Dummies®	by Douglas Hergert	ISBN: 1-56884-093-4	$19.95 USA/$26.95 Canada
Visual Basic 3 For Dummies®	by Wallace Wang	ISBN: 1-56884-076-4	$19.95 USA/$26.95 Canada
Visual Basic "X" For Dummies®	by Wallace Wang	ISBN: 1-56884-230-9	$19.99 USA/$26.99 Canada
Visual C++ 2 For Dummies®	by Michael Hyman & Bob Arnson	ISBN: 1-56884-328-3	$19.99 USA/$26.99 Canada
Windows® 95 Programming For Dummies®	by S. Randy Davis	ISBN: 1-56884-327-5	$19.99 USA/$26.99 Canada

SPREADSHEET

1-2-3 For Dummies®	by Greg Harvey	ISBN: 1-878058-60-6	$16.95 USA/$22.95 Canada
1-2-3 For Windows® 5 For Dummies, 2nd Edition	by John Walkenbach	ISBN: 1-56884-216-3	$16.95 USA/$22.95 Canada
Excel 5 For Macs® For Dummies®	by Greg Harvey	ISBN: 1-56884-186-8	$19.95 USA/$26.95 Canada
Excel For Dummies, 2nd Edition	by Greg Harvey	ISBN: 1-56884-050-0	$16.95 USA/$22.95 Canada
MORE 1-2-3 For DOS For Dummies®	by John Weingarten	ISBN: 1-56884-224-4	$19.99 USA/$26.99 Canada
MORE Excel 5 For Windows® For Dummies®	by Greg Harvey	ISBN: 1-56884-207-4	$19.95 USA/$26.95 Canada
Quattro Pro 6 For Windows® For Dummies®	by John Walkenbach	ISBN: 1-56884-174-4	$19.95 USA/$26.95 Canada
Quattro Pro For DOS For Dummies®	by John Walkenbach	ISBN: 1-56884-023-3	$16.95 USA/$22.95 Canada

UTILITIES

Norton Utilities 8 For Dummies®	by Beth Slick	ISBN: 1-56884-166-3	$19.95 USA/$26.95 Canada

VCRS/CAMCORDERS

VCRs & Camcorders For Dummies™	by Gordon McComb & Andy Rathbone	ISBN: 1-56884-229-5	$14.99 USA/$20.99 Canada

WORD PROCESSING

Ami Pro For Dummies®	by Jim Meade	ISBN: 1-56884-049-7	$19.95 USA/$26.95 Canada
MORE Word For Windows® 6 For Dummies®	by Doug Lowe	ISBN: 1-56884-165-5	$19.95 USA/$26.95 Canada
MORE WordPerfect® 6 For Windows® For Dummies®	by Margaret Levine Young & David C. Kay	ISBN: 1-56884-206-6	$19.95 USA/$26.95 Canada
MORE WordPerfect® 6 For DOS For Dummies®	by Wallace Wang, edited by Dan Gookin	ISBN: 1-56884-047-0	$19.95 USA/$26.95 Canada
Word 6 For Macs® For Dummies®	by Dan Gookin	ISBN: 1-56884-190-6	$19.95 USA/$26.95 Canada
Word For Windows® 6 For Dummies®	by Dan Gookin	ISBN: 1-56884-075-6	$16.95 USA/$22.95 Canada
Word For Windows® For Dummies®	by Dan Gookin & Ray Werner	ISBN: 1-878058-86-X	$16.95 USA/$22.95 Canada
WordPerfect® 6 For DOS For Dummies®	by Dan Gookin	ISBN: 1-878058-77-0	$16.95 USA/$22.95 Canada
WordPerfect® 6.1 For Windows® For Dummies, 2nd Edition	by Margaret Levine Young & David Kay	ISBN: 1-56884-243-0	$16.95 USA/$22.95 Canada
WordPerfect® For Dummies®	by Dan Gookin	ISBN: 1-878058-52-5	$16.95 USA/$22.95 Canada

Windows is a registered trademark of Microsoft Corporation. Mac is a registered trademark of Apple Computer. OS/2 is a registered trademark of IBM. UNIX is a registered trademark of AT&T. WordPerfect is a registered trademark of Novell. The "...For Dummies Book Series" logo, the IDG Books Worldwide logos, Dummies Press, and The Fun & Easy Way are trademarks, and ---- For Dummies and ... For Dummies are registered trademarks under exclusive license to IDG Books Worldwide, Inc., from International Data Group, Inc.

For scholastic requests & educational orders please call Educational Sales at 1. 800. 434. 2086

FOR MORE INFO OR TO ORDER, PLEASE CALL ▶ 800. 762. 2974

For volume discounts & special orders please call Tony Real, Special Sales, at 415. 655. 3048

Fun, Fast, & Cheap!™

10/31/95

The Internet For Macs® For Dummies® Quick Reference
by Charles Seiter

ISBN:1-56884-967-2
$9.99 USA/$12.99 Canada

Windows® 95 For Dummies® Quick Reference
by Greg Harvey

ISBN: 1-56884-964-8
$9.99 USA/$12.99 Canada

Photoshop 3 For Macs® For Dummies® Quick Reference
by Deke McClelland

ISBN: 1-56884-968-0
$9.99 USA/$12.99 Canada

WordPerfect® For DOS For Dummies® Quick Reference
by Greg Harvey

ISBN: 1-56884-009-8
$8.95 USA/$12.95 Canada

Title	Author	ISBN	Price
DATABASE			
Access 2 For Dummies® Quick Reference	by Stuart J. Stuple	ISBN: 1-56884-167-1	$8.95 USA/$11.95 Canada
dBASE 5 For DOS For Dummies® Quick Reference	by Barrie Sosinsky	ISBN: 1-56884-954-0	$9.99 USA/$12.99 Canada
dBASE 5 For Windows® For Dummies® Quick Reference	by Stuart J. Stuple	ISBN: 1-56884-953-2	$9.99 USA/$12.99 Canada
Paradox 5 For Windows® For Dummies® Quick Reference	by Scott Palmer	ISBN: 1-56884-960-5	$9.99 USA/$12.99 Canada
DESKTOP PUBLISHING/ILLUSTRATION/GRAPHICS			
CorelDRAW! 5 For Dummies® Quick Reference	by Raymond E. Werner	ISBN: 1-56884-952-4	$9.99 USA/$12.99 Canada
Harvard Graphics For Windows® For Dummies® Quick Reference	by Raymond E. Werner	ISBN: 1-56884-962-1	$9.99 USA/$12.99 Canada
Photoshop 3 For Macs® For Dummies® Quick Reference	by Deke McClelland	ISBN: 1-56884-968-0	$9.99 USA/$12.99 Canada
FINANCE/PERSONAL FINANCE			
Quicken 4 For Windows® For Dummies® Quick Reference	by Stephen L. Nelson	ISBN: 1-56884-950-8	$9.95 USA/$12.95 Canada
GROUPWARE/INTEGRATED			
Microsoft® Office 4 For Windows® For Dummies® Quick Reference	by Doug Lowe	ISBN: 1-56884-958-3	$9.99 USA/$12.99 Canada
Microsoft® Works 3 For Windows® For Dummies® Quick Reference	by Michael Partington	ISBN: 1-56884-959-1	$9.99 USA/$12.99 Canada
INTERNET/COMMUNICATIONS/NETWORKING			
The Internet For Dummies® Quick Reference	by John R. Levine & Margaret Levine Young	ISBN: 1-56884-168-X	$8.95 USA/$11.95 Canada
MACINTOSH			
Macintosh® System 7.5 For Dummies® Quick Reference	by Stuart J. Stuple	ISBN: 1-56884-956-7	$9.99 USA/$12.99 Canada
OPERATING SYSTEMS:			
DOS			
DOS For Dummies® Quick Reference	by Greg Harvey	ISBN: 1-56884-007-1	$8.95 USA/$11.95 Canada
UNIX			
UNIX® For Dummies® Quick Reference	by John R. Levine & Margaret Levine Young	ISBN: 1-56884-094-2	$8.95 USA/$11.95 Canada
WINDOWS			
Windows® 3.1 For Dummies® Quick Reference, 2nd Edition	by Greg Harvey	ISBN: 1-56884-951-6	$8.95 USA/$11.95 Canada
PCs/HARDWARE			
Memory Management For Dummies® Quick Reference	by Doug Lowe	ISBN: 1-56884-362-3	$9.99 USA/$12.99 Canada
PRESENTATION/AUTOCAD			
AutoCAD For Dummies® Quick Reference	by Ellen Finkelstein	ISBN: 1-56884-198-1	$9.95 USA/$12.95 Canada
SPREADSHEET			
1-2-3 For Dummies® Quick Reference	by John Walkenbach	ISBN: 1-56884-027-6	$8.95 USA/$11.95 Canada
1-2-3 For Windows® 5 For Dummies® Quick Reference	by John Walkenbach	ISBN: 1-56884-957-5	$9.95 USA/$12.95 Canada
Excel For Windows® For Dummies® Quick Reference, 2nd Edition	by John Walkenbach	ISBN: 1-56884-096-9	$8.95 USA/$11.95 Canada
Quattro Pro 6 For Windows® For Dummies® Quick Reference	by Stuart J. Stuple	ISBN: 1-56884-172-8	$9.95 USA/$12.95 Canada
WORD PROCESSING			
Word For Windows® 6 For Dummies® Quick Reference	by George Lynch	ISBN: 1-56884-095-0	$8.95 USA/$11.95 Canada
Word For Windows® For Dummies® Quick Reference	by George Lynch	ISBN: 1-56884-029-2	$8.95 USA/$11.95 Canada
WordPerfect® 6.1 For Windows® For Dummies® Quick Reference, 2nd Edition	by Greg Harvey	ISBN: 1-56884-966-4	$9.99 USA/$12.99/Canada

Microsoft and Windows are registered trademarks of Microsoft Corporation. Mac and Macintosh are registered trademarks of Apple Computer. UNIX is a registered trademark of AT&T. WordPerfect is a registered trademark of Novell. The "...For Dummies Book Series" logo, the IDG Books Worldwide logos, Dummies Press, The Fun & Easy Way, and Fun, Fast, & Cheap! are trademarks, and ---- For Dummies and ... For Dummies are registered trademarks under exclusive license to IDG Books Worldwide, Inc., from International Data Group, Inc.

For scholastic requests & educational orders please call Educational Sales at 1. 800. 434. 2086

FOR MORE INFO OR TO ORDER, PLEASE CALL ▶ 800. 762. 2974

For volume discounts & special orders please call Tony Real, Special Sales, at 415. 655. 3048

PC PRESS

IDG BOOKS WORLDWIDE

10/31/95

Windows® 3.1 SECRETS™
by Brian Livingston
ISBN: 1-878058-43-6
$39.95 USA/$52.95 Canada
Includes software.

MORE Windows® 3.1 SECRETS™
by Brian Livingston
ISBN: 1-56884-019-5
$39.95 USA/$52.95 Canada
Includes software.

Windows® GIZMOS™
by Brian Livingston
& Margie Livingston
ISBN: 1-878058-66-5
$39.95 USA/$52.95 Canada
Includes software.

Windows® 3.1 Connectivity SECRETS™
by Runnoe Connally,
David Rorabaugh,
& Sheldon Hall
ISBN: 1-56884-030-6
$49.95 USA/$64.95 Canada
Includes software.

Windows® 3.1 Configuration SECRETS™
by Valda Hilley
& James Blakely
ISBN: 1-56884-026-8
$49.95 USA/$64.95 Canada
Includes software.

Internet SECRETS™
by John Levine
& Carol Baroudi
ISBN: 1-56884-452-2
$39.99 USA/$54.99 Canada
Includes software.

Internet GIZMOS™ For Windows®
by Joel Diamond,
Howard Sobel,
& Valda Hilley
ISBN: 1-56884-451-4
$39.99 USA/$54.99 Canada
Includes software.

Network Security SECRETS™
by David Stang
& Sylvia Moon
ISBN: 1-56884-021-7
Int'l. ISBN: 1-56884-151-5
$49.95 USA/$64.95 Canada
Includes software.

PC SECRETS™
by Caroline M. Halliday
ISBN: 1-878058-49-5
$39.95 USA/$52.95 Canada
Includes software.

WordPerfect® 6 SECRETS™
by Roger C. Parker
& David A. Holzgang
ISBN: 1-56884-040-3
$39.95 USA/$52.95 Canada
Includes software.

DOS 6 SECRETS™
by Robert D. Ainsbury
ISBN: 1-878058-70-3
$39.95 USA/$52.95 Canada
Includes software.

Paradox 4 Power Programming SECRETS,™ 2nd Edition
by Gregory B. Salcedo
& Martin W. Rudy
ISBN: 1-878058-54-1
$44.95 USA/$59.95 Canada
Includes software.

Paradox 5 For Windows® Power Programming SECRETS™
by Gregory B. Salcedo
& Martin W. Rudy
ISBN: 1-56884-085-3
$44.95 USA/$59.95 Canada
Includes software.

Hard Disk SECRETS™
by John M. Goodman,
Ph.D.
ISBN: 1-878058-64-9
$39.95 USA/$52.95 Canada
Includes software.

WordPerfect® 6 For Windows® Tips & Techniques Revealed
by David A. Holzgang
& Roger C. Parker
ISBN: 1-56884-202-3
$39.95 USA/$52.95 Canada
Includes software.

Excel 5 For Windows® Power Programming Techniques
by John Walkenbach
ISBN: 1-56884-303-8
$39.95 USA/$52.95 Canada
Includes software.

 ...SECRETS®

 INFO WORLD TECHNICAL BOOKS

Windows is a registered trademark of Microsoft Corporation. WordPerfect is a registered trademark of Novell. ----SECRETS, ----GIZMOS, and the IDG Books Worldwide logos are trademarks, and ...SECRETS is a registered trademark under exclusive license to IDG Books Worldwide, Inc., from International Data Group, Inc.

For scholastic requests & educational orders please call Educational Sales, at 1. 800. 434. 2086

FOR MORE INFO OR TO ORDER, PLEASE CALL ▶ 800 762 2974

For volume discounts & special orders please call Tony Real, Special Sales, at 415. 655. 3048

10/31/95

"A lot easier to use than the book Excel gives you!"

Lisa Schmeckpeper, New Berlin, WI, on PC World Excel 5 For Windows Handbook

Official Hayes Modem Communications Companion
by Caroline M. Halliday

ISBN: 1-56884-072-1
$29.95 USA/$39.95 Canada
Includes software.

1,001 Komputer Answers from Kim Komando
by Kim Komando

ISBN: 1-56884-460-3
$29.99 USA/$39.99 Canada
Includes software.

PC World DOS 6 Handbook, 2nd Edition
by John Socha, Clint Hicks, & Devra Hall

ISBN: 1-878058-79-7
$34.95 USA/$44.95 Canada
Includes software.

PC World Word For Windows® 6 Handbook
by Brent Heslop & David Angell

ISBN: 1-56884-054-3
$34.95 USA/$44.95 Canada
Includes software.

PC World Microsoft® Access 2 Bible, 2nd Edition
by Cary N. Prague & Michael R. Irwin

ISBN: 1-56884-086-1
$39.95 USA/$52.95 Canada
Includes software.

PC World Excel 5 For Windows® Handbook, 2nd Edition
by John Walkenbach & Dave Maguiness

ISBN: 1-56884-056-X
$34.95 USA/$44.95 Canada
Includes software.

PC World WordPerfect® 6 Handbook
by Greg Harvey

ISBN: 1-878058-80-0
$34.95 USA/$44.95 Canada
Includes software.

QuarkXPress For Windows® Designer Handbook
by Barbara Assadi & Galen Gruman

ISBN: 1-878058-45-2
$29.95 USA/$39.95 Canada

Official XTree Companion, 3rd Edition
by Beth Slick

ISBN: 1-878058-57-6
$19.95 USA/$26.95 Canada

PC World DOS 6 Command Reference and Problem Solver
by John Socha & Devra Hall

ISBN: 1-56884-055-1
$24.95 USA/$32.95 Canada

Client/Server Strategies™: A Survival Guide for Corporate Reengineers
by David Vaskevitch

ISBN: 1-56884-064-0
$29.95 USA/$39.95 Canada

"PC World Word For Windows 6 Handbook is very easy to follow with lots of 'hands on' examples. The 'Task at a Glance' is very helpful!"

Jacqueline Martens, Tacoma, WA

"Thanks for publishing this book! It's the best money I've spent this year!"

Robert D. Templeton, Ft. Worth, TX, on MORE Windows 3.1 SECRETS

Microsoft and Windows are registered trademarks of Microsoft Corporation. WordPerfect is a registered trademark of Novell. ----STRATEGIES and the IDG Books Worldwide logos are trademarks under exclusive license to IDG Books Worldwide, Inc., from International Data Group, Inc.

10/31/9

Macworld® Mac® & Power Mac SECRETS™, 2nd Edition
by David Pogue & Joseph Schorr

HOT!

This is the definitive Mac reference for those who want to become power users! Includes three disks with 9MB of software!

WINNERS 1994-95
TECHNICAL PUBLICATIONS AND ART COMPETITIONS OF THE SOCIETY FOR TECHNICAL COMMUNICATION

ISBN: 1-56884-175-2
$39.95 USA/$54.95 Canada

Includes 3 disks chock full of software.

NEWBRIDGE BOOK CLUB SELECTION

Macworld® Mac® FAQs™
by David Pogue

HOT!

Written by the hottest Macintosh author around, David Pogue, *Macworld Mac FAQs* gives users the ultimate Mac reference. Hundreds of Mac questions and answers side-by-side, right at your fingertips, and organized into six easy-to-reference sections with lots of sidebars and diagrams.

ISBN: 1-56884-480-8
$19.99 USA/$26.99 Canada

Macworld® System 7.5 Bible, 3rd Edition
by Lon Poole

ISBN: 1-56884-098-5
$29.95 USA/$39.95 Canada

NATIONAL BESTSELLER!

Macworld® ClarisWorks 3.0 Companion, 3rd Edition
by Steven A. Schwartz

ISBN: 1-56884-481-6
$24.99 USA/$34.99 Canada

NATIONAL BESTSELLER!

Macworld® Complete Mac® Handbook Plus Interactive CD, 3rd Edition
by Jim Heid

BMUG SPRING 1995 CHOICE PRODUCT

ISBN: 1-56884-192-2
$39.95 USA/$54.95 Canada

Includes an interactive CD-ROM.

NEWBRIDGE BOOK CLUB SELECTION

Macworld® Ultimate Mac® CD-ROM
by Jim Heid

ISBN: 1-56884-477-8
$19.99 USA/$26.99 Canada

CD-ROM includes version 2.0 of QuickTime, and over 65 MB of the best shareware, freeware, fonts, sounds, and more!

Macworld® Networking Bible, 2nd Edition
by Dave Kosiur & Joel M. Snyder

ISBN: 1-56884-194-9
$29.95 USA/$39.95 Canada

Macworld® Photoshop 3 Bible, 2nd Edition
by Deke McClelland

ISBN: 1-56884-158-2
$39.95 USA/$54.95 Canada

Includes stunning CD-ROM with add-ons, digitized photos and more.

WINNERS 1994-95
TECHNICAL PUBLICATIONS AND ART COMPETITIONS OF THE SOCIETY FOR TECHNICAL COMMUNICATION

NEW!

Macworld® Photoshop 2.5 Bible
by Deke McClelland

ISBN: 1-56884-022-5
$29.95 USA/$39.95 Canada

NATIONAL BESTSELLER!

Macworld® FreeHand 4 Bible
by Deke McClelland

ISBN: 1-56884-170-1
$29.95 USA/$39.95 Canada

Macworld® Illustrator 5.0/5.5 Bible
by Ted Alspach

ISBN: 1-56884-097-7
$39.95 USA/$54.95 Canada

Includes CD-ROM with QuickTime tutorials.

Mac is a registered trademark of Apple Computer. Macworld is a registered trademark of International Data Group, Inc. ----SECRETS, and ----FAQs are trademarks under exclusive license to IDG Books Worldwide, Inc., from International Data Group, Inc.

For scholastic requests & educational orders please call Educational Sales, at 1. 800. 434. 2086

FOR MORE INFO OR TO ORDER, PLEASE CALL ▶ 800. 762. 2974

For volume discounts & special orders please ca Tony Real, Special Sales, at 415. 655. 3048

MACWORLD® PRESS

10/31/95

"Macworld Complete Mac Handbook Plus CD covered everything I could think of and more!"

Peter Tsakiris, New York, NY

"Very useful for PageMaker beginners and veterans alike— contains a wealth of tips and tricks to make you a faster, more powerful PageMaker user."

Paul Brainerd, President and founder, Aldus Corporation

"Thanks for the best computer book I've ever read—Photoshop 2.5 Bible. Best $30 I ever spent. I love the detailed index....Yours blows them all out of the water. This is a great book. We must enlighten the masses!"

Kevin Lisankie, Chicago, Illinois

"Macworld Guide to ClarisWorks 2 is the easiest computer book to read that I have ever found!"

Steven Hanson, Lutz, FL

"...thanks to the Macworld Excel 5 Companion, 2nd Edition occupying a permanent position next to my computer, I'll be able to tap more of Excel's power."

Lauren Black, Lab Director, Macworld Magazine

**Macworld®
QuarkXPress
3.2/3.3 Bible**
*by Barbara Assadi
& Galen Gruman*

ISBN: 1-878058-85-1
$39.95 USA/$52.95 Canada

*Includes disk with
QuarkXPress XTensions
and scripts.*

**Macworld®
PageMaker 5
Bible**
by Craig Danuloff

ISBN: 1-878058-84-3
$39.95 USA/$52.95 Canada

*Includes 2 disks with
PageMaker utilities, clip art,
and more.*

**Macworld®
FileMaker Pro
2.0/2.1 Bible**
by Steven A. Schwartz

ISBN: 1-56884-201-5
$34.95 USA/$46.95 Canada

*Includes disk with ready-to-run
data bases.*

**Macworld®
Word 6 Companion,
2nd Edition**
by Jim Heid

ISBN: 1-56884-082-9
$24.95 USA/$34.95 Canada

**NEWBRIDGE
BOOK CLUB
SELECTION**

**Macworld®
Guide To Microsoft®
Word 5/5.1**
by Jim Heid

ISBN: 1-878058-39-8
$22.95 USA/$29.95 Canada

**Macworld®
ClarisWorks 2.0/2.1
Companion,
2nd Edition**
by Steven A. Schwartz

ISBN: 1-56884-180-9
$24.95 USA/$34.95 Canada

**Macworld® Guide To
Microsoft® Works 3**
by Barrie Sosinsky

ISBN: 1-878058-42-8
$22.95 USA/$29.95 Canada

**Macworld®
Excel 5 Companion,
2nd Edition**
*by Chris Van Buren
& David Maguiness*

ISBN: 1-56884-081-0
$24.95 USA/$34.95 Canada

**NEWBRIDGE
BOOK CLUB
SELECTION**

**Macworld® Guide To
Microsoft® Excel 4**
by David Maguiness

ISBN: 1-878058-40-1
$22.95 USA/$29.95 Canada

Microsoft is a registered trademark of Microsoft Corporation. Macworld is a registered trademark of International Data Group, Inc.

For scholastic requests & educational orders please call Educational Sales, at 1. 800. 434. 2086

FOR MORE INFO OR TO ORDER, PLEASE CALL ▶ 800. 762. 2974

For volume discounts & special orders please call Tony Real, Special Sales, at 415. 655. 3048

PROFESSIONAL PUBLISHING GROUP

IDG BOOKS WORLDWIDE

10/31/95

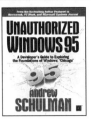

Unauthorized Windows® 95: A Developer's Guide to Exploring the Foundations of Windows "Chicago"
by Andrew Schulman

ISBN: 1-56884-169-8
$29.99 USA/$39.99 Canada

Unauthorized Windows® 95 Developer's Resource Kit
by Andrew Schulman

ISBN: 1-56884-305-4
$39.99 USA/$54.99 Canada

Best of the Net
by Seth Godin

ISBN: 1-56884-313-5
$22.99 USA/$32.99 Canada

Detour: The Truth About the Information Superhighway
by Michael Sullivan-Trainor

ISBN: 1-56884-307-0
$22.99 USA/$32.99 Canada

PowerPC Programming For Intel Programmers
by Kip McClanahan

ISBN: 1-56884-306-2
$49.99 USA/$64.99 Canada

Foundations™ of Visual C++ Programming For Windows® 95
by Paul Yao & Joseph Yao

ISBN: 1-56884-321-6
$39.99 USA/$54.99 Canada

Heavy Metal™ Visual C++ Programming
by Steve Holzner

ISBN: 1-56884-196-5
$39.95 USA/$54.95 Canada

Heavy Metal™ OLE 2.0 Programming
by Steve Holzner

ISBN: 1-56884-301-1
$39.95 USA/$54.95 Canada

Lotus Notes Application Development Handbook
by Erica Kerwien

ISBN: 1-56884-308-9
$39.99 USA/$54.99 Canada

The Internet Direct Connect Kit
by Peter John Harrison

ISBN: 1-56884-135-3
$29.95 USA/$39.95 Canada

Macworld® Ultimate Mac® Programming
by Dave Mark

ISBN: 1-56884-195-7
$39.95 USA/$54.95 Canada

The UNIX®-Haters Handbook
by Simson Garfinkel, Daniel Weise, & Steven Strassmann

ISBN: 1-56884-203-1
$16.95 USA/$22.95 Canada

Learn C++ Today!
by Martin Rinehart

ISBN: 1-56884-310-0
34.99 USA/$44.99 Canada

Type & Learn™ C
by Tom Swan

ISBN: 1-56884-073-X
34.95 USA/$44.95 Canada

Type & Learn™ Windows® Programming
by Tom Swan

ISBN: 1-56884-071-3
34.95 USA/$44.95 Canada

Windows is a registered trademark of Microsoft Corporation. Mac is a registered trademark of Apple Computer. UNIX is a registered trademark of AT&T. Macworld is a registered trademark of International Data Group, Inc. Foundations of ----, Heavy Metal, Type & Learn, and the IDG Books Worldwide logos are trademarks under exclusive license to IDG Books Worldwide, Inc., from International Data Group, Inc.

For scholastic requests & educational orders please call Educational Sales, at 1. 800. 434. 2086

FOR MORE INFO OR TO ORDER, PLEASE CALL ▶ 800 762 2974

For volume discounts & special orders please ca Tony Real, Special Sales, at 415. 655. 3048

DUMMIES PRESS™ PROGRAMMING BOOKS

10/31/95

**COMPUTER
BOOK SERIES
FROM IDG**

For Dummies
who want
to program...

**Delphi Programming
For Dummies®**
by Neil J. Rubenking

ISBN: 1-56884-200-7
$19.99 USA/$26.99 Canada

**Access Programming
For Dummies®**
by Rob Krumm

ISBN: 1-56884-091-8
$19.95 USA/$26.95 Canada

TCP/IP For Dummies®
*by Marshall Wilensky &
Candace Leiden*

ISBN: 1-56884-241-4
$19.99 USA/$26.99 Canada

HTML For Dummies®
by Ed Tittel & Carl de Cordova

ISBN: 1-56884-330-5
$29.99 USA/$39.99 Canada

**Windows® 95 Programming
For Dummies®**
by S. Randy Davis

ISBN: 1-56884-327-5
$19.99 USA/$26.99 Canada

**Mac® Programming
For Dummies®**
by Dan Parks Sydow

ISBN: 1-56884-173-6
$19.95 USA/$26.95 Canada

**PowerBuilder 4 Programming
For Dummies®**
by Ted Coombs & Jason Coombs

ISBN: 1-56884-325-9
$19.99 USA/$26.99 Canada

Visual Basic 3 For Dummies®
by Wallace Wang

ISBN: 1-56884-076-4
$19.95 USA/$26.95 Canada

Covers version 3.

ISDN For Dummies®
by David Angell

ISBN: 1-56884-331-3
$19.99 USA/$26.99 Canada

Visual C++ "2" For Dummies®
*by Michael Hyman &
Bob Arnson*

ISBN: 1-56884-328-3
$19.99 USA/$26.99 Canada

Borland C++ For Dummies®
by Michael Hyman

ISBN: 1-56884-162-0
$19.95 USA/$26.95 Canada

C For Dummies,® Volume I
by Dan Gookin

ISBN: 1-878058-78-9
$19.95 USA/$26.95 Canada

C++ For Dummies®
by Stephen R. Davis

ISBN: 1-56884-163-9
$19.95 USA/$26.95 Canada

**QBasic Programming
For Dummies®**
by Douglas Hergert

ISBN: 1-56884-093-4
$19.95 USA/$26.95 Canada

**dBase 5 For Windows®
Programming For Dummies®**
by Ted Coombs & Jason Coombs

ISBN: 1-56884-215-5
$19.99 USA/$26.99 Canada

Windows is a registered trademark of Microsoft Corporation. Mac is a registered trademark of Apple Computer. Dummies Press, the "...For Dummies Book Series" logo, and the IDG Books Worldwide logos are trademarks, and ----For Dummies, ... For Dummies and the "...For Dummies Computer Book Series" logo are registered trademarks under exclusive license to IDG Books Worldwide, Inc., from International Data Group, Inc.

For scholastic requests & educational orders please call Educational Sales, at 1. 800. 434. 2086   **FOR MORE INFO OR TO ORDER, PLEASE CALL ▶ 800 762 2974**   For volume discounts & special orders please call Tony Real, Special Sales, at 415. 655. 3048

Order Center: **(800) 762-2974** *(8 a.m.–6 p.m., EST, weekdays)*

Quantity	ISBN	Title	Price	Total

Shipping & Handling Charges

	Description	First book	Each additional book	Total
Domestic	Normal	$4.50	$1.50	$
	Two Day Air	$8.50	$2.50	$
	Overnight	$18.00	$3.00	$
International	Surface	$8.00	$8.00	$
	Airmail	$16.00	$16.00	$
	DHL Air	$17.00	$17.00	$

*For large quantities call for shipping & handling charges.
**Prices are subject to change without notice.

Ship to:

Name _____

Company _____

Address _____

City/State/Zip _____

Daytime Phone _____

Payment: ☐ Check to IDG Books Worldwide (US Funds Only)

☐ VISA   ☐ MasterCard   ☐ American Express

Card # _____ Expires _____

Signature _____

Subtotal _____

CA residents add
applicable sales tax _____

IN, MA, and MD
residents add
5% sales tax _____

IL residents add
6.25% sales tax_____

RI residents add
7% sales tax_____

TX residents add
8.25% sales tax_____

Shipping_____

Total _____

Please send this order form to:

IDG Books Worldwide, Inc.
7260 Shadeland Station, Suite 100
Indianapolis, IN 46256

Allow up to 3 weeks for delivery.
Thank you!

IDG BOOKS WORLDWIDE, INC.
END-USER LICENSE AGREEMENT

READ THIS. You should carefully read these terms and conditions before opening the software packet(s) included with this book ("Book"). This is a license agreement ("Agreement") between you and IDG Books Worldwide, Inc. ("IDGB"). By opening the accompanying software packet(s), you acknowledge that you have read and accept the following terms and conditions. If you do not agree and do not want to be bound by such terms and conditions, promptly return the Book and the unopened software packet(s) to the place you obtained them for a full refund.

1.   **License Grant.** IDGB grants to you (either an individual or entity) a nonexclusive license to use one copy of the enclosed software program(s) (collectively, the "Software") solely for your own personal or business purposes on a single computer (whether a standard computer or a workstation component of a multiuser network). The Software is in use on a computer when it is loaded into temporary memory (RAM) or installed into permanent memory (hard disk, CD-ROM, or other storage device). IDGB reserves all rights not expressly granted herein.

2.   **Ownership.** IDGB is the owner of all right, title, and interest, including copyright, in and to the compilation of the Software recorded on the disk(s) or CD-ROM ("Software Media"). Copyright to the individual programs recorded on the Software Media is owned by the author or other authorized copyright owner of each program. Ownership of the Software and all proprietary rights relating thereto remain with IDGB and its licensers.

3.   **Restrictions On Use and Transfer.**

   (a)   You may only (i) make one copy of the Software for backup or archival purposes, or (ii) transfer the Software to a single hard disk, provided that you keep the original for backup or archival purposes. You may not (i) rent or lease the Software, (ii) copy or reproduce the Software through a LAN or other network system or through any computer subscriber system or bulletin-board system, or (iii) modify, adapt, or create derivative works based on the Software.

   (b)   You may not reverse engineer, decompile, or disassemble the Software. You may transfer the Software and user documentation on a permanent basis, provided that the transferee agrees to accept the terms and conditions of this Agreement and you retain no copies. If the Software is an update or has been updated, any transfer must include the most recent update and all prior versions.

4.   **Restrictions On Use of Individual Programs.** You must follow the individual requirements and restrictions detailed for each individual program in Appendix D of this Book. These limitations are also contained in the individual license agreements recorded on the Software Media. These limitations may include a requirement that after using the program for a specified period of time, the user must pay a registration fee or discontinue use. By opening the Software packet(s), you will be agreeing to abide by the licenses and restrictions for these individual programs that are detailed in Appendix D and on the Software Media. None of the material on this Software Media or listed in this Book may ever be redistributed, in original or modified form, for commercial purposes.

5.   Limited Warranty.

(a)   IDGB warrants that the Software and Software Media are free from defects in materials and workmanship under normal use for a period of sixty (60) days from the date of purchase of this Book. If IDGB receives notification within the warranty period of defects in materials or workmanship, IDGB will replace the defective Software Media.

(b)   IDGB AND THE AUTHORS OF THE BOOK DISCLAIM ALL OTHER WARRANTIES, EXPRESS OR IMPLIED, INCLUDING WITHOUT LIMITATION IMPLIED WARRANTIES OF MERCHANTABILITY AND FITNESS FOR A PARTICULAR PURPOSE, WITH RESPECT TO THE SOFTWARE, THE PROGRAMS, THE SOURCE CODE CONTAINED THEREIN, AND/OR THE TECHNIQUES DESCRIBED IN THIS BOOK. IDGB DOES NOT WARRANT THAT THE FUNCTIONS CONTAINED IN THE SOFTWARE WILL MEET YOUR REQUIREMENTS OR THAT THE OPERATION OF THE SOFTWARE WILL BE ERROR FREE.

(c)   This limited warranty gives you specific legal rights, and you may have other rights that vary from jurisdiction to jurisdiction.

6.   Remedies.

(a)   IDGB's entire liability and your exclusive remedy for defects in materials and workmanship shall be limited to replacement of the Software Media, which may be returned to IDGB with a copy of your receipt at the following address: Software Media Fulfillment Department, Attn.: *Photoshop Tech Support*, IDG Books Worldwide, Inc., 7260 Shadeland Station, Ste. 100, Indianapolis, IN 46256, or call 1-800-762-2974. Please allow three to four weeks for delivery. This Limited Warranty is void if failure of the Software Media has resulted from accident, abuse, or misapplication. Any replacement Software Media will be warranted for the remainder of the original warranty period or thirty (30) days, whichever is longer.

(b)   In no event shall IDGB or the authors be liable for any damages whatsoever (including without limitation damages for loss of business profits, business interruption, loss of business information, or any other pecuniary loss) arising from the use of or inability to use the Book or the Software, even if IDGB has been advised of the possibility of such damages.

(c)   Because some jurisdictions do not allow the exclusion or limitation of liability for consequential or incidental damages, the above limitation or exclusion may not apply to you.

7.   U.S. Government Restricted Rights. Use, duplication, or disclosure of the Software by the U.S. Government is subject to restrictions stated in paragraph (c)(1)(ii) of the Rights in Technical Data and Computer Software clause of DFARS 252.227-7013, and in subparagraphs (a) through (d) of the Commercial Computer—Restricted Rights clause at FAR 52.227-19, and in similar clauses in the NASA FAR supplement, when applicable.

8.   General. This Agreement constitutes the entire understanding of the parties and revokes and supersedes all prior agreements, oral or written, between them and may not be modified or amended except in a writing signed by both parties hereto that specifically refers to this Agreement. This Agreement shall take precedence over any other documents that may be in conflict herewith. If any one or more provisions contained in this Agreement are held by any court or tribunal to be invalid, illegal, or otherwise unenforceable, each and every other provision shall remain in full force and effect.

HOW TO USE THE
CD-ROM

The *Photoshop Tech Support* companion CD-ROM can be used in both the Macintosh and Windows environments. Macintosh users can access files using the Finder. Windows 95 or NT 4.0 users can access files with My Computer or Windows Explorer.

System Requirements

Macintosh: System 7.0 or later, at least 8MB of RAM, at least 20MB of hard disk space, a 68040 or PowerPC processor, and at least a 640¥480 256-color display.

Windows 95 or NT 4.0: An 80486 or Pentium processor with 16MB of RAM, at least 20MB of hard disk space, and at least a 640¥480 256-color display.

Usage Instructions

Read Appendix D for a complete description of the CD-ROM's contents and installation/usage instructions for the various products. (Also refer to the main Read Me file on the CD-ROM for updated information about the contents of the disc.)

In fact, whenever you see a file called "Read Me" in a folder, be sure to read it. It's a message from the creator of the product that usually contains important information about installing the software and often lists new features and enhancements made since the last version came out — as well as known bugs that either exist or have been fixed from earlier editions.